Emotions in the Practice of Psychotherapy

Emotions in the Practice of Psychotherapy

Clinical Implications of Affect Theories

Robert Plutchik

American Psychological Association
Washington, DC

Published by
American Psychological Association
750 First Street, NE
Washington, DC 20002

Copies may be ordered from
APA Order Department
P.O. Box 92984
Washington, DC 20090-2984

In the U.K., Europe, Africa, and the Middle East, copies may be ordered from
American Psychological Association
3 Henrietta Street
Covent Garden, London
WC2E 8LU England

Typeset in Goudy by EPS Group Inc., Easton, MD

Printer: Automated Graphics Systems, White Plains, MD
Cover Designer: NiDesign, Baltimore, MD
Technical/Production Editor: Jennifer Powers

The opinions and statements published are the responsibility of the authors, and such opinions and statements do not necessarily represent the policies of the APA.

Library of Congress Cataloging-in-Publication Data
Plutchik, Robert.
    Emotions in the practice of psychotherapy : clinical implications of affect theories / Robert Plutchik.
        p. cm.
    ISBN 1-55798-694-0 (cloth : alk. paper)
        1. Emotions.   2. Psychotherapy.   I. Title.

    RC489.E45 P58 2000
    616.89'14—dc21

                                                                        00-041612

British Library Cataloguing-in-Publication Data
A CIP record is available from the British Library.

Printed in the United States of America
First Edition

Dedicated with love to
my granddaughters
Lauren and Michelle Silva,
who have brought much joy
to my September years

The problem in therapy is always how to move
from an ineffectual intellectual appreciation
of a truth about oneself to some
emotional experience of it.

It is only when therapy enlists deep emotions
that it becomes a powerful force for change.

—Irvin D. Yalom

CONTENTS

PREFACE

Early in my life I learned that all people use their emotions in varying ways to help them deal with life's problems. I discovered that smiles and laughter went a long way toward enhancing relationships among friends, family members, students, and colleagues. I also saw that when people became angry they sometimes got their way, and that when they looked sad, others often tried to be nice to them. I discovered that falling in love felt good and that being abandoned felt terrible. When I eventually had children of my own, I was thrilled with the experiences of their growth and development and anguished when problems befell them.

After getting an undergraduate degree in physics and a graduate degree in experimental and physiological psychology, I eventually found myself doing research on emotion. This research was primed during a period of primate brain research at the National Institute of Mental Health where our research group was examining the effects of electrical brain stimulation on emotional and motivational behavior. Later studies of manic–depressive illness at the Psychiatric Institute in New York City led me into clinical research in psychiatric hospitals and finally to a plethora of studies at the Albert Einstein College of Medicine, where I spent 25 interesting and stimulating years.

During my research, I came to realize that the study of emotions should involve at least three broad facets. One facet is concerned with defining the concept of emotion, showing its relations to other ideas and areas of study, and stimulating the gathering of new knowledge. The second facet should be concerned with issues of emotion measurement and concepts related to emotion (e.g., attachment, stress, and personality). The third facet should be concerned with what to do when our emotions create problems for us—in other words, the area of emotional dysfunction and change.

In my previous writings on emotion I have tried to deal primarily with the first two facets. I have developed a theory of emotion, which I call a *psychoevolutionary theory* because I believe that emotions are relevant to all living organisms and have highly adaptive purposes. I have tried to show that emotions communicate information and intentions from one individual to another, regulate social interactions, and increase the chances of survival in the face of life's adversities. I have also tried to show that emotions are systematically related to other areas of research usually considered as quite separate from basic research on emotions. These other areas include the study of personality, personality disorders and other mental disorders, ego defenses, and coping styles, to name a few. Over the years I have also tried to develop appropriate and theory-based ways to measure emotions and the concepts derived from them. Both of these facets are considered to some degree in this book.

However, in the present volume, I have tackled the third facet of affect theory in more depth: its relevance to problems of emotional disorders and to the treatment of these disorders. In this book I examine the relations between emotions and symptoms of emotional disorders. I review current affect theories that have particular relevance to clinical work, and I examine how emotions may be related to personality disorders. I have selected personality disorders (or Axis II disorders) because there are good theoretical reasons, to be described later, for considering personality disorders to be extreme derivatives of personality traits, which in turn, are derived from emotions.

A number of examples are taken from psychodynamic psychotherapy not because I believe it to be the most effective form of therapy but because it is one form of effective psychotherapy that I have studied in my research and clinical work. Much of what I present has clear relevance for other forms of therapy, such as cognitive–behavioral therapy and family therapy, because all deal fundamentally with emotions.

Two central issues described here are therapist tactics used for uncovering emotions and the complex problems of therapeutic communication. Although many ideas reflect psychodynamic theory, uncovering emotions and communicating therapeutically are central to all forms of effective treatment. I also include a discussion of tests and scales used to measure emotions and related concepts. I hope that this presentation serves as an impetus to further research that focuses on emotions and their importance in the psychotherapeutic enterprise.

There is both theory and practice in the following pages. I hope that the material presented is useful to clinicians, to students planning to be clinicians, and to those who are interested in research on psychotherapy. Above all, I would like to emphasize that the ideas presented in the following pages do not represent another school of therapy. It is time we reduced the list of therapeutic schools rather than increased them. Perhaps the recognition of emotions as a central aspect of the therapeutic process will help bring this about.

It is difficult to appropriately express my indebtedness to others in connection with the writing of this book. Some influences are clearly evident, whereas others are subtle and possibly hidden in the recesses of my consciousness. I have gotten ideas from colleagues, books, and clients, and it is now impossible to clearly disentangle the labyrinth of sources. They have become fused, like the colors of a portrait or the notes of a fugue.

However, I would like to thank a few people who have contributed to my thinking. Byram Karasu, chairman of the Psychiatry Department at the Albert Einstein College of Medicine, has sensitized me to the nuances of therapeutic communication, and Henry Kellerman has broadened my knowledge of the subtleties of expression of defense mechanisms. I would also like to express my sincere appreciation to my good friend, Carlos Climent (at the University of Cali, Colombia), and my daughter, Lori Plutchik, both psychiatrists, who have given me the benefit of their expertise and suggestions.

A number of people have read all of the manuscript and have contributed in many ways to its final preparation. Margaret Schlegel, development editor at the Books Program of the American Psychological Association, provided detailed and illuminating comments about all aspects of the manuscript; I am grateful to her. Finally, I would like to express my deepest appreciation to my wife, Anita, for her continuing emotional support as well as her acute insights, which often helped me avoid ambiguities of expression and thought.

Emotions in the Practice of Psychotherapy

INTRODUCTION

Clinical work is generally concerned with emotional disorders, emotional illness, and emotions that have gone awry. This is true whether the clinician is a psychodynamic therapist, a cognitive–behavioral therapist, or a family systems coach. All clinicians know that emotions are critical in the change process, yet many lack a practical understanding of how to use their knowledge of emotions to make psychotherapy more effective.

Most theories of emotion are based on laboratory research or research conducted with college students. Few bridges have been built between theory and research on emotions and the psychotherapeutic enterprise. The exceptions to this include the work by Leslie Greenberg, Leigh Vaillant, Richard Lazarus, and others. In this book, I review their work briefly but I focus primarily on constructing a bridge between the work that I have done over the past 30 years on emotion and the tactics and strategies that one may use to recognize and uncover emotions in the therapeutic setting.

It is important to emphasize that I am not presenting a new school of psychotherapy. My focus is entirely on the role of emotions in mental health and illness, a role that transcends any particular way of doing therapy. I believe that such an examination of emotions has considerable relevance for psychologists in general but particularly for clinicians, those who are studying to become clinicians, and those who have a special interest in research on psychotherapy.

Because of the universal relevance of emotions to life as well as to psychotherapy, I sometimes had difficulty in deciding on which issues to focus. I finally decided to include chapters that deal with different aspects of emotion in which I felt I could make a special contribution. The material in the book is a hybrid of empirical research, theoretical models, and clinical experience. Four ideas are the driving forces behind the development of this book: (a) emotions are of central importance in the process of psychotherapy, (b) ambiguities exist in our conceptions of emotions, (c) few systematic theories of emotion are of wide relevance to clinical problems, and (d) the implications for therapy of systematic theories of emotions must be made explicit. To give readers a preliminary sense of this content, I present a brief description of each chapter.

CHAPTER 1: EMOTIONS IN OUR LIVES

Psychologists have found the study of emotion to be one of the most confused areas in the social sciences. Many different and conflicting definitions of the concept exist; none of the theories that have been proposed to explain emotions enjoys universal acceptance. According to some theories, emotions are disruptive and blind rational thought, so individuals are taught as children to control their emotions. Other theories posit that emotions are adaptations that help individuals deal with adversities and other important life events.

In psychotherapy, clients or patients describe problems with their emotions; for example, too much sadness, anger, hate, or regret and too little love, trust, or compassion. Therapists, such as Benjamin, Ellis, Kellerman, and Spezzano, who have written about emotions and psychotherapy believe that emotions are the least studied and most misunderstood aspect of therapy. Both psychodynamic and cognitive therapists recognize the need to understand emotions if they are to understand behavioral dysfunction and therapeutic change.

CHAPTER 2: SYMPTOMS AND EMOTIONS

I believe that most psychiatric symptoms are actually disorders of emotion. A detailed examination of the *Diagnostic and Statistical Manual of Mental Disorders* (4th ed.; DSM–IV; American Psychiatric Association, 1994) reveals that most symptoms that define the various diagnostic categories are, in fact, descriptions of excessive emotions (e.g., panic) or decreased emotions (e.g., flat affect). Within each diagnosis, at least one or more symptoms refer explicitly to emotional states. From the point of view of patients, however, not all symptoms (e.g., loneliness, lack of meaning in life) fall neatly into *DSM* categories, although they still imply the existence of emotions that must be addressed.

Different theoretical approaches interpret symptoms in different ways. Behavioral approaches try to alleviate the symptoms by focusing directly on them, using such techniques as systematic desensitization. In other approaches, symptoms are assumed to be an expression of something else, and successful treatment requires dealing with that "something else" (e.g., conflicts, self-estrangement, childhood fixations, or repressed drives). That "something else" may involve lack of skills, for example, or inability to communicate effectively with important people in one's lives. It is of great importance to recognize that symptoms are not necessarily stable; many come and go during the course of psychotherapy. The chapter concludes with a description of five ways by which emotions may generate symptoms. It also notes that despite great divergence in theory among different schools, there is considerable overlap of goals. All clinicians believe that increases in hopefulness, trust, and relatedness to others are positive signs of change.

CHAPTER 3: THEORIES OF EMOTION

There are many reasons for the confusion and diversity in theorizing about emotions. One is that people learn to censor and inhibit the expression of their feelings and assume that other people do also. Others learn to exaggerate their emotions and to use this exaggeration to gain important resources that they do not know how to obtain otherwise. This means that subjective reports of emotion cannot be taken at face value. Another reason is the impact of the philosophy of behaviorism, which posits that inner states cannot be reliably observed and are therefore outside the realm of scientific psychology. A third major reason is the diversity of historical traditions concerned with emotions. These traditions range from Darwin's (1872/1965) evolutionary approach to emotions, to William James's (1884) psychophysiological viewpoint, to the Freudian psychodynamic tradition (S. Freud & J. Breuer, 1895/1936) , and the more recent cognitive tradition (e.g., Heider, 1958). These traditions have focused on different aspects of the complex state called an *emotion*.

The remainder of the chapter reviews a number of clinically relevant theories of emotion. Although all clinicians write about emotions to some degree, I chose those authors who have specifically tried to develop general approaches to affect as applied to clinical practice. The result is that I have included a number of psychoanalytic theories (represented by Brenner, 1974; Freud, 1926/1959; Rado, 1975; and Spezzano, 1993), Tomkins's (1962) theory of affects as the primary motivational system, Vaillant's (1997) theory of affect restructuring, Richard Lazarus's (e.g., 1991) theory of core relational themes, and Greenberg's (Greenberg & Paivio, 1997) theory of emotional schemes. All of these authors recognize that emotions are attempts to adapt to challenging aspects of one's environments, that emotions are not always available to introspection, and that emotions are related to the meanings people give to events.

CHAPTER 4: A PSYCHOEVOLUTIONARY THEORY OF EMOTION

The psychoevolutionary theory of emotions, sometimes referred to as the *circumplex model,* consists of three interrelated models. The *structural* model assumes that properties of emotion (i.e., intensity, similarity, and polarity) can be represented by a three-dimensional cone-shaped structure. It also assumes that there are eight basic emotions, that they exist as bipolar pairs, and that a cross-section of the model leads to a circumplex or circular set of relations among emotions. I describe empirical studies that support these ideas and show that by mixing or blending primary emotions it is possible to create hundreds of terms representing the language of affect.

The *sequential* model is based on the idea that emotions are complex, circular feedback systems that function to communicate information and influence the chances of individual survival. The components of this complex system are cognitions, feeling states, physiological changes, impulses to action, defenses against such impulses, and functional behavior, which affects the event that started this circular process going in the first place.

The *derivatives* model is based on the assumption that emotions are intimately and systematically related to personality traits, personality disorders, and ego defenses. Empirical studies are cited to show that the circumplex model applies to these and other domains. The chapter concludes with several evolutionarily based definitions of emotion.

CHAPTER 5: EMOTIONS AND PERSONALITY DISORDERS

The hypothesis is developed that for each basic emotion dimension, there is a group of personality traits, and that extremes of personality traits result in personality disorders. For example, the emotion of disgust is associated with the personality traits of hostile, scornful, and rebellious. When these traits exist in extreme form the individual possessing them may be diagnosed as having a paranoid personality disorder. This general idea has been proposed by a number of clinicians. Empirical data are summarized showing that various personality disorders are comorbid and that such comorbidity implies a circumplex structure for personality disorders. An empirically derived circumplex of personality disorders is then presented on the basis of similarity scaling methods. It is then compared with eight other circumplex models obtained by empirical methods to demonstrate considerable overlap. An empirical circumplex for impulses to action is also given. The chapter concludes with a number of implications of circumplex models for clinical practice with regard to people diagnosed with personality disorders.

CHAPTER 6: EMOTIONS, DECEPTION, EGO DEFENSES, AND COPING STYLES

Self-deceptions are commonly seen in patients and nonpatients alike, and clinicians are aware that most people are faulty observers of their own affective states. Deception enables individuals to get other people to see them as they wish to be seen, so that their interests can be better served. From an evolutionary point of view, the ability to present one's self in socially desirable ways and to believe in the self-image has powerful reinforcing value; it is related both to popularity and reproductive success.

Because deception is an aspect of ego defenses, I review at length the history of the concept of defenses. Ego defenses are basically primitive, unconscious reactions to a sense of helplessness in the face of painful reality. They are characterized by pressure from the past, magical thinking, and gratification by subterfuge. In contrast, coping styles are flexible, open to choice, and focused on realistic compromises between wishes and affects.

Ego defenses can also be described by means of a circumplex model, and empirical data are given to support this argument. My theory is based on the idea that each basic ego defense is associated with certain personality traits, with certain social needs, with a particular method for satisfying these needs, and with a particular function. For example, the defense of projection is associated with the traits of blame and fault-finding, with the need to identify imperfections in others, with the method of hypercriticality, and with the function of decreasing feelings of inferiority, shame, and personal imperfections. The chapter concludes with a description of eight basic coping styles.

CHAPTER 7: THERAPIST TACTICS FOR UNCOVERING EMOTIONS

Various tactics and strategies are described that clinicians may use to understand emotions, encourage the appropriate expression of emotions, and manage emotions outside of the therapy session when they appear. Examples of such tactics are identifying precisely the stimuli that trigger emotions, identifying the basic emotion components that underlie each emotion, and examining impulses to action. I discuss 16 primary tactics and additional therapist interventions for uncovering and managing emotions.

CHAPTER 8: PSYCHOTHERAPY AND EXISTENTIAL ISSUES

Every individual faces certain universal existential issues over the course of his or her life. These issues have been described as related to the fear of death, the sense of loneliness, the absence of structure, and the feeling of the meaninglessness of life. Another way to describe such existential issues is in terms of the struggle to find a place in the ladder of life (hierarchical issues), to discover one's own boundaries (territorial issues), to develop a sense of self (identity issues), and to accept the fact that life is finite (temporality issues). I discuss the relations of these ideas to emotions and suggest some clinical implications. The chapter concludes with a discussion of the underlying questions with which patients are concerned in the course of their therapeutic work: Who am I? How did I get to be me? What rewards do I get out of being me? What do I want in life? How can I reach my goals?

CHAPTER 9: THERAPEUTIC COMMUNICATION

Twenty distinctions are explored between social conversations and therapeutic communication. For example, social conversation is usually directed at maintaining a relationship that may continue indefinitely. Therapeutic communication tries to produce a desired change (e.g., a decrease in symptoms) so that the relationship can end. In social conversation each person tends to take turns being the focus of attention. In psychotherapy, the focus of attention is usually on the patient and his or her life, emotions, and experiences.

I then examine the nature of therapeutic dialogue by reviewing selected literature in the field. Those who have written about the subject agree that therapist interventions that create shame, guilt, or blame in the patient; anger at the therapist; or a decrease in self-esteem are undesirable. Through an examination of some transcript material, one finds that patient communications are often unclear, ambiguous, or partially incoherent. Nevertheless, conversations usually go on as if the participants are either unaware of the partial incoherence or are able to ignore them. From this starting point, a model of patient–therapist interactions is presented which has the character of a complex feedback system. The patient–therapist interaction involves a complex translation process containing descriptive, theoretical, and diagnostic information. Empirical data are then given on how experienced clinicians might respond to brief statements of patient communications. From this and other material, I compiled a list of 15 broad therapist response categories that cover most of the types of interventions that therapists use.

APPENDIX: MEASUREMENT IMPLICATIONS OF AFFECT THEORY

A comprehensive emotion theory should have implications not only for the practice of psychotherapy, but for the measurement of affect as well. Further research on the complex interplay of emotion, communication, and psychotherapy depends on having a valid way of measuring emotions. For example, cognitive theories try to find ways to describe the conceptual triggers of emotional reactions and use self-report methods to do so. Evolution-based theories tend to focus on expressive behaviors of humans and animals, whereas psychoanalytic theories imply that emotions can best be measured by projective and drawing techniques.

The appendix focuses on a number of measurement scales that have been developed on the basis of the psychoevolutionary theory described earlier in the book. Because of the detailed nature of the descriptions, this material is placed in an appendix; I hope that researchers as well as clinicians find it valuable. Two adjective checklists are described along with some empirical evidence for their usefulness. The Emotions Profile Index (Plutchik & Kellerman, 1974) is described as a way of measuring both emotions and personality traits. This scale is based on paired affect words from which the respondent selects the best description of himself or herself. Scoring is done by means of a circumplex with eight sectors. Extensive empirical data have been obtained through use of this test. Another personality test based on the theory is the Personality Profile (Conte, Plutchik, Picard, Galanter, & Jacoby, 1991). It has been developed in two versions: (a) a series of single trait terms with an intensity rating scale and (b) a series of brief trait descriptions with an intensity rating scale. This test has been used with a number of clinical samples and has shown both good reliability and discriminative power.

Another type of scale based on the theory was developed to measure ego defenses because of their intimate connections to emotions. The Life Style Index (Conte & Apter, 1995) has been used with a number of clinical populations and has revealed some interesting relations between ego defenses and anxiety, self-esteem, alcoholism, suicidality, violence, and other conditions. It is part of the family of scales implied by the psychoevolutionary theory.

The final test described in the appendix, The AECOM Coping Scales (Josepho & Plutchik, 1994) measures the eight derivative dimensions of coping implied by the theory. These include such dimensions as mapping, blame, help-seeking, minimization, and reversal. A number of studies are described that have used this test. Relations have been obtained between coping styles and interpersonal problems, suicide risk, rehospitalization, alcoholism, business management styles, and parenting styles. Copies of each of these tests are included. I hope that students, experienced researchers, and clinicians find these instruments of value in their work.

CONCLUSION

Most importantly, I hope that the readers of this book are receptive to my attempt to relate emotion theory, therapeutic practice, and test construction and that this integration contributes to their research as well as their current therapeutic practice.

1

EMOTIONS IN OUR LIVES

Affects are our biologically endowed mechanisms to help us cope with existence.

—Leigh McCullough Vaillant

Many events in our everyday life trigger strong emotional reactions. Despite the ubiquity of such experiences, however, it is sometimes difficult to find the right words to describe our emotions, and so we resort to metaphors: "I have butterflies in my stomach," "I have a lump in my throat," "I feel bottled up."

Although many clinicians express the importance of understanding and uncovering emotions in psychotherapy, the issue has been somewhat neglected by psychotherapists. This chapter provides examples of the importance of emotions in everyday life, and in the process of psychotherapy, and describes some of the ambiguities that exist in clinical conceptions of emotions.

Consider the following:

- A young man, fueled by hatred of the government, parks a truck full of explosives alongside a federal building. In the ensuing blast the building is destroyed; so too are almost 200 lives.
- A young mathematical prodigy learns of Pascal's theorem, a mathematical statement that was said to have been proved (although never written down) by the 17th-century mathematician. The modern prodigy yearns to solve the problem. Years later, after he has become a professor, he devotes more

than 7 years in secrecy to the problem and finally solves it. During an interview by reporters about his great achievement, he joyously breaks down in tears.

- At a soccer match in Europe, supporters of the losing team rush onto the field, tear up the stadium, and trample 20 people to death. They profess loyalty to their team and seek revenge on the victors.
- In Africa, in a poverty-stricken country containing two culturally diverse Black groups, a civil war erupts over access to power. In the resulting devastation, hundreds of thousands of people are murdered in horrible ways by the military arms of both sides.
- A child falls through the snow into a frozen river and clings desperately to a piece of ice. A stranger, passing by, sees the child and rushes out onto the ice, risking his life to save the child.
- A teenager overhears his mother tell his older brother that the younger brother will not amount to anything. Filled with disappointment and anger, the young man goes on to West Point and eventually becomes chief of staff of the U.S. Army. After World War II he successfully carries out a plan, named after him, that helps to rebuild a shattered Europe.
- A young nun devotes her life to the care of severely ill children and adults in India. She risks her life, yet her belief in God and her compassion and love are stronger than her fear of death.

EMOTIONS IN EVERYDAY LIFE

We all recognize the examples in the preceding paragraphs as expressions of powerful emotions at work in extraordinary circumstances. We can understand at least some of the emotions described because we can empathize with others and because we ourselves have experienced most of these emotions, perhaps less dramatically, in our own lives.

Despite what we intuitively know about emotions and their obvious importance in life, we might have some difficulty finding exactly the right words if we are asked to describe or define them. We might be uncertain of the best ways to describe what we think we are feeling. *Thinking about feeling* is not the same as *feeling*, and the language we use to reconstruct inner experiences is not always up to the task. Sometimes poets and novelists, with their subtle evocations of language and metaphor, catch the nuances of feeling better than we ourselves can.

This is the way the poet Emily Dickinson describes her feelings of despair.

My life closed twice before its close;
It yet remains to see
If Immortality unveil
A third event to me,

So huge, so hopeless to conceive,
As these that twice befell.
Parting is all we know of heaven,
And all we need of hell.

In anothr poem she talks of her unrequited love without once using the word *love*.

[1]If you were coming in the fall,
I'd brush the summer by
With half a smile and half a spurn,
As housewives do a fly.

If I could see you in a year,
I'd wind the months in balls,
And put them each in separate drawers,
Until their time befalls.

If only centuries delayed,
I'd count them on my hand,
Subtracting till my fingers dropped
Into Van Diemen's land.

If certain, when this life was out,
That yours and mine should be,
I'd toss it yonder like a rind,
And taste eternity.

But now, all ignorant of the length
Of time's uncertain wing,
It goads me, like the goblin bee,
That will not state its sting.

Another example of the use of metaphors to describe emotional states is provided by the vocabulary of drunkenness. Drunkenness is a universal experience in the sense that it can be found in all cultures, most people

---

[1]Reprinted by permission of the publishers and the Trustees of Amherst College from "The Poems of Emily Dickinson," Ralph W. Franklin, ed., Cambridge, MA: The Belknap Press of Harvard University Press, copyright 1951, 1955, 1979 by the President and Fellows of Harvard College.

have experienced some degree of it in their own lives, and many different words and expressions are used to describe the experience. In 1737, Benjamin Franklin compiled a list of 228 terms for being drunk. The *Dictionary of American Slang* (1975) lists 353 terms, and the *American Thesaurus of Slang* (1953) lists almost 900 terms. Examples of synonyms for *drunkenness* include the following: *crashed, bombed, crocked, gassed, plastered, tanked, looped, floating, glassy eyed, gone, juiced, lit, loaded, mellow, pickled, potted, smashed, soused, stewed, tight, high,* and *zonked.* Many of the terms are forceful or even violent words (e.g., *crashed, bombed*), whereas others (e.g., *floating, mellow*) suggest a pleasant state. Emotion terms are similar in their expression of different levels of intensity of feeling, in their partial expression of complex inner states, and in that a limited class of stimuli trigger them.

Patients with posttraumatic stress disorder frequently use metaphors to describe their tumultuous inner states:

> I am a time bomb ticking, ready to explode.
> I feel like I am caught up in a tornado.
> I feel like I am in a cave and can't get out.
> I feel like a pressure cooker. (Meichenbaum, 1994, pp. 112–113)

Meichenbaum also pointed out that patients who improve begin to use other metaphors to express their emotions. For example, they say things like "I like to be the author of my own stories" or "I want to move out of whirlpools and into still waters."

If one turns to the writings of psychologists for help in pinning down our amorphous conceptions of emotion, we are disappointed to learn that the study of emotions is one of the most confused chapters in the social sciences. The dozens of definitions of the term *emotion* have little in common. A number of theories have been proposed to try to help explain what emotions are, yet none is universally accepted. In some theories, emotions are regarded as disruptive; under states of emotion, such theories claim humans lose their ability to reason and are blinded by urges to act, and as a result people need to be taught, from the time of childhood, to control their emotions.

Other theories conceive of emotions as ways that nature has organized humans to solve life problems. Joy and anger, fear and sadness are not merely disruptions of organized rational daily lives, but are also adaptations to help people deal with emergencies or especially important events. For example, anger often intimidates others and gets them to do what the person wants; sadness often brings nurturance and comfort.

Some theories claim that some emotions (joy, trust) are positive or good for people, whereas other emotions (anger, fear, sadness) are negative or bad. Yet people everywhere are happily engaged in difficult and dangerous sports; they jump out of airplanes with parachutes, they swim to great depths under the ocean, they volunteer to try new experimental drugs, and they look forward to reading certain books and seeing tragedies on the stage that make them sad. Such things are puzzling if one assumes that some emotions are bad, and one is led to wonder how evolution has allowed so-called negative emotions to persist over countless generations. If they were bad, why do they still exist?

Language is a complex structure that has evolved over thousands of years. Within each language there are many historical elements. The words of the English language, for example, stem from Latin, Greek, German, and French roots and, to lesser degrees, from various other sources. Over the centuries, a multiplicity of meanings may become attached to a word. In addition, if a word becomes used in a scientific or technical context, it is often given a new or modified meaning. This is true for emotion words as well as all other terms.

To illustrate this last point, consider the word *anxiety*. Most people would agree that this is an emotion word, yet the definitions of the term are diverse. Webster's *International Unabridged Dictionary* states that the word *anxiety* comes from a Latin root which means "to cause pain or to choke." It then provides three definitions: (a) "a painful uneasiness of the mind respecting an impending or anticipated ill"; this emphasizes subjective feelings; (b) "a pathological state of restlessness and agitation with a distressing sense of oppression about the heart"; this focuses on behavior and physiology; and (c) based on psychoanalytic theory, "an expectancy of evil or of danger without adequate ground, explained as a transformed emotion derived from repressed libido." The last definition evidently is based on theory and not on subjective experience. These examples illustrate the complexity of people's ideas about emotions and help explain why there has been so much confusion in the field. These examples also suggest that clinicians might try to define emotions as part of a body of theory and not only as subjective experience.

One additional point is that the meanings of words are given not only by explicit definitions, but also by listing related words or synonyms. Thus, to understand a word like anxiety, it is useful to list such related words as *fear, worry, foreboding, concern, dread, uneasiness, apprehension*, and even *eagerness*. However, the dictionary adds one other important way to help understand emotions; it lists antonyms as well as synonyms. In this case, words such as *bold, calm*, and *confident* are given as antonyms for *anxiety*. This practice implies that the concept of opposites (antonyms) or bipolarity is a useful way to describe at least one aspect of emotions, an idea that is examined in detail in chapter 4.

EMOTIONS IN PSYCHOTHERAPY

Problems in life imply emotions of one kind or another. Conflicts between parents and children or between spouses arouse strong feelings.

Loss of jobs, status, position, connections, and attachments to others engender grief and depression. Feelings of hate, revenge, and regret often linger for years in a person's mind and become major issues in psychotherapy. In fact, many people who enter therapy describe problems with their emotions (e.g., too much sadness or anger; too little love or trust).

Psychotherapy is concerned with the treatment of emotional disorders. Despite this obvious fact, many clinicians admit to a sense of confusion or frustration with regard to their understanding of emotions. Although they constantly deal with emotions in their day-to-day practices, they are not always sure of the most efficient way to conceptualize emotions or how to use their knowledge to make psychotherapy more effective.

To illustrate these points, I examine what some clinicians have written about emotions. "Psychiatrists deal mainly with gross emotions and alien thoughts because they are easy to recognize and because patients complain about them . . . patients seek psychotherapy because of grief, pain, anxiety, depression and doubt" (Weisman, 1965, p. 80). He added: "Psychoanalysis attempts to revive traces of past events only because of their emotional relevance to the present" (p. 93).

Vaillant (1997) observed that "It is emotional change that is necessary . . . yet emotional change is the least studied and most misunderstood area in the field" (p. 1). She added that a "focus on affects and attachment has not been adequately addressed as a source of pathology in either traditional psychodynamic theory or cognitive theory" (p. 16), and she concluded that "people have a terrible time understanding and handling emotions" (p. 190). Within this same tradition, Nathanson (1996) wrote that "no matter how it is described or understood, all psychotherapy involves emotion" and that "no clinical evaluation in psychiatry, psychology or other psychotherapy can be considered complete if it neglects the world of affect and emotion" (p. 35).

Writing within an experiential tradition, Greenberg, Rice, and Elliott (1993) stated that

> psychotherapists have long concerned themselves with working with people's emotions. Theories of psychotherapy, however, have unfortunately failed to produce adequate theories of emotional functioning or comprehensive means of assessing emotion in therapy. Emotion for too long fell into the background in attempts at understanding dysfunction and therapeutic change. (p. 499)

Therapists working within the cognitive–behavioral tradition also are concerned with the ambiguities in clinical notions about emotions. For example, Lewis and Haviland (1993) wrote

> No one would deny the proposition that in order to understand human behavior, one must understand feelings . . . [and] the interest in emotions has been enduring. However, within the discipline of psychology

at least, the study of feeling and emotions has been somewhat less than respectable. (p. ix)

In many forms of psychoanalytic psychotherapy, the concern with affects is of primary importance, yet confusions exist here, too. Knapp (1981) noted that the psychoanalytic study of emotions is "fitful, largely unfocused" (p. 415). Spezzano (1993), a psychoanalyst, observed that psychoanalysis has never had a systematic theory of affects; he then attempted to develop a clinical synthesis. He points out that "Affects are difficult to access. The unconscious processes that produce affective states are never fully available even to the conscious scrutiny of the patient in whom they have occurred, much less to the analytic observer and listener" (p. ix). His theory includes the ideas that

> psychological life begins for all of us with affect, [and] all human beings either constantly experience the world through the organizing force of specific feelings or are basically oriented to the world by their constant seeking of certain specific feelings ... analysts think predominantly in terms of their patients' affective lives and talk to patients predominantly about their affective lives. (p. 118)

His theory is discussed in more detail in chapter 3. It is worth noting that Albert Ellis (1962), the originator of rational therapy, eventually changed the name of his therapy to *rational–emotive therapy*.

These examples—and many more could be added—are presented to emphasize the importance of emotions in the process of psychotherapy, the ambiguities that exist in the conceptions of emotions, and the limited existence of systematic theory. These observations are the driving force behind the development of the present book.

NOTES ON TERMINOLOGY

Patient or Client

It is not surprising that the person who seeks psychotherapeutic treatment is called a *patient*. The field of psychiatry developed in a medical setting as a derivative of care for people with severe mental illnesses. The psychodynamic tradition has also been largely dominated by psychiatrists who consider all people who come for treatment as patients, even those with relatively minor problems. This tradition has continued to the present day, and most clinicians, regardless of whether they are psychiatrists, psychologists, or social workers, usually refer to the people who seek treatment as *patients*.

However, with the development of Carl Rogers's (1951) client-centered therapy in the 1940s, a different framework was suggested.

Rogers's use of the term *client* rather than *patient* was intended to establish a more equal relationship between the therapist and person seeking treatment. Rather than assume that the therapist is an expert (like a physician) who diagnoses and treats patients, Rogers preferred to have the clinician take a role that required neither giving instructions to the patient nor interpreting the patient's remarks, and control of the pace and direction of therapy was to remain largely in the patient's hands.

In recent years, the use of the term *client* has become increasingly popular even in the case of therapies that are quite directive (e.g., behavior therapy). This may reflect a wish to relate therapy to American egalitarian ideals. The current psychotherapy literature frequently includes the terms *patient* and *client*, and they are often used interchangeably. In this book, both terms are used to refer to individuals who are in treatment. The individuals who provide treatment are referred to as *therapists*, *clinicians*, or *psychotherapists*.

Emotion or Affect

Although the terms *emotion* and *affect* are widely used in clinical practice, an aura of ambiguity surrounds their meanings. Generally, academic psychologists are much more likely to use the term *emotion* in their writings, whereas clinicians are more inclined to use the term *affect*. All introductory psychology textbooks have a chapter on emotion but not on affect. In clinical writings, the word *affect* is used; *emotion* is used to denote an emotional disorder or emotional problems.

Is there any way to establish meaningful distinctions between these terms? Over the years some efforts have been made mainly by clinicians to distinguish between the terms. In a textbook of psychotherapy, Langs (1990), a psychiatrist, defined *affects* as "manifest and surface communications" (p. 295). He discussed emotions only in the context of *emotional disturbances*, which he defined as "all forms of psychologically and emotionally founded disorders. The emotional disturbances range from characterological pathology to psychosis and neurosis. They also include psychosomatic and other psychologically founded physical disorders" (p. 726). Langs suggested that emotional disturbances include disturbances in affect such as anxiety, depression, boredom, and anger, implying that affects are the subjective feelings associated with dysfunction.

In contrast, the clinicians Greenberg and Paivio (1997) stated that

> affect refers to an unconscious biological response to stimulation. It involves autonomic, physiological, motivational, and neural processes involved in the evolutionary adaptive behavioral response system. Affects do not involve reflective evaluation. They just happen, whereas both emotions and feelings are conscious products of these unconscious affective processes. (p. 7)

Given these confusing and overlapping definitions, it is no wonder that a computer expert who tried to develop a computer program that simulates human emotions defined *emotions* and *affects* as interchangeable terms (Picard, 1997).

Two other clinicians have discussed this issue. Vaillant (1997) has partly based her views on Tomkins's (1992) affect theory. She suggested that the word *emotion* refers to inner bodily experiences, which include drives, affects, and pain. Affect, therefore, is a subtype of emotion, but is hard to distinguish from emotions. Tomkins admitted that it is difficult to define affects, to know how many there are, and to know how they differ from one another.

In his "clinical synthesis" in *Affect in Psychoanalysis*, Spezzano (1993) used affect almost exclusively and seldom referred to emotions. (In fact, the word *emotion* is not even included in his index.) However, he does provide a number of statements about what affects are. He described *affects* as internal states that create a demand for action. People, however, are not the final authorities on their own affective states because verbal reports of affects are often inconsistent with behavior.

This brief review of recent writings related to affect and emotion suggests that there is considerable ambiguity in the description of these terms. More often than not there appears to be extensive overlap in the uses of these terms. My own preference is to use *emotion* as the more general concept and to use *affect* more specifically in connection with clinical work. However, given the substantial overlap that exists, I do not attempt to legislate how these terms should be defined but simply follow precedent and use them more or less interchangeably.

WHAT THIS BOOK IS ABOUT

This book is not an attempt to add a new therapeutic system or "school" to the dozens that now exist. It is an attempt to clarify our understanding of emotions so that clinicians can do what they do best with an increased insight into one fundamental aspect of their work. With that aim in mind, I review some key ideas about what psychotherapy is all about, with an emphasis on the question of what symptoms are and what the therapeutic dialogue attempts to do. In a separate chapter, I review several contemporary theories of emotion in terms of their relevance to psychotherapy. Another chapter is concerned with some ideas dealing with the nature of the therapeutic dialogue and their implications for the psychotherapy process.

I elaborate on the psychoevolutionary view of emotion and discuss its many implications for therapy. These deal with such issues as the relations between emotions and personality, personality disorders, and defenses. The concept of the circumplex is discussed particularly in relation to issues of diagnosis of personality disorders. Implications for the measurement of the emotions are also presented. The relationships between existential crises and emotions are discussed.

The volume is based on empirical evidence, theory, and research methodology, as well as my own clinical insights and those of other practitioners. I hope that the ideas presented help clinicians practice with a better grasp of the role of emotions and help clinical researchers better understand how to measure and relate emotions to the phenomena that they are studying.

2

SYMPTOMS AND EMOTIONS

> All dis-ease is not disease.
> —Viktor E. Frankl

Individuals who seek psychotherapy enter treatment with certain symptoms or presenting problems. Common among them are feelings of depression, anxiety, suicidal feelings, and interpersonal conflicts. The *Diagnostic and Statistical Manual of Mental Disorders* (*DSM;* see, e.g., the 4th ed., *DSM–IV;* American Psychiatric Association, 1994), created largely by psychiatrists, represents one attempt to standardize the diagnoses and symptoms that characterize patients seeking treatment. Examination of such diagnoses reveals that many include a description of disturbed emotional functioning such as feelings of hopelessness, flat affect, worry, guilt, arrogance, aggressiveness, and exaggerated expressions of emotion.

Some therapeutic approaches focus primarily on symptoms and their alleviation. Others assume that symptoms have meanings and that explorations of the implied meanings reduce the symptoms. A number of meanings of symptoms have been proposed. Symptoms are sometimes seen as a reflection of interpersonal conflicts, as a reflection of existential conflicts, as an expression of unfulfilled longing for nurturant and protective attachment, as expressions of underlying affect scripts, as indicators of interpersonal power struggles, and as chronic exaggerations of innate behavior potentials. Emotions become symptoms when there is too much of an emotion, when there is too little of an emotion, when interpersonal relations are unsatisfactory, when strong emotions are in conflict, and when parts of the emotion chain are disconnected.

In this chapter, I examine a number of perspectives on the nature of symptoms as they relate to emotions, including those of the *DSM,* the patient, and the clinician. I describe how different theoretical models interpret the meaning of symptoms. I conclude the chapter by describing the goals of therapy and how they are related to changes in emotional functioning.

BENEFITS OF PSYCHOLOGICAL SERVICES

All psychotherapy begins with symptoms or problems. Usually the problems are recognized by the individual who seeks the treatment, but sometimes treatment is initiated at the request (or order) of another person. This occurs, for example, in the case of delinquents referred for therapy by the court or children brought for therapy by their parents.

The American public generally accepts the idea that psychological services may be beneficial. In a 1957 government survey, 50% of the U.S. population reported that they believed that they might benefit from psychological services, and about 14% had actually sought help from a mental health source, a family physician, or clergyman (Gurin, Veroff, & Field, 1960). In a replication of this survey in 1976 (both of which involved more than 2,000 respondents each), 59% reported that they might benefit from psychological services, and 26% had actually sought help (Kulka, Veroff, & Douvan, 1979). In 1995, *Consumer Reports* obtained mail survey data on utilization of mental health services from 22,000 respondents in the United States. About 18% reported seeking help for emotional problems in the past 3 years from a mental health services provider. These data suggest that large numbers of people recognize the potential benefits of psychotherapy and that many have used such services (VandenBos, 1996).

WHAT IS A SYMPTOM?

The question "what is a symptom?" seems to be simple, yet a careful examination of the issue reveals a surprising degree of complexity. Our first thought is that symptoms are such things as depression, anxiety, suicidal feelings, and uncontrollable anger, all of which are expressions of emotions. Viktor Frankl (1975), the logotherapist, wrote that the "neurotic triad" consists of depression, addiction, and aggression. A psychoanalyst, Weisman (1965), wrote that patients seek psychotherapy because of grief, pain, anxiety, depression, and doubt. Another clinician suggested that people seek psychotherapy because of loneliness, self-contempt, impotence, migraine headaches, sexual compulsivity, obesity, hypertension, grief, a love obsession, mood swings, and depression (Yalom, 1989).

Given such a range of symptoms, or at least such a range of reasons for entering therapy, is there some way to characterize the basic symptoms that lead individuals to seek psychotherapy? One possible approach is to turn to the community of therapists who are believed to have the authority to make decisions about the nature of diagnoses. Over the past 50 years North American psychiatrists have made efforts to standardize diagnoses through the DSM (*Diagnostic and Statistical Manual of Mental Disorders*) system, whereas World Health Organization (WHO) psychiatrists have carried out a similar endeavor with the ICD system (*International Classification of Diseases*, see, e.g., ICD-10; WHO, 1994). Despite the differences between the two systems in some details, there is considerable overlap between them.

Symptoms in DSM–IV

What does the DSM system say about how to define symptoms? More than 1,000 people participated in the preparation of the DSM–IV (American Psychiatric Association, 1994). Thirteen work groups were formed, each of which was responsible for a particular section. Empirical research was reviewed by each group and then critiqued by hundreds of advisers. Twelve field trials were carried out at 70 sites with 6,000 individuals to compare alternative formulations of symptoms. The final result is an 800-page manual that describes more than 50 broad categories of mental disorder and hundreds of subcategories. These include not only the "traditional" categories such as schizophrenia and mood- and substance-related disorders, but also such new categories as "caffeine-related disorders," "nicotine-related disorders," and "learning disorders." Psychiatrists define each mental disorder as a clinically significant syndrome

> that occurs in an individual and that is associated with present distress (e.g., a painful symptom) or disability (i.e., impairment in one or more important areas of functioning) or with a significantly increased risk of suffering death, pain, disability, or an important loss of freedom. (American Psychiatric Association, 1994, p. xxi)

To obtain a clearer idea of the DSM system, one should look more closely at the way in which the major disorders are described. The DSM–IV describes each disorder and states the number of symptoms that define it. The symptom descriptions for a given category range from 1 to 13, with a median of 7. For example, the dysthymic disorder (for adults) is characterized in the following way:

> A. Depressed mood for most of the day, for more days than not, as indicated either by subjective account or observation by others, for at least two years.

B. Presence, while depressed, of two (or more) of the following:
   (1) poor appetite or overeating
   (2) insomnia or hypersomnia
   (3) low energy or fatigue
   (4) low self-esteem
   (5) poor concentration or difficulty making decisions
   (6) feelings of hopelessness.
C. During the two-year period of the disturbance, the person has never been without the symptoms in criteria A and B for more than two months at a time.
D. The symptoms cause clinically significant distress or impairment in social, occupational, or other important areas of functioning. (Four additional criteria are negative; that is, no psychosis, no manic episode, no drug reaction, etc.) (p. 349)

It is evident from this description that a dysthymic disorder is clearly a disorder of emotion. The symptoms given are either directly about affects or imply the existence of affects (e.g., insomnia). Almost all the *DSM–IV* diagnoses include one or more affect disturbances. Here are some examples.

- *Generalized anxiety disorder*: "Anxiety, worrying, or physical symptoms cause clinically significant distress or impairment in social, occupational, or other important areas of functioning" (p. 436).
- *Obsessive–compulsive disorder*: "Person has recurrent and persistent thoughts, impulses, or images (obsessions) that are experienced as intrusive and inappropriate and that cause marked anxiety or distress" (p. 422).
- *Panic attack*: "A discrete period of intense fear or discomfort, in which the fear of dying developed abruptly and reached a peak within ten minutes" (p. 395).
- *Manic episode*: "Expressive involvement in pleasurable activities that have a high potential for painful consequences (e.g., engaging in unrestrained buying sprees, sexual indiscretions, or foolish business investments)" (p. 338).
- *Manic–depressive episode*: "Feelings of worthlessness or excessive or inappropriate guilt nearly every day" (p. 327).
- *Schizophrenia*: "Flat or inappropriate affect" (p. 288).
- *Obsessive-compulsive personality disorder*: "Shows rigidity and stubbornness" (p. 673).
- *Dependent personality disorder*: "Has difficulty expressing disagreement with others because of fear of loss of support or approval" (p. 668).
- *Avoidant personality disorder*: "Views self as socially inept, personally unappealing, or inferior to others" (p. 665).

- *Narcissistic personality disorder*: "Shows arrogant, haughty behaviors or attitudes" (p. 661).
- *Histrionic personality disorder*: "Shows self-dramatization, the-
  atricality, and exaggerated expressions of emotion" (p. 658).
- *Borderline personality disorder*: "Shows an affective instability
  due to a marked reactivity of mood (e.g., intense episodic
  dysphoria, irritability, or anxiety usually lasting a few hours
  and only rarely more than a few days)" (p. 654).
- *Antisocial personality disorder*: "Shows irritability and aggressiveness, as indicated by repeated physical fights or assaults"
  (p. 650).
- *Schizotypal personality disorder*: "Shows inappropriate or con-
  stricted affect" (p. 645).
- *Schizoid personality disorder*: "Shows emotional coldness, de-
  tachment, or flattened affectivity" (p. 641).
- *Paranoid personality disorder*: "Perceives attacks on his or her
  character or reputation that are not apparent to others, and
  is quick to react angrily or to counterattack" (p. 638).

These examples suggest that within each diagnosis there is at least one or
more symptoms that explicitly refer to emotional states. In addition, as will
be shown in chapter 4, references to personality traits are implicit references to emotions.

Symptoms From the Perspective of Patients

Although the *DSM* system represents a kind of norm, many clinicians
carry out their therapeutic activities without much reference to it. This is
simply because the symptoms and problems for which individuals seek psychotherapy are diverse and bear only a limited relation to the formal *DSM*
diagnoses. In addition, many individuals meet the criteria for two or more
diagnoses; thus, overlap of symptoms is common (Plutchik, 1997).

Patients who seek the help of psychoanalysts typically complain of
fears, avoidances, inhibitions, or repudiated wishes (Weisman, 1965). Vaillant (1997), a clinician, lists such problems as severe shyness, chronic late-
ness, acting-out behavior, high levels of interpersonal distrust, a lack of
friends, chronic job problems, and lack of intimate relationships as reasons
for seeking treatment. Chronic dissatisfaction is another reason for treatment (Karasu, 1992). Both Frankl (1975) and Yalom (1989) maintained
that feelings of aimlessness and lack of meaning in life are sources of distress
that lead an individual to seek psychotherapy; so, too, are problems of
intimacy and difficulties in getting along with other people (parents, teachers, supervisors, members of the opposite sex; Yalom, 1995). A psychoanalyst described symptoms in this way: "The client presents a problem: her

child is difficult, her husband drinks, his daughter is anorectic, his wife too controlling" (Maranhao, 1986, p. 91). Such descriptions point to events or people outside of the patient as the problem, and many patients would be pleased to be told how they should handle such "difficult people." Mahoney (1996) concluded that "anger, anxiety, depression, disgust, hate, embarrassment, guilt and shame are the most frequent concerns of psychotherapy patients" (p. 243). From the point of view of the patient, reasons for entering therapy do not fall neatly into DSM categories. Although these examples of presenting complaints are based largely on psychodynamic sources, they apply equally to cognitive–behavioral and other clinicians (Ellis, 1981).

Problems and symptoms are defined by the patient, but the clinician's views may not necessarily be the same as the patient's views. Therapists are usually guided by their theories and presuppositions, and what they consider to be symptoms may be quite different from what patients consider to be symptoms. The patient's chief complaint often turns out not to be what the clinician considers the most important complaint. For example, a person who cannot touch doorknobs without using paper or gloves may be said to have a compulsion related to fear of germs. He or she may feel comfortable with the compulsion and feel no need to change (i.e., the symptom is *ego syntonic*), or he or she may experience this behavior as a troublesome, unwanted intrusion in his or her life and would like to see it changed (i.e., the symptom is *ego dystonic*). The same general issue arises with alcoholic individuals, some of whom accept their drunkenness as a tolerable part of their lives, whereas others may be upset and troubled with their behavior and seek change. In such cases, clinicians may consider the patients problems to center around issues of anxiety, shame, dependency, and certain family relationships.

HOW CLINICIANS INTERPRET SYMPTOMS: THEORETICAL MODELS

Many clinicians believe that it is important to distinguish among (a) a symptom, (b) its cause, (c) its meaning, and (d) its function. For example, depression is considered a symptom of psychological dysfunction. The cause of depression may be a significant loss, a biochemical change in the brain, or both. The meaning of depression has been described as a cry for help (which need not necessarily be verbal); the function of depression has been suggested to be a way of mobilizing social support from other members of one's community. These kinds of interpretations are not always obvious and may need to be discovered through extensive clinical experience and theory. In this chapter, I consider the different views that exist among clinicians concerning the meaning of symptoms. Later, in chapter 4, I examine the question of the function of symptoms.

Different clinicians focus on different aspects of these four alternatives. The various theories attempt to make sense of symptoms in terms of these possibilities. I illustrate these ideas by looking at some of the writings of clinicians on the interpretation of symptoms.

THE MEANING OF SYMPTOMS

Psychodynamic Approaches

From a psychodynamic point of view, a symptom is the manifestation of an underlying conflict (Karasu, 1992); the symptom stands for something else that has been repressed (Maranhao, 1986). Sigmund Freud (see Fenichel, 1945b) viewed life as a constant struggle between instincts (or drives) and wishes or external demands. Such conflicts lead to various kinds of compromises that result in symptoms.

Psychoanalysts believe that their theories deal with basic human nature, which they interpret as meaning the deposits of evolution in the form of genetically-based or instinctual drives. Such drives are insistent, variable, and acquire their objects through learning, and they are primarily sexual or aggressive in nature (Mishne, 1993). Freud also noted that conflicts and compromises occur in everyday life but that the differences between normal and pathological compromises depend on the degree of exclusiveness and fixation of the resulting behavior.

Sandor Rado, a psychoanalyst, considered psychopathology to be an overreaction of "emergency emotions." For example, fear, rage, and disgust are emergency reactions that attempt to restore the individual to safety through such behaviors as withdrawal, attack, and rejection. Rado (1969) suggested that four types of miscarried repair mechanisms underlie most psychopathological behavior: (a) a phobic reaction to dangers that determines avoidance or retreat behaviors, (b) a riddance response (rejection, disgust) evoked by pain, (c) an attempt to coerce other people through the use of aggressive behaviors, and (d) self-coercion that is produced by guilt or shame.

Another analyst, David Shapiro, claimed that Freud's greatest achievement was his discovery of self-estrangement and its many manifestations. Patients may be caught up by "irresistible impulses" or the need to carry out a ritual against their own will. They may have strong, uncontrollable emotions that are strange to them. They may experience conflicts between different emotions; for example, they may have temper outbursts toward important people in their lives yet wish for close attachments, or they may wish to be thought of as generous yet recognize their greed or selfishness. All symptoms, in fact, are believed to be products of conflicts of which the patients are often unaware.

Insight-oriented psychotherapy is primarily concerned with self-awareness, self-understanding, and personality changes. The assumption is that by identifying the underlying conflicts, symptoms gradually disappear and are less likely to recur. This kind of therapy focuses on unconscious intrapsychic conflicts, on early childhood conflicts, and on family dynamics. In the course of such therapy, the patient is likely to develop new symptoms or experience an exacerbation of old ones and to develop a "transference neurosis." In such cases, the patient may begin to see the therapist as wonderful and perfect. At the same time, periods of ambivalence occur, and the patient alternates between submissiveness and rebellion. "Whenever the patient begins to develop symptoms in respect to the relationship with the therapist, therapy has really begun, and inquiry into these symptoms will open the path to the central issues" (Yalom, 1989; p. 99).

In some sense, patients get worse before they get better. During the course of psychodynamic treatment, patients must experience corrective emotional experiences. From a psychodynamic viewpoint, the therapist is to remain empathic, but at the same time, neutral, non-gratifying, and anonymous (Mishne, 1993). A crucial marker of the progress of treatment is that patients increasingly expose their frailties but are not hurt within the therapeutic context.

Existential Therapy: Symptoms as Derivatives of Existential Crises

Irvin Yalom (1989, 1995) is a group and individual psychotherapist who calls his approach *existential therapy*. In his book *Love's Executioner and Other Tales of Psychotherapy* (1989), he described an elderly patient who came to him because of an impotence problem. Yalom, however, believed that the real task of therapy was to improve the way that the patient related to others. Therapy moved along not because it greatly improved the patient's sexual performance but because it gave the patient an opportunity to reminisce, "to keep alive the halcyon days of previous sexual triumphs" (p. 156). A cognitive–behavioral approach would probably have focused on the sexual dysfunction and would have measured success in terms of its alleviation.

Yalom (1989) believed that psychotherapy is not basically about repressed drives or about attempts to repair childhood traumas, but rather about anxiety that results from inadequately dealing with life's existential issues; namely, the inevitability of death for ourselves and those we love, the problems connected with controlling our lives, the ultimate loneliness that we each bear, and the need to find meaning in a chaotic world. He stated that patients do not always know which of these existential issues underlies the particular symptoms with which they enter therapy. The problem in therapy, he argued, "is always how to move from an ineffectual, intellectual appreciation of a truth about oneself to some emotional experience of it. It is only when therapy enlists deep emotions that it becomes a powerful force for change" (p. 35). Carl Rogers (1965) pointed out that "in a very true sense the client never knows what the problem is until it is well on its way to resolution" (p. 104), and Masterson (1976) stated that the early presentation of one's problems is often "wrapped in romantic camouflage" (p. 9).

Short-Term Integrative Therapy: Core Themes Implied by Symptoms

Leigh McCullough Vaillant has written extensively on short-term integrative therapy. Her work (e.g., 1997) has emphasized the role of ego defenses in limiting patients' access to their own inner troubles. She believed that both traditional psychodynamic and cognitive theory have not focused sufficiently on painful affects and disturbed attachments as sources of pathology. One characteristic of all patients is an inhibition of the full range of their emotions; they may be able to express anxiety but not anger, or they may be able to be violent but not affectionate or sad. Most patients also have a deep unfulfilled longing for nurturant and protective attachment. Vaillant's approach in short-term therapy is to focus on core themes, to manage resistance, to clarify defenses, to deal with anxiety that is produced, and then to help the patient build new skills and relationships.

Vaillant (1997) also assumed that patients suffer from "missing capabilities," all of which involve inadequate handling of one's own affects. She listed five:

(1) Inability to calm one's extreme tension states.
(2) Inability to defend oneself from assault.
(3) Inability to avoid frequent disappointments.
(4) Inability to work out conflicts with others.
(5) Inability to tolerate frustrations in life. (p. 352)

Such missing capabilities are also symptoms with which clinicians deal.

Affect Scripts and Symptoms

Based on the work of Sylvan Tomkins (1995), some clinicians have suggested that symptoms reflect or express underlying "affect scripts" (Nathanson, 1996). From an evaluation of patients' behavior, their past history, and their emotional reactions to historical and recent events, clinicians may be able to infer certain characteristic affect patterns that guide patients' reactions to life events. Some patterns are reasonably adaptive, whereas others are maladaptive. For example, an individual who persistently withdraws from social situations, who seldom is able to make personal requests of others, and who is easily intimidated and so engages in activities that he or she would rather not do, may have an affect script that is centered around anxiety. Such a script determines how the patient reacts to a wide variety of life situations. As Stone (1996) put it, "No clinical evaluation in psychiatry, psychology, or other psychotherapy can be considered complete if it neglects the world of affect and emotion" (p. 35).

Symptoms That Imply Power Relationships

Jay Haley (1984) believed that symptoms are indirect expressions of a struggle for power in a personal relationship. The individual who struggles but who is unable to gain control over the relationship is likely to develop one set of symptoms such as anxiety, dysthymia, panic attacks, and agoraphobia, whereas the more dominant and controlling member of the relationship may become arrogant, aggressive, paranoid, or narcissistic. These kinds of patterns are seen more readily in group or family therapy, but they may be revealed in any therapeutic relationship because all therapeutic settings involve relationships of unequal power.

Haley believed that direct educational techniques are of little value but that homework assignments and recommendations to try various activities are appropriate strategies. His theory is that changes in the power interactions in a couple or in a family often change dysfunctional patterns of relating into more adaptive ones (Haley, 1984). Haley's ideas have implications for emotions. The concern with power and control as underlying symptoms suggests a connection between symptoms and implied fear and anger. It focuses on the ubiquitous hierarchical relations between people and the emotions produced by struggles for power and control. This idea is elaborated in chapter 8.

Symptoms and Evolutionary Psychology

In recent years there has been an increasing interest among psychologists and psychiatrists in an evolutionary view of human psychopathology. Stevens and Price (1996), both psychiatrists, have written *Evolutionary Psychiatry*, which attempts to apply both Darwinian and Jungian ideas to the understanding of psychopathology.

From their evolutionary point of view, a psychiatric disorder is a pattern of behavior that may have been adaptive under evolutionary ancient conditions but that is not adaptive in a contemporary context. An individual patient's history must be understood as not only a personal predicament, but as also being related to general human propensities. For example, depression is interpreted to be an adaptive response to a major loss,

TABLE 2.1
Eight Role Functions and Their Expression in Both "Usual" and "Unusual" Contexts

Role	Usual human expression	Unusual human expression
Nurturing, giving	Parenting, caregiving	Kidnapping without financial aims
Nurturing, receiving	Normal offspring behavior	Dependency
Sexual	Love, intercourse	Perversions, rape
Dominance striving	Leadership	Mania or hypomania
Submissive acceptance	Follower, becoming a member of the audience	Loss of values
Submissive withdrawal	Low-ranking member of a group	Depression
Attack	Persecution of others	Paranoia
Spacing	Isolated living	Schizoid behavior

Note. From *Evolutionary Psychiatry: A New Beginning* (p. 28), by A. Stevens and J. Price, 1996, New York: Routledge. Copyright 1996 by Routledge. Reprinted by permission.

whereas anxiety is an adaptive response to a grave danger. One task of the clinician is to identify the exact nature of the adaptive value of the emotion as well as the often hidden or repressed images that trigger the loss and danger responses in a particular person. "Rather than representing discrete disease entities, symptoms like depression, anxiety, etc. are better understood as chronic exaggerations of innate behavioral potentials with which all human beings are equipped by virtue of their humanity" (p. 47).

These authors cited Gardner (1988), who posited that humans have at least eight propensities to engage in social roles. These propensities are assumed to be innate and are stimulated by certain features of our environment to produce appropriate behavior. Such behaviors evolved to increase the chances of individual survival and to increase the likelihood that one's genes would be transmitted to the next generation.

These eight role potentials (which are all related to communication between individuals) are listed in Table 2.1. Gardner suggested that a psychiatric symptom or disorder may be related to each of these "normal" or usual role potentials, and some are suggested in the table. It is evident that these role functions overlap to various degrees, and it is assumed that each is related to underlying neural structures and systems. It is not likely, however, that these eight roles are a complete list of human behavioral potentials.

Stevens and Price (1996) argued that "psychopathology results when the environment fails, either partially or totally, to meet one (or more) archetypal needs in the developing individual" (p. 34). They provided detailed analyses of how different pathological conditions can be conceptualized as disorders of attachment, rank, spacing, or reproduction, and they attempted to show how each symptom is a potentially adaptive process that has gone awry generally in an exaggerated or inhibited form.

Symptoms as Symbols

In a book concerned with the nature of therapeutic discourse, Maranhao (1986), a psychoanalyst, discussed the nature of symptoms in relation to emotions (Maranhao, 1986). In Freud's early work, Freud believed that many patients had experienced sexual molestation in their childhood. The effects of such traumas were so painful that the idea or memory of it had been repressed. However, the affects associated with the experiences could not be fully repressed and were then acted out in the form of hysterical symptoms such as inappropriate crying, sudden changes in facial expression, or muscular or sensory losses of function. According to psychoanalytic theory, the formation of symptoms is a compromise between drives, affects, ego functions, and reality.

In a sense, symptoms are symbols of other events. As Maranhao (1986) put it, "the symbol is a dummy replacing an affect that had its flow thwarted by censorship" (p. 87). Unacceptable affects are camouflaged to prevent the ideas associated with them from becoming conscious. A patient who expresses hostility against all forms of authority may in fact have a hidden hatred for his father. Psychoanalysts attempt to get patients to reveal the symbols and then, through a combination of theory and experience, interpret the symbols as aspects of underlying affects. Analysts believe that correct interpretations lead to strong release of emotions. Insight must be grounded on emotions, rather than result from rational agreement with suggestions made by the therapist. Psychoanalysts have, in fact, concluded that "psychoanalysis can be viewed usefully as being primarily a theory of affects" (Spezzano, 1993, p. 35).

Symptoms as Emotions Gone Awry

This chapter has examined the nature of symptoms. As discussed, it appears that experts define symptoms of disorders, and that diagnostic labels are simply clusters of symptoms. Many symptoms are clearly about emotions and their vicissitudes, whereas others can be seen as being related to emotions in a more indirect way. In the actual practice of psychotherapy, patients enter with a wide range of presenting problems, many of which are not part of the psychiatric nomenclature. These include feelings of desperation and demoralization as well as poor coping skills. Many patients with less severe disturbances do not meet the criteria for the DSM–IV diagnoses (e.g., four out of seven symptoms), yet they feel unhappy, disappointed with life, and experience feelings of meaninglessness and ennui.

They seek psychotherapeutic treatment without meeting formal diagnostic criteria. Even though most diagnostic terms are meant to be purely descriptive, various connotations about causality are implied. A term such as *borderline personality disorder* usually implies severe pathology, origins in childhood, and great difficulty in treatment. In addition, there is little homogeneity in this label, and some patients with the disorder are able to enter group or individual therapy and benefit from it, whereas others cannot (Yalom, 1995). Terms such as *disorder*, *dysfunction*, and *psychopathology* elicit images of deficiency and sometimes create a negative attitude on the part of the clinician (Furman & Ahola, 1992).

Patients sometimes have difficulty describing their symptoms to therapists, and symptoms come and go during the course of therapy. Some patients prefer to stay in therapy even when their presenting problems have disappeared.

Of great importance is the fact that psychotherapists often see symptoms in a different way than patients do. Symptoms are seen as symbols or expressions of "something else," and that something else is determined largely by theory. Psychoanalysts see the meaning of symptoms in underlying conflicts (usually unconscious). Other clinicians see symptoms in terms of an individual's inadequate coping with life's existential crises. Some see symptoms as resulting from missing capabilities in individuals, which limit their ability to cope with frustrations or interpersonal conflicts. Other clinicians claim that the presence of symptoms points to underlying affect scripts that determine how individuals react to a wide variety of life situations. Symptoms can also be interpreted to reflect struggles for power in the hierarchical relations characteristic of all relationships. Clinicians also may interpret symptoms as reflecting the failure of the environment to meet the developing individual's basic, innate needs or propensities.

Given this diversity of theoretical models concerning the meaning of symptoms, it is obviously difficult, if not impossible, to claim that one interpretation is true and the others are false. It seems perfectly possible that all are true to some degree but that each clinician may choose to focus his or her strategies on one or another of these possibilities. It is also likely that any psychotherapy that progresses long enough deals with all these issues: underlying conflicts, existential crises, missing capabilities, affect scripts, power struggles, and unmet biological propensities.

EMOTIONS AND THEIR VICISSITUDES

One may formulate the notion of emotions and their relations to symptoms in a more precise way (Plutchik, 1993). There are at least five alternatives.

1. Patients may experience certain emotions, such as depression, anxiety, or anger, too often or too strongly. This is probably the major reason why individuals seek psychotherapy. However, other emotions may also exist too strongly or occur too often that are less often seen as factors initiating therapy. Examples include disgust (in the form of rejection, blame, or hostility), trust (in the form of excessive gullibility), and joy (in the form of hypomania or mania). Patients generally express a wish to be able to reduce the intensity or frequency of such emotions.

2. Patients may experience certain emotions too weakly or infrequently. They may complain that they cannot show affection or love, or get angry, or be assertive. In such cases patients would like to increase the frequency or intensity of these emotions. Such problems are often encountered in patients with posttraumatic stress disorder, who often have a restricted range of affect related to the trauma that they experienced.

3. Sometimes patients describe their problems in interpersonal terms. They experience difficulty in getting along with people —their spouses, lovers, parents, children, friends, supervisors, or co-workers. When such complaints are examined closely, it becomes evident that emotions are at the heart of these problems as well. Parents make them feel guilty, bosses make them feel resentful, children disappoint them, and lovers create anxiety. The interpersonal relations trigger emotional reactions that individuals find difficult to handle. When coping is difficult or impossible, an individual may become "emotionally disturbed."

4. Emotions may become part of psychopathology when two or more emotions are aroused simultaneously, producing severe conflict. Psychoanalysts point out that this is a common occurrence and that patients are often not aware of the extent to which this is true. An example of such conflicting emotions is a simultaneous activation of fear and anger, reactions that are not uncommon in the relations between children and parents or supervisors and co-workers. Other common conflicts occur between trust toward a friend, parent, or spouse and suspicions that lead to feelings of rejection, or between impulses toward independence and dominance and feelings of dependence, submissiveness, and wishes to be cared for. Shapiro has called the neurotic character a personality in conflict.

5. Emotions do not apply only to the subjective reports that adults give about their feelings; emotions are recognized in children, infants, patients with mental retardation or psychosis, and "normal" individuals who have repressed certain feelings. All theoreticians believe that emotions involve a cognitive or appraisal process (R. S. Lazarus, 1991) as well as impulses to action (Plutchik, 1980a).

Emotions appear to involve a chain of events that include appraisals, subjective feelings, impulses to action, and goal-directed behaviors. Sometimes a disconnection occurs between different parts of this complex, emotional chain of events. Thus, for example, it is possible to have "free-floating anxiety" without an awareness of the source of the anxiety (i.e., without an appropriate cognitive appraisal). It is possible to be depressed without knowing why one is depressed or angry without being aware of the source of the anger. It is even possible to have the physical signs of a panic attack without any subjective feelings of fear or anxiety (Kurschner & Beitman, 1990). Psychiatrists report "masked anxiety" or "masked depression" conditions in which signs of anxiety or depression exist without the individual being aware of them. Moreover, "psychosomatic equivalents" are sometimes reported in which a physical illness appears in place of, or in reaction to, strong emotions (Karasu & Plutchik, 1978).

In summary, emotions become symptoms or create symptoms in one or more of the following five ways: (a) when there is too much of an emotion, (b) when there is too little of an emotion, (c) when interpersonal relations are unsatisfactory, (d) when strong emotions are in conflict, and (e) when parts of the emotion chain are disconnected (e.g., feelings from behaviors). It is thus evident that emotions gone awry are intimately related to symptoms.

SYMPTOMS, EMOTIONS, AND THE GOALS OF PSYCHOTHERAPY

Freud once wrote that the aim of psychoanalysis is to change neurotic misery into ordinary unhappiness. Yalom (1989) put it differently: The aim of therapy is the assumption of responsibility for one's life predicament. Generally most clinicians assume that a goal of psychotherapy, at the very least, is to reduce or eliminate the symptom or problem for which the patient entered therapy. However, if the clinician believes that the patient's symptoms reflect underlying conflicts, fixations, traumas, and power struggles, then the goals of therapy become more complex and are designed to deal in some way with these issues. If successful, the therapy produces changes not only in the presenting symptoms but also in self-esteem, per-

EXHIBIT 2.1
Goals of Psychotherapy: A Sampling

McGlashan and Miller (1982)
1. Increase self-esteem and one's sense of self as a responsible agent.
2. Improve object relatedness to peers and family members.
3. Increase one's frustration tolerance and capacity to control drive states.
4. Raise one's developmental level as expressed by trust, assertiveness, and sexuality.
5. Experience the full range of affects.
6. Cope with problems through the use of more mature defenses.
7. Be able to tolerate ambivalence.
8. Increase one's power of self-observation and analysis.
9. Decrease symptoms of emotional distress.

Strayhorn (1988)
1. Increase closeness and feelings of trust.
2. Handle separation from as well as rejection by close others.
3. Handle interpersonal conflicts.
4. Deal with frustration and unfavorable events.
5. Enjoy approval, compliments, and attention.
6. Deny current gratification for the sake of future gain.
7. Be able to play and be spontaneous.
8. Increase ability to verbalize feelings.
9. Develop long-term goals.

Prochaska, Norcross, and DiClemente (1994)
1. Increase knowledge of oneself.
2. Increase one's power and ability to change.
3. Increase public commitment to self-change.
4. Find behaviors that counter one's own undesirable behavior.
5. Restructure one's environment to decrease probability of problem-causing events.
6. Reward oneself for increasing desirable behavior.
7. Express and experience feelings about one's problems and solutions.

Yalom (1995)
1. Accept personal responsibility for one's own interpersonal world.
2. Develop feelings of caring, closeness, and compassion.
3. Obtain insight into one's interpersonal patterns of behavior, motivations, and genetic sources.
4. Increase feelings of hopefulness.
5. Increase ability to offer support and reassurance to others.
6. Ventilate feelings along with cognitive awareness.
7. Recognize that ultimately there is no escape from some of life's pain or from death.

sonality, coping ability, and emotions. The result of such views has been to increase the number of goals of psychotherapy held by clinicians. These can be extensive and may include many aims. A comparison of a number of therapists' views is shown in Exhibit 2.1.

Examination of this exhibit reveals how important emotional changes are in the judgment of clinicians. For example, McGlashan and Miller (1982) included as goals the ability to experience the full range of affects and the decrease of symptoms of emotional distress. Strayhorn (1988) emphasized the increase of closeness and feelings of trust as well as the ability to enjoy compliments. Prochaska, Norcross, and DiClemente (1994) included the expressing and experiencing of feelings (affects) about one's problems. Yalom (1995) stated that two major goals of psychotherapy are to increase feelings of hopefulness and to be able to ventilate feelings along with cognitive awareness. Many of the other goals listed imply a need to change certain emotions if a client is to be considered to have benefited from psychotherapy. In the next chapter, I demonstrate why emotions are so central to the therapeutic enterprise.

3

THEORIES OF EMOTION

Everyone could in fact be right if each one did not insist on being the only one to be right.

—Manfred Eigen and Ruthhild Winkler

Although a number of theories of emotion have been described in the literature, relatively few have direct bearing on clinical practice. This is even true of the clinical literature, which has many references to emotions in clients but few general theories of emotion. In this chapter, I trace the five major historical traditions in the study of emotion and then give a rationale for selecting eight clinicians—Freud, Rado, Brenner, Spezzano, Tomkins, Vaillant, Lazarus, and Greenberg—who have attempted to provide a theory of affect that is directly applicable to clinical work. Their views are described in detail.

Despite the obvious importance of emotions in daily life, the topic of emotion has not received the attention that it deserves. Most textbooks of psychology have only a brief chapter on emotions, and few universities offer any courses specifically devoted to this topic. Clinical writings have also been relatively limited in their discussions of emotion.

Academicians have had a great deal of difficulty even agreeing on a definition of the term. Kleinginna and Kleinginna (1981) sought to create a consensus on how emotions should be defined; in their survey, they identified 92 definitions found in various textbooks, dictionaries, and other sources. In a review of the relevant literature, I identified 24 theories of emotion (Plutchik, 1980b). In a similar overview, Strongman (1987) described 30 approaches to a theory of emotion. Most of these theories tend to be somewhat narrow in focus and are usually concerned with one or two major issues, for example, how the autonomic nervous system changes during emotional reactions or what cognitions or appraisals are associated with emotions. These issues are important, but a satisfactory theory of emotion should be broad and general and should deal with a large number of interesting questions.

WHY IS THERE SUCH CONFUSION AND DIVERSITY IN THE STUDY OF EMOTIONS?

There are many reasons for the confusion that exists about the nature of emotions. One such reason is that most people have learned to be cautious about accepting at face value other people's comments about their feelings. This is because we are aware that we censor our thoughts and feelings and assume that other people do, too. We learn to grin and bear it in embarrassing situations. We learn to smile even when we are sad or angry, and we learn to put on a "poker face." We do these things to avoid criticisms from others and to try to receive respect and acceptance.

A second reason is that behaviorism has had a strong effect on the thinking of psychologists for nearly half a century. Behaviorists held the view that the only truly reliable objective information obtainable about living creatures was information about their behavior (and preferably simple behavior). This attitude led to a preoccupation with conditioned responses; emotions, on the other hand, were considered to be inner states that could not be reliably observed and were therefore outside the realm of scientific psychology.

A third reason for the confusion about emotions stems from the fact that psychoanalysts have pointed out that subjective reports of emotions cannot always be accepted at face value. Not only are some emotions repressed (and thus are unavailable to introspection), but others are frequently modified or distorted by ego defenses.

A fourth reason concerns the language of emotions. A number of studies have attempted to get judges (college students or professors) to identify English words that express emotions (e.g., Averill, 1975; Clore, Ortony, & Foss, 1987; Shields, 1984; Storm & Storm, 1987). With the exception of relatively few terms, there is much disagreement on precisely which words pertain to emotion and exactly what they mean.

A fifth reason for the confusions and disagreements about emotions is a reflection of the fact that our concepts about emotions are derived from a number of different historical traditions.

EXHIBIT 3.1
The Five Historical Traditions Related to Emotions

The Evolutionary Tradition
- Key person: Charles Darwin (1809–1882)
- Key publication: *The Expression of the Emotions in Man and Animals* (1872/1965)
- Key ideas: Emotional expressions are communications of intentions in emergency situations and tend to increase the chances of survival.

The Psychophysiological Tradition
- Key person: William James (1842–1910)
- Key publication: *What Is Emotion* (1884)
- Key idea: Emotions are subjective feelings based on the awareness of internal autonomic changes associated with actions.

The Neurological Tradition
- Key person: Walter B. Cannon (1871–1945)
- Key publication: *Bodily Changes in Pain, Hunger, Fear and Rage* (1929)
- Key idea: Emotions are subjective feelings resulting from hypothalamic arousal and are usually associated with acts of fight or flight.

The Psychodynamic Tradition
- Key person: Sigmund Freud (1856–1939)
- Key publication: *Studies on Hysteria* (1895/1936, with J. Breuer)
- Key idea: Emotions are complex states involving conflicts, early experiences, and personality traits and defenses. They can only be inferred on the basis of various kinds of indirect evidence.

The Cognitive Tradition
- Key person: Fritz Heider (1896–1988)
- Key publication: *The Psychology of Interpersonal Relations* (1958)
- Key idea: The beliefs of individuals, particularly their goals, their casual attributions, and their expectations, all influence their emotions. The presence of emotions may also influence beliefs.

HISTORICAL TRADITIONS CONCERNING EMOTIONS

There are five historical traditions concerning emotions: evolutionary, psychophysiological, neurological, psychodynamic, and cognitive. See Exhibit 3.1 for the key ideas associated with each.

The Evolutionary Tradition

Charles Darwin created not only a theory of evolution but a theory of emotion as well (Darwin, 1872/1965). He recognized that the process of evolution applies not only to anatomical structures, but also to an animal's "mind" and expressive behavior. Based on studies of animals, human infants, and adults in various cultures, he concluded that expressive behaviors serve an adaptive function in the lives of animals. They act as signals and preparations for actions. They communicate information from one animal to another about what is likely to happen. Therefore, they affect the chances of survival of the individual demonstrating the behavior.

Darwin also believed that most emotional expressions are unlearned.

His work expanded the study of emotion from the study of subjective feelings to the study of behavior within a biological, evolutionary context. It became scientifically legitimate to ask the question, "In what way does a particular emotion or behavior pattern function in aiding survival?" The evolutionary view of emotions has influenced the work of many contemporaries, particularly the ethologists.

The Psychophysiological Tradition

Twelve years after Darwin (1872/1965) published his book on emotions, the American psychologist–philosopher William James published an article (1884) in which he presented a new way of looking at emotion and at the same time founded a second major tradition in the psychology of emotion. His concern was principally with the sequence issue; that is, what comes first, the feeling of emotion or the physiological changes in emotion? He concluded, "common sense says we lose our fortune, are sorry and weep; . . . [My] hypothesis . . . is that we feel sorry because we cry, angry because we strike, afraid because we tremble" (James, 1890, p. 1066).

Over the past 100 years or so, many psychologists have attempted to prove or disprove James's hypothesis. It has stimulated researchers to study autonomic changes in relation to emotion and has led to important advances in the understanding of autonomic physiology, lie detection, and arousal.

The Neurological Tradition

A few years after William James died, another Harvard professor, medical researcher Walter Cannon, began to publish a series of studies dealing with the effect of stress on autonomic changes in animals. This work formed the basis of his critique of James's theory and his development of an alternative view of emotions.

Cannon (1929) reported that removal of certain parts of the brain in cats produced states of sham rage that might last 2 or 3 hours. His studies showed that the neural structure associated with the display of rage is located in the hypothalamus of the brain and that this area might be thought of as the "seat" of the emotions. This work stimulated a large number of studies concerned with the role in emotion of neurological structures. Researchers later discovered the importance of the limbic system as well as many other brain areas. In addition, the study of the biochemistry of the brain in relation to emotion and psychiatric illness is a direct consequence of this early work in the neurological tradition.

The Psychodynamic Tradition

Near the beginning of the 20th century, Sigmund Freud and Josef Breuer (1895/1936) published a book, *Studies on Hysteria*, that described the development of his new theory of the origin of psychiatric illness. At the same time, Freud laid the foundation for a theory of emotion.

Freud initially used hypnosis for the treatment of his patients, but he gradually gave up this method and substituted free associations as the best way to help patients identify their repressed memories and emotions. The aim of therapy was no longer to "abreact" an emotion whose expression had been blocked, but to uncover repressions and to replace them with acts of judgment. Over a period of many years, Freud and his associates built a complex theory of the origin and development of neuroses. Explicit or implicit in psychoanalytic writings is a theory of drives, affects, stages of emotional development, aberrations of development, conflict, mind, and personality.

Despite extensive writings in psychoanalysis, an explicit general theory of emotion was not articulated until very recently (Spezzano, 1993), although even now psychoanalysts lack agreement about the nature of emotions.

The Cognitive Tradition

The fifth of the major historical traditions dealing with emotions is relatively recent and may be identified initially with the work of Fritz Heider (1958). Heider was a social psychologist who maintained that different cognitive processes, such as causal attributions, sense of what "ought" to be, and goals all influence our emotions. He also recognized that sometimes the presence of emotion alters our cognitions, so that cognition and emotion are related to one another through a kind of circular feedback process.

Heider's analyses were mostly anecdotal or theoretical, but many investigators have been stimulated by his work to study the cognitive side of emotional reactions. This interest is quite strong in contemporary psychology, and many recent contributions (see, for example, the discussion of the work of Lazarus in this chapter) have been made to the understanding of emotions.

SOME THEORETICAL IMPLICATIONS

It should now be evident why the study of emotion has been so difficult. The language of emotion is ambiguous; self-censorship often takes place when reporting emotions; intellectual movements such as behaviorism and psychoanalysis have questioned (for different reasons) the validity of reports of emotional states; and different historical traditions have focused on quite different aspects of the complex state called an emotion.

Despite these obstacles, many efforts have been made, particularly in recent years, to develop theories of emotion. However, some have focused on evolutionary aspects, some on brain function, some on autonomic physiology, some on cognitive aspects, and some on psychotherapeutic issues. Many of these theories have been reviewed previously (Plutchik, 1980a, 1994). Because the focus of this book is on clinical implications of emotion theories, this chapter is concerned with those theories that have specific implications for understanding clinical problems.

The selection of the most clinically relevant emotion theories is not without controversy. Although most clinicians discuss the emotions of their patients, relatively few, however, have made an explicit attempt to present a comprehensive theory of affects. Even Freud's theory of affect (see Plutchik, 1994) was primarily about anxiety rather than affect in general.

In my judgment, the most important contributors to a general psychoanalytic theory of affect are Rado, Brenner, and Spezzano, all of whom have written books about emotions within a psychoanalytic context. This is not true of other important psychodynamic contributors such as Horney, Sullivan, and Malan. There are many nonpsychoanalytic theories of emotion in existence (for a description, see Plutchik, 1980a); most deal with academic issues such as the role of autonomic changes in subjective reports, and few have direct relevance to clinical practice. In my judgment, recent books by Tomkins, L. Vaillant, R. Lazarus, and Greenberg deal most directly with emotions as applied to the practice of psychotherapy, and this is why they are described in this chapter.

What is common to all of the authors that I have selected for discussion is that they all recognize that emotions are central to therapy and that emotions are usually attempts to adapt to challenging aspects of the environment, particularly the human environment. Most recognize that emotions are not always available to introspection and that people misjudge their own feelings. The reader should bear in mind that these authors discuss emotions in relation to psychotherapy; they do not necessarily present general theories of treatment or particular schools of practice.

SOME CLINICALLY RELEVANT THEORIES OF EMOTION

Sigmund Freud: Affects as the Reason for Repression

As a result of his studies of hysterical patients, Freud (Freud, & Breuer, 1895/1936) concluded that his patients were suffering from memories that they had forgotten or actively repressed. This happened with memories that had a strong emotion attached to them, even though the patient might not be aware of the emotion. The hysterical symptom, Freud hypothesized, acts as a kind of disguised representation of the repressed emotion. At first, he believed that the patient could eliminate the symptom only by an intense expression of the repressed emotion, a process he called *catharsis*. However, he changed his mind about the need for catharsis after he found that cures obtained with the use of hypnosis were unreliable, but he continued to believe in his theory of the origin of symptoms. In fact, he gradually came to the conclusion that repression of emotionally charged memories was the basis for all neurotic symptoms and not only those associated with hysteria.

Freud's theories of anxiety may be examined as an example of his view of affects. The concept of anxiety took a number of different forms in Freud's writings, and they were not all consistent. Freud proposed (see Fenichel, 1946) that anxiety represented a reaction related to an inability to cope with an overwhelming stress. Such a condition first occurs in every individual's life at the time of birth when the sudden massive stimulation of the environment creates a birth trauma. This trauma produces an archaic discharge syndrome, which Freud referred to as *primary anxiety*, the prototype for the occurrence of secondary anxiety reactions later in a person's life.

Freud presented a second hypothesis about anxiety in 1915. He proposed (1915/1957) that affects were primarily a form of energy that required some kind of direct or indirect expression. If repression or inhibition of affect existed, then the energy of the emotion had to be expressed in the form of neurotic overflow mechanisms such as phobias, obsessions, or compulsive rituals. Thus, Freud saw anxiety as the consequence of repression of emotion. He also assumed that the emotions involved were always related to conflicts over the sexual drive.

However, in 1926, in his book *Inhibitions, Symptoms and Anxiety*, Freud formulated a new conception of the nature of anxiety. Instead of anxiety being the result of a conversion of the energy of the affect, he now interpreted it to be the result of the ego's evaluation of dangerous aspects of the external or internal environment. Examples of dangerous types of events that psychoanalysis has been primarily concerned with include birth, hunger, absence of mother, loss of love, castration, conscience, and death. In terms of Freud's later formulation, anxiety was not the result of repression but the reason for repression. Evaluations by the ego determine whether internal impulses or external events are to be considered dangerous. This decision, in turn, determines the subsequent emotional response.

This psychoanalytic interpretation of emotion, as exemplified by anxiety, had several implications. It raised the question of whether an emotion could be unconscious; that is, whether an individual could experience an emotion and not be aware of it. Although Freud wrote about unconscious guilt and unconscious anxiety, he was dissatisfied with this idea, because he considered an emotion to be a response process. In *The Unconscious* (1915), he wrote,

> It is surely of the essence of an emotion that it should enter consciousness. So for emotion, feelings, and affects to be unconscious would be quite out of the question. But in psychoanalytic practice we are accustomed to speak of unconscious love, hate, anger, etc., and find it impossible to avoid even the strange conjunction, "unconscious consciousness of guilt". . . . Strictly speaking . . . there are no unconscious affects in the sense in which there are unconscious ideas . . . . (p. 110)

Only when Freud developed his later interpretation of anxiety did he resolve the dilemma. He finally concluded that the evaluation of an event can be unconscious even though the response process is not (e.g., a free-floating anxiety is evident, but the source of it, i.e., the evaluation, is not recognized).

A second implication concerns the question of how to recognize emotion in others. If it is true that emotions may be repressed, how can the analyst identify something that even the patient cannot identify?

Freud assumed that various displacements and transformations may occur in the expression of an emotion but that indirect signs of its presence are always noticeable. For example, if someone continually frowns, grinds his or her teeth, and has dreams in which people are being murdered, we might conclude that this person is angry even if he or she denies it. Freud relied heavily on dreams, free associations, slips of the tongue, postures, facial expressions, and voice quality to arrive at judgments about a person's repressed emotions. In other words, in the Freudian psychodynamic tradition, an *emotion* is a complex state of the individual that one infers on the basis of various classes of behavior. Although subjective feelings may provide a clue to a person's emotions, they are only one type of evidence among many others. An emotion is not synonymous with a verbal report of a supposed introspective state.

A third implication of the psychodynamic tradition is that emotions are seldom if ever found in a pure state. Any emotion has a complex history, with elements that go as far back as infancy. An emotion may have several drive sources and may include a mixture of feelings and reactions. The very idea of psychoanalysis implies an attempt to determine the elements of the complex state.

Sandor Rado: A Theory of Emergency Affects

Sandor Rado was trained in Europe as a psychoanalyst but spent many years as director of a major psychoanalytic training center in the United

States. Although his training background was classical, he has made innovative contributions to analytic theory, particularly in the area of affects.

Rado (1969) suggested that at least seven important affect patterns may be identified: escape, combat, submission, defiance, brooding, expiation, and self-damage. He then developed a multilevel theory of emotion based on evolutionary considerations. He hypothesized that there are four psychological levels of control. The first, the *hedonic level*, refers simply to the effects of pleasure and pain in organizing and selecting forms of behavior. This primitive mode of control is present in all organisms, even the very lowest. Its effect is to move an individual toward a source of pleasure and away from a cause of pain.

Contact with a bad or dangerous object usually leads to pain, which is simply a primitive, emergency signal indicating that injury has already occurred. "This signal arrangement, developed at an early stage of evolutionary history, is the very basis upon which the entire organization of emergency behavior has evolved" (Rado, 1969, p. 26).

Just as the effect of pleasure is to produce an incorporation response, the effect of pain is to produce a riddance response. Mental pain or anticipated pain may precipitate riddance behavior just as readily as does bodily pain, but some attempts at riddance are less effective and may even be pathological. For example, the defense mechanism of repression is a form of riddance response and acts to exclude painful thoughts or emotions from awareness. Some patients who have a psychosis and are in delusional states have been known to suddenly remove a vital organ (e.g., eye or genitalia) through self-mutilation and have perceived this riddance as a way of avoiding painful sights or feelings.

In the second level of control, the *brute-emotional level*, as organisms evolved distance receptors with a corresponding development of the central nervous system, they also evolved new ways to organize and select patterns of behavior. These new methods of control are the basic emotions of fear, rage, love, and grief. Just as pleasure and pain move the organism toward or away from stimuli in the environment, these emotions provide a more controlled way to do the same thing (e.g., anger organizes patterns of combat or attack). These emotions create the possibility of anticipation of future events, because an animal that evaluates an environmental event as threatening may fearfully run away or angrily attack. In a sense, the overt behavior amplifies whatever feeling states exist in the organism.

The third level of integration, the *emotional-thought level*, is associated with a notable increase in encephalization of the brain. In this level of control, emotions are more restrained and more mixed. Derivative emotions appear, such as apprehension, annoyance, jealousy, and envy. The goal of ruling and exploiting replaces the goal of destruction associated with anger. Defense mechanisms such as repression become used more frequently. The number of emotions exhibited is much greater than four basic ones.

The fourth level of regulation of action, the *unemotional thought level*, involves the mastery of events by rational, intellectual means alone. Rado (1969) then defined *emotion* as "the preparatory signal that prepares the organism for emergency behavior. . . . The goal of this behavior is to restore the organism to safety" (p. 27).

As a practicing psychoanalyst, Rado regarded these ideas as meaningful only in relation to their role in the treatment of patients. He therefore wrote at some length about the practical implications of his views and claimed that disordered behavior is fundamentally an overreaction. A person who experiences pain, fear, rage, or other emergency emotions tries to get rid of the cause by withdrawal, submission, or combat. These emergency reactions often do not work and instead create an extreme, somewhat rigid style of behavior.

Rado's conceptions of emotions are original and thought provoking, evidently influenced by Cannon's (1929) ideas on fight and flight as emergency reactions. Some of his ideas, such as those relating to the social communication value of emotions, are similar to Darwin's. Fundamentally, however, he wrote within the Freudian tradition that acknowledges the existence of unconscious and mixed emotions whose characteristics can only be inferred on the basis of indirect evidence.

Charles Brenner: Affect as Hedonic State Plus Concept

Charles Brenner is a well-known psychoanalyst and a former president of the American Psychoanalytic Association. His work is strongly based on classical psychoanalytic thinking, and his theoretical proposals have only cautiously moved away from this traditional body of concepts.

Brenner (1974) viewed Freud's theory of affects as being largely limited to anxiety and Freud's focus as being on emotions as processes of motor discharge. In recent years, psychoanalysts have become increasingly concerned with so-called "ego psychology" and have tried to clarify the role of ideas in relation to action. Brenner's aim has been to develop a theory of affects that is congruent with contemporary ego psychology.

Like all psychoanalysts, Brenner (1974) believed that conscious, subjective reports of emotions (affects) are often unreliable. This is simply because most affect states are characterized by mixtures of both pleasant and unpleasant feelings, as well as expectations or memories of both good and bad events. Such ambivalence is the rule rather than the exception. In addition, part or all of these affects may be repressed or modified, and thus a conscious report is seldom what it seems. As an example, he presented the idea of overcoming a rival, which may produce a feeling of pleasure and triumph but may also involve a feeling of pity or compassion for the rival and an expectation of punishment for having defeated him or her.

To relate affects to ego psychology, Brenner (1974) defined an *affect* as "a sensation of pleasure, unpleasure, or both, plus the ideas, both conscious and unconscious, associated with that sensation" (p. 536). From this point of view, anxiety is a feeling of unpleasure, associated with specific ideas of danger. He distinguished between the different words related to anxiety in terms of the intensity of the unpleasure or the degree of certainty of the danger. For example, if the danger is imminent, the affect is called *fear*. If the unpleasure is intense, the affect is labeled *panic*. If the unpleasure is mild and the danger uncertain, the affect is described as *worry*. These ideas are summarized in Table 3.1.

Once an individual develops an unpleasant affect such as anxiety, for whatever reason, certain consequences follow. In accordance with the operation of the so-called pleasure principle, the individual attempts to reduce the degree of unpleasure either by actions such as withdrawal from the situation or by unconscious mental operations called *ego defenses*. Examples of ego defenses are repression, by which the individual becomes unaware of the unpleasant feelings; denial, which implies ignoring the existence of the event; and displacement, which means deflection of the affect toward nonthreatening objects.

Brenner pointed out that the theory that applies to anxiety as an affect also applies to the affect of depression. Whereas *anxiety* is defined as

TABLE 3.1
Labeling of Affects in Terms of Hedonic Tone and Idea

Label	Hedonic Tone	Idea
Anxiety	Unpleasure	Danger
Fear	Unpleasure	Imminent danger
Panic	Intense unpleasure	Imminent danger
Worry	Mild unpleasure	Uncertain danger
Sadness	Unpleasure	Object loss or physical injury
Loneliness	Unpleasure	Longing for lost object
Despair	Unpleasure	No hope of relief from loss
Misery	Intense unpleasure	No hope of relief from loss
Discontent	Mild unpleasure	No hope of relief from loss
Shame	Unpleasure	Public defeat or failure
Embarrassment	Mild unpleasure	Public defeat or failure
Happiness	Pleasure	Fantasy or experience of gratification
Ecstasy	Intense pleasure	Fantasy or experience of instinctual gratification
Triumph	Pleasure	Defeat of rival

From "On the Nature and Development of Affects: A Unified Theory," by C. Brenner, 1974, *Psychoanalytic Quarterly, 43*, 532–556. Copyright 1974 by Psychoanalytic Quarterly, Inc. Used with permission.

feelings of unpleasure connected with the idea that something bad is about to happen, *depression* is defined as feelings of unpleasure associated with the idea that something bad has already happened. The something bad

> may be a narcissistic injury or humiliation; it may be a person or other object one has lost; it may be a bad deed one has committed or a brutal punishment one is suffering; it may involve physical pain, mental anguish or both. (Brenner, 1975, p. 11)

Brenner stated that the experience of loss need not be based on a real loss; even a fantasized loss may bring about the affect of depression.

In regard to both depression and anxiety, the appearance of the affect triggers some kind of ego defense such as repression, denial, or projection. These defenses function to reduce the feelings of unpleasure. However, ego defenses are seldom completely efficient in reducing a danger or a loss; the final result is always a compromise between the affect and the reaction to the affect (the defense). A symptom, such as a phobia, or a personality trait, such as submissiveness, may express the compromise.

These ideas are represented schematically in Figure 3.1. The perception of a situation as dangerous or as implying a personal loss leads to the development of the affects of anxiety or depression or both. Because these affects are unpleasant, various ego defenses (depending on the individual's personal history) then begin to act to reduce the feelings of unpleasure. Because most defenses are not entirely successful, a compromise results. The compromise involves the formation either of a symptom or of a character trait.

What are some of the practical, clinical implications of these views? For one thing, Brenner (1975) insisted that there is no such thing as free-floating, or content-less, anxiety.

> When a patient complains of anxiety, but has no conscious knowledge of what it is that he fears, analysts assume that the nature of his fear, the "something bad" that is about to happen, as well as all the other associated ideas are unconscious. They assume that it is repression and other defenses that are responsible for the fact that the patient himself is unable to say what it is he fears, to give any content to his anxiety. (p. 18)

Second, in line with the theory that affects trigger ego defenses that function to minimize the unpleasant affect, the presence of overt anxiety or depression indicates a failure of defense. It means that the individual has been unsuccessful in reducing the unpleasant affect. This condition implies that the therapist should examine the problem of why the ego defenses are not working. Such an examination may provide insights into personality dynamics that the therapist may not otherwise recognize. A third implication of Brenner's views relates to the use of the term *depression*. He pointed out that it has been used in two senses: as an affect state and as

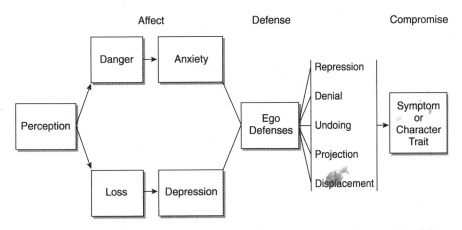

Figure 3.1. A psychoanalytic point of view of the sequence of events involving affects and their consequences.

a diagnostic label. The diagnostic label of *depression* refers to a heterogeneous group of symptoms, conflicts, and origins. The therapist should try to separate the role of danger from that of object loss and should try to identify the defenses and personality traits that reflect the compromises individuals make in handling the vicissitudes of life.

Brenner's concept of affects as hedonic states plus ideas is an important addition to the psychoanalytic literature. It leads to new insights about the role of ego defenses and some practical therapeutic ideas.

Charles Spezzano: Psychoanalysis as the Communication and Interpretation of Affect

The most extensive discussion of affect from a psychodynamic perspective has been presented by Charles Spezzano, a psychoanalyst in private practice on the West Coast, in the book *Affect in Psychoanalysis* (1993). He maintained that, despite earlier inconsistencies of theory and lack of attention to the topic, psychoanalysis is primarily a theory of affect. Most clinicians think, talk, and interpret in terms of affects. Affects do not need to be verbally identified by the patient for them to be known or recognized by the clinician. Empathic understanding is a common experience in psychotherapy.

Spezzano identified several characteristics of affect:

- Affect states are both informative and adaptive.
- Affects are forms of information about unconscious inner states.
- Affects are clues to drives and social relations.
- Affects are transient.
- Basic affects include at least rage, anxiety, sex, and excitement that combine in various ways to create more complex states like jealousy.

- Psychological life begins with affects before the development of ideas and the recognition of objects.
- Affects interact with each other. For example, anxiety inhibits sexual excitement.
- Affects are modes of communication and action predisposition. In other words, affects imply action; for example, fear implies escape, shame implies hiding.
- We all have predispositions to maximize or minimize specific emotions.
- Neuroses are unconscious strategies for managing one's affective life.

Spezzano argued that affects have an intimate relationship to drives or motives. To achieve safety and survival, individuals are born with the capacity to feel anxiety. To procreate, individuals are born with the potential to feel sexual excitement and affection. To withdraw from a hopeless situation, individuals are born with the capacity to withdraw and feel depressed. Affective meanings are implied in all human experience although their unconscious sources often make them difficult to identify. Children experience the need or drive for nurturance, safety, power, curiosity, control, and autonomy. The emotions are the methods by which such drives are satisfied.

With regard to issues of treatment, Spezzano proposed that the development of symptoms is always an attempt to regulate one's own affects. For example, he believed that narcissism is a perversion of both sexual excitement and curiosity. Narcissism involves a central conflict between security and risky choices. Narcissistic persons tend to have feelings of certainty and perfection as defensive reactions to unsatisfactory events.

In therapy, clinicians recognize that patients are not the final authorities on their own affective states.

> They claim that they are feeling nothing while simultaneously saying and doing things that would be hard to imagine being done or said by someone who felt nothing. They can also claim they feel one affect while talking or acting in ways we more commonly expect from people feeling a different affect. (p. 53)

Affects are inferred from complex sources of information, only one of which is patient verbalizations.

Psychoanalysis also has some interesting things to say about the relations between emotions and personality or character. It is a common clinical experience to encounter patients who feel anxious, angry, or guilty most of the time. Such persisting states of emotion are constantly being generated because they keep the patient ready to deal with threats to his or her needs for psychic safety. The process becomes circular because a person in (for example) a state of anxious expectation finds an endless supply of possible dangers. Such persisting states may be described as moods or, if persistent enough, as personality traits or character.

Patients enter therapy with a wish to avoid situations that make them more anxious or ashamed. They resist revealing bad feelings or humiliations. They try to protect their character traits that have produced as much security and self-esteem as they can handle without taking more risks than they can tolerate. Traits are interpreted as compromises between affective risks and affective security. Traits may be thought of as simultaneously inhibiting and expressing competing desires. Therapy, in a sense, takes over the task of regulating the patient's affects, a task that is normally done by the patient's traits.

Patients often enter therapy with feelings of mistrust, anger, fear, and sexual excitement. Therapists should try to identify such states, conflicts, and resistances and to assess the relative strengths of conflicting impulses and affects. Ideally, the psychoanalytic therapy situation should be a space in which patients can safely play with affects: to discover them, to express them, to change them, and to use them to help identify the unconscious processes out of which they came.

Sylvan S. Tomkins: Affects as the Primary Motivational System

Sylvan S. Tomkins, formerly a professor of psychology at Harvard and at Rutgers, (1962) hypothesized that there are eight basic emotions. The positive ones are interest, surprise, and joy; the negative ones are anguish, fear, shame, disgust, and rage. These basic emotions are innately patterned responses to certain types of stimuli, and individuals express them through a wide variety of bodily reactions, particularly through facial responses. For each distinct affect, there are assumed to be specific programs stored in subcortical areas of the brain. There is therefore a genetic, species-related basis for the expression of the basic emotions.

Much of the theory's emphasis is on the distinctions between the affect system and the motivational system. Most psychologists take for granted the idea that motives, such as hunger and sex, strongly drive a person to action. In contrast, Tomkins believed that motives are primarily signals of bodily need and that emotions then amplify these signals. As an illustration, he pointed out that oxygen deprivation (anoxia) creates a need for oxygen, but the affect of fear creates the sense of urgency or panic. In World War II, pilots who neglected to wear oxygen masks at 30,000 feet suffered gradual oxygen deprivation. Although the need was present, the slow process of deprivation did not produce an awareness of the need, and no panic occurred. Without the emotion being present, the pilots took no action and lost their lives.

The affect system is more general than the drive system. Drives are primarily concerned with getting certain objects into or out of the body and tend to have a rhythmic pattern. Affects can become associated with almost any stimuli (through learning) and can exist for long or short periods of time. Affects are stronger than drives, according to Tomkins; to get a person to act, all we need do is create an emotional state (e.g., joy, anger, or shame), regardless of his or her state of drive. A person who is frightened by a car runs, regardless of whether he or she is hungry or thirsty.

These ideas seemed academic and not clearly related to clinical issues, but in recent years several clinicians have attempted to develop these concepts so as to be useful in a therapeutic context. The most detailed elaboration may be found in the work of Leigh McCullough Vaillant (1997).

Leigh McCullough Vaillant: Affect Restructuring

Leigh McCullough Vaillant was concerned with the central concept of defenses. Trained as a psychodynamic therapist, she has conducted extensive research on short-term dynamic psychotherapy. Clinicians see many examples of emotions gone wrong. Rage, for example, is not necessarily an adaptive effort to overcome barriers but may also be a defense against grief and longing. Pain and distress lead to acting out, a form of defensive behavior. Vaillant suggested that one feeling can be substituted for another, and in such cases, one emotion can act as a defense that prevents the appearance of another emotion.

Fundamental to interpersonal relations is the need for attachment. When attachment is inhibited or prevented, it produces grief and anger; when satisfied, attachment produces joy and tenderness. When severe conflict exists attachment produces anxiety, which in turn can lead to defensiveness, guilt, and shame. This schema can work backward as well. A knowledge of the patient's defenses can provide useful information about the existence of core conflicts. Vaillant found this concept to be so important that she went further and argued that every symptom is a form of defensive behavior. Because defenses are so important to patients, they need to be grieved before they can be relinquished. Giving up comforting behavior such as stinginess or sarcasm implies that some other valuable but more mature behavior has to be substituted. The ratio of affect expressed in psychotherapy to defenses expressed has turned out to be a moderate predictor of improvement (Taurke et al., 1990).

Vaillant's (1997) model of affects has the following key assumptions.

- Human nature is benign unless provoked.
- Psychodynamic theory must include the full range of affects and not be limited to the three or four most commonly encountered.
- "Affects constitute our biologically endowed basic motivational system and, in contrast to drives, are amenable to psychotherapeutic change" (p. 424).

- Affects may be adaptive or maladaptive.
- Core conflicts are the major sources of affect patterns; knowledge of and inferences about such patterns guide treatment interventions.
- Explicit use of both operant and respondent conditioning are major elements of therapeutic change.
- Change takes place through the systematic desensitization of anxiety.
- Change takes place through acquiring new knowledge and skills.
- Emotions shared by patients and therapists have powerful beneficial effects.

Vaillant (1997) argued that emotions are usually very useful to individuals. They have evolved to direct behavior to adaptive ends; that is, "to cry when sad . . . , to laugh when happy, to seek out what is interesting, to withdraw from what is threatening, and to feel calmness and joy when all goes well" (p. 30). When things do not go well and conflicts develop, emotions become part of our defensive system and they act to protect the self. Examples of such defensive, modified affects are severe shyness, chronic politeness, acting out, distrust, excessive compliance, social isolation, chronic failure of relationships, and vagueness and circumstantiality in verbal interactions. Defenses protect the patient by avoiding what is unpleasant. In fact, the more severe the underlying conflict, the greater the benefit to the individual in avoiding the conflict.

One final point may be made about this theory of emotions. Vaillant believed that each primary emotion has both an adaptive aspect and a maladaptive aspect. This may be illustrated in the case of sorrow. Adaptive sadness is associated with feelings of closeness to others, with hope for the future, and with responsive compassion in an observer or listener. In contrast, maladaptive sadness is associated with self-pity, with feelings of hopelessness, and with helpless feelings in an observer. These ideas are summarized in Table 3.2.

TABLE 3.2
Adaptive and Maladaptive Forms of Sadness

Adaptive	Maladaptive
Concern for self	Self-blame, self-pity, self-attack
Hopeful about the future	Hopeless about the future
Good memories are accessible	Bad memories dominate
Feels close to others	Feels distant from others
Observer feels compassion	Observer feels helpless or irritated
Sadness comes to an end	Sadness persists

Note. From *Changing Character: Short-Term Anxiety-Regulating Psychotherapy for Restructuring Defenses, Affects, and Attachments*, by L. M. Vaillant, 1997, New York: Basic Books. Copyright 1997 by Basic Books. Reprinted by permission.

Richard Lazarus: Coping With Emotions

Richard Lazarus, a professor emeritus of psychology at the University of California in Berkeley, has been concerned during much of his career with the relations between stress and coping in adults (Lazarus, 1991). This research gradually led him to realize that stress and coping are part of a larger area of study of the emotions.

According to Lazarus, the study of emotion must include the study of cognition, motivation, adaptation, and physiological activity. Emotions involve appraisals of the environment and of the individual's relationships with others and his or her attempts at coping with them. Lazarus therefore referred to his theory as a "cognitive–motivational–relational" (Lazarus, 1991, p. 87) system of explanation with the focus being on the person–environment relationship.

The central idea of the theory is the concept of *appraisal*, which refers to a decision-making process through which an individual evaluates the personal harms and benefits existing in each interaction with the environment. *Primary appraisals* concern the relevance of the interaction for one's goals, the extent to which the situation is goal congruent (i.e., thwarting or facilitating of personal goals), and the extent of one's own ego involvement (or degree of commitment). *Secondary appraisals* are those in which the individual makes decisions about blame or credit, one's own coping potential, and future expectations. In this view, emotions are discrete categories, each of which can be placed on a weak-to-strong continuum. Several emotions can occur at the same time, because of the multiple motivations and goals involved in any particular encounter, and each emotion involves a specific action tendency (e.g., anger with attack, fear with escape, shame with hiding).

A key ingredient of his concept of secondary appraisal is the idea of coping, which refers to ways of managing and interpreting conflicts and emotions. According to Lazarus, there are two general types of coping processes. The first is *problem-focused coping*, which deals with conflicts by direct action designed to change the relationship (e.g., fighting if threatened). The second is *emotion-focused* (or *cognitive*) *coping*, which deals with conflicts by reinterpreting the situation (e.g., denial in the face of threat). The concept of appraisal implies nothing about rationality, deliberateness, or consciousness.

Another important aspect of Lazarus's theory is the concept of core relational themes. A *core relational theme* is defined as the central harm or benefit that occurs in each emotional encounter. For example, the core relational theme for anger is "a demeaning offense against me and mine;" for guilt it is "having transgressed a moral imperative;" and for hope it is "fearing the worst but yearning for better" (Lazarus & Lazarus, 1994, p. 20). One implication of these ideas is that emotion always involves cognition. As Shakespeare said, "There is nothing either good or bad, but thinking makes it so."

Is appraisal necessary for all emotional reactions, or can emotions occur without appraisal? Lazarus discussed this at some length and concluded that "appraisal is a necessary and sufficient cause of the emotions, and that the emergence of different emotions in infants and young children at different ages reflects the growth of understanding about self and world" (Lazarus & Lazarus, 1994, p. 214). Appraisals determine emotional states.

Lazarus has elaborated his ideas about psychopathology (Lazarus & Lazarus, 1994). He concluded that emotions result from the meanings we attribute to life events and depend fundamentally on what is important to us. "Life and death issues—who and what we are and will be—are the main sources of human anxiety and our emotional life" (p. 5). For an emotion to occur, an individual must appraise a situation as being personally harmful or beneficial. If there is no appraisal of harm or benefit, no emotion is aroused.

A key hypothesis in his writings is that each emotion is like a script with a distinctive dramatic plot. For example, in the case of shame, the dramatic plot is not having lived up to one's personal ideals. In the case of jealousy the plot is that an individual is threatened with a loss of another person's affection. The dramatic plot that generates pride is a condition that increases one's sense of importance.

With regard to therapy, Lazarus emphasized the role of cognition in re-interpreting situations so that the scripts may be changed. He suggested that we pay attention to our daily emotions and the thoughts we engage in before and during these emotions. He emphasized the role of coping behavior in dealing with stresses, frustrations, and subjective discomforts, and he believed that we should try to spend less energy protecting our self-image and justifying our behavior.

Leslie S. Greenberg: Experiencing Emotion in Psychotherapy

Leslie S. Greenberg, a professor of psychology at York University in Toronto, Canada, and his colleagues have written extensively about the role of emotions in psychotherapy. Rather than accept the view that the task of therapy is to examine early historical events in the life of the client, formulate hypotheses about internal dynamics, or discover unconscious motivations, Greenberg and his associates argued that the goal of therapy is primarily to understand the moment-by-moment emotional experiences of a client (Greenberg, Rice, & Elliott, 1993). The basic aim is to help clients become aware of their emotional schemes that guide their own behavior.

These ideas are based on a view of emotion that considers them to be adaptive and whose biological function is to increase the chances of survival. Emotions are based on appraisals made by each individual of his or her encounters. Emotions act to establish, maintain, or disrupt an individual's relations with the environment, particularly the environment of other people. Many emotions, although not all, have unique action tendencies; for example, impulses to attack when angry, to run away if frightened, or to seek contact if joyful. However, complex emotions such as jealousy or pride are believed to have no characteristic facial expressions or action tendencies (Greenberg & Korman, 1994).

The emotion system integrates information across the variety of information-processing domains and, as such, is the most complex subsystem humans possess. Emotions, Greenberg believed, provide a constant readout of an individual's current state and one therefore of central concern to psychotherapy. Clients need to be brought to conscious awareness of their emotions whenever possible to help improve their orientation to the environment and to help them mobilize their efforts for goal-directed action (Greenberg & Safran, 1990).

The process of psychotherapy involves at least four aspects or phases: (a) bonding with the client; (b) evoking the emotions that reflect "emotion schemes," which express how individuals think about themselves; (c) exploring emotion schemes in detail through examination of the idiosyncratic meanings that situations hold for each person; and (d) restructuring the emotions through various therapeutic interventions. An example of the restructuring of emotions is through use of role-playing techniques to encourage the client to resolve unfinished family relations. Another aspect of this process is to help individuals accept their emotions in whatever form they appear, with the goal of eventually achieving some degree of control over their modes of expression. Some of the active techniques used by the therapist to achieve these goals is to focus on the present, to analyze facial and bodily expressions, to encourage the intensification of specific emotions, and to focus on goals and future plans (Greenberg & Paivio, 1997).

CONCLUSION

This chapter has directed attention to theories of emotion that relate most directly to the clinical enterprise. Clinicians believe that psychotherapy is concerned primarily with the repair of emotional disorders. Clinicians believe that emotions are related to interpersonal conflicts, that they can be both adaptive and maladaptive, that they can be related to personality and defenses, and that they are deeper and more complex than is revealed by verbal reports alone. Recognizing and explaining emotions are basic functions of the psychotherapy process. The following chapter will begin examining another view of emotions and their relations to psychotherapy that considers emotion within a broad evolutionary framework.

4

A PSYCHOEVOLUTIONARY THEORY OF EMOTION

Behavior in general cannot be understood except in the framework of evolution.

—K. Breland and M. Breland

I begin by describing a theory that I have called a *psychoevolutionary theory of emotion,* which consists of three models. The *structural* model assumes that there are eight primary emotion dimensions (like primary colors) that vary in intensity, similarity, and polarity. They can be conceptualized by means of a three-dimensional analog model, a cross section of which is a circumplex. Mixtures of the primary emotions produce terms that have been described as *personality traits*. This suggests an intimate connection between emotions and personality traits.

The *sequential* model defines the major components of an emotional reaction, which include cognitions, feelings, neural changes, impulses to action, goal-directed behavior, defenses, and coping styles. These elements are related to one another through a series of feedback loops. This model implies that emotions are complex, behavioral, homeostatic feedback systems, whose functions are to communicate information and increase the chances of individual survival.

The *derivatives* model posits that several conceptual domains, such as personality, personality disorders, and ego defenses, are systematically derived from emotion and that they have a particular pattern of relations among them.

Some important similarities between emotions and personality traits are discussed. Both use a similar and highly overlapping language, both serve communication functions in interpersonal relations, and both regulate the relations among individuals. I conclude the chapter by offering several different but overlapping definitions of the term *emotion* based on an evolutionary framework.

ORIGINS OF THE PSYCHOEVOLUTIONARY THEORY OF EMOTION

In its beginnings (Plutchik, 1962), the psychoevolutionary theory of emotion emphasized ideas taken from the academic research literature and the Darwinian or evolutionary historical tradition. As it developed over the years in a series of articles and books (Plutchik, 1970, 1980b, 1984, 1989, 1990, 1993, 1994, 1995, 1997), I have attempted to relate emotions to clinical issues (Plutchik, 1966, 1967, 1987, 1988, 1990, 1993) and the cognitive tradition (Plutchik, 1977, 1980b, 1983). The theory also deals with the Jamesian view concerning the sequence issue, but I believe that the sequence of events in an emotional reaction is more complex than William James envisioned.

Despite criticisms of Darwin's ideas over the years, evolutionary thinking has been described as the cornerstone of contemporary biology and is increasingly influencing the thinking of psychologists (Barkow, Cosmides, & Tooby, 1992). In addition, the Freudian perspective also influenced the development of the psychoevolutionary theory of emotion. Many of these Freudian ideas have received reasonable confirmation in the research literature (Fisher & Greenberg, 1996; Westen, 1998). For example, Westen provided an extensive review of the literature that supports five basic psychodynamic propositions. The first is that much of mental life is unconscious, so people may develop symptoms or show behaviors that are inexplicable to themselves. It is also recognized that many cognitive processes, including defenses and coping styles, are carried out unconsciously. The second postulate is that many mental processes operate in parallel systems so that conflicts—between feelings and motives, between conscious and unconscious processes—often occur. When such conflicts occur, the result is usually compromise. "From a developmental perspective, conflict is virtually built into human existence" (Westen, 1998, p. 345).

The third postulate assumes that both childhood experiences and genetics play a major role in personality formation and underlie many types of behavior. These ideas have been well-documented. The fourth postulate is that cognitive interpretations of oneself and judgments about other people influence social interactions. Interactions are greatly influenced by the emotional significance of decisions made about other people. The final postulate is that mature, independent development requires that individuals learn to regulate their sexual and aggressive drives. Westen (1998) concluded that these postulates, once controversial, have been largely verified and are the bases for current psychodynamically oriented therapies.

THE PSYCHOEVOLUTIONARY THEORY OF EMOTION

A desirable theory of emotion should not only provide a meaningful definition of the term *emotion*, but should also guide our research, suggest new insights, show connections between apparently diverse domains, assist in the development of methods of measurement, and provide some clinical insights useful to those professionals concerned with recognizing, changing, and ameliorating emotional problems. This is what this theory has attempted to do, and the next few chapters reveal the extent to which it has done so. The theory described in this chapter is neither a new school of treatment nor an alternative to psychodynamic therapies or cognitive–behavioral ones. It is an attempt to understand the nature of emotions in the broadest sense possible and to show the possible relevance of affect theory to clinical issues.

Over the years, the psychoevolutionary theory has developed three major interrelated models, which together constitute the theory. These models are called the *structural*, the *sequential*, and the *derivatives* models. Each model deals with different fundamental questions.

The Structural Model

The language of emotions includes an implicit intensity dimension. For most words in the emotion lexicon, it is usually possible to find other words that suggest either a more intense or a weaker version of that emotion. For example, more intense versions of *anger* would be *rage* and *fury*, whereas less intense forms of *anger* would be *annoyance* and *irritation*. Similarly, a clear intensity difference exists between *pensiveness*, *sadness*, and *grief*. The implication of these examples is that most (perhaps all) emotions exist at points along implicit intensity dimensions.

A second point is that emotions vary in how similar they are to one another. This characteristic is clearly evident in the case of synonyms such as *fear* and *fright* (which may simply reflect close points along the intensity dimension), but it is also true for the major dimensions themselves. The dimension of anger, for example, is more similar to the dimension of disgust (dislike, loathing) than it is to the dimension of joy (cheerfulness, elation). It is, in fact, possible to study systematically the degree of similarity of the various emotion dimensions, or primary emotions.

A third important characteristic that is part of our experience of emotions is their bipolar nature. In everyday experience we tend to think about emotions in terms of opposition; we talk about happiness and sadness, love and hate, fear and anger. Thus, one may conclude that the language of emotions implies at least three characteristics of emotions: (a) they vary in intensity, (b) they vary in degree of similarity to one another, and (c) they express opposite or bipolar feelings or actions.

It is possible to combine these three ideas of intensity, similarity, and polarity of emotions by means of a simple three-dimensional geometric model that looks like a cone. The vertical dimension represents intensity of emotion, any cross-sectional circle represents similarity of emotions, and bipolarity is reflected by opposite points on the circle. This cone-shaped model looks very much like the well-known color solid that describes the relations among colors, and in fact many observers over the years have remarked on the similarity between emotions and colors in terms of their general properties (e.g., intensity, hue, and complementarity; Plutchik, 1980a).

To these ideas is added one important concept to complete the structural model. From at least the time of Descartes (1596–1650), philosophers have assumed that there is a small number of primary emotions and that all others are derived from them. Descartes listed 6; Spinoza, 3; Hobbes, 7; McDougall, 7; and Cattell, 10 (Plutchik, 1980). In more recent years, investigators have proposed from 3 to 11 emotions as primary. All include fear, anger, and sadness, and most include joy, love, and surprise (Kemper, 1987).

If we combine the idea of primary emotions with the three characteristics of the language of emotion, we can conceptualize a three-dimensional structure with eight slices representing the (assumed) basic emotions. This is shown in Figure 4.1 The idea that there are 8 basic emotions is a theoretical one but should be evaluated partly in terms of the inferences and insights to which it leads, the research it suggests, and the extent to which empirical data are consistent with it.

If we imagine a cross section through this three dimensional structure which may be called an emotion solid, we obtain an emotion circle as shown in Figure 4.2 for a midlevel cross section on the intensity dimension. A number of studies summarized in Plutchik (1980b) and Plutchik and Conte (1997) support this circular or circumplex set of interrelations among emotions. Table 4.1 provides a listing of the empirically determined angular locations of a large number of emotion concepts. For example, starting with the emotion *accepting* arbitrarily set at 0°, the word *apathetic* is 90° away from it, whereas *revolted* is opposite on the circumplex at 181°. The word *adventurous* is at 270° and is therefore opposite the term *apathetic*. Many other pairs of opposites are found on the circle.

If there are 8 basic emotion dimensions (each with a number of synonymous or related terms), how can we account for the total language of

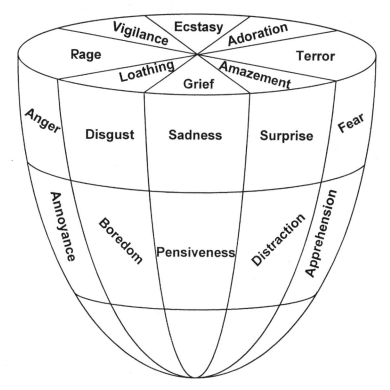

Figure 4.1. A multidimensional model of the emotions (prepared by Roy Plutchik).

emotions? Various published research (see Plutchik, 1994) implies that the total number of emotion words is a few hundred at most and that they tend to fall into families on the basis of similarity. If we follow the pattern used in color theory and research, we can obtain judgments about what results when 2 or more emotions are combined. When this was done, the results were clear; the college student judges agreed that a mixture of *joy* and *acceptance* produces the mixed emotion of *love*. The blending of *disgust* and *anger* produces the mixed emotional state of *hatred* or *hostility*. Such mixtures have been called *primary dyads* in the theory (Plutchik, 1962). Table 4.2 shows a number of other examples. By mixing two or more emotions at different intensity levels it is possible to create hundreds of terms representing the language of emotions.

Another important idea stemming from the structural model is that many of the terms that judges used in describing mixtures of the emotions are words that are typically used to describe personality traits. In fact, most of the terms used to describe emotions are also used to describe personality traits. For example, words such as *gloomy, resentful, anxious,* or *calm* can describe personality traits as well as emotional feelings. The distinction between emotional states and personality traits is largely arbitrary (Allen

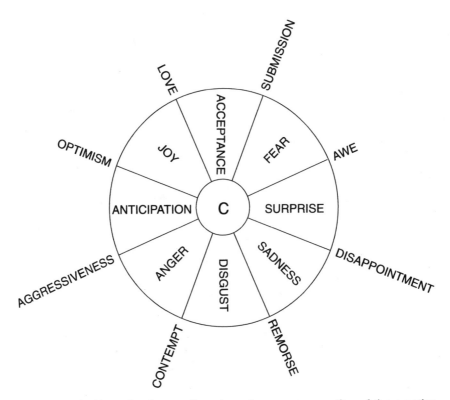

Figure 4.2. A circumplex for emotions based on a cross-section of the emotion solid. Primary dyads are formed by combining adjacent pairs of basic emotions.

& Potkay, 1981). Often the same adjective checklist can be used to measure both states and traits by a simple change in instructions. If the research participants are asked how they feel *now* or how they felt within the past few days or so, they are being asked about emotional states or moods. If, however, they are asked to describe how they *usually* feel, they are being asked about personality traits. Thus, according to this theory, emotions and personality traits are intimately connected, and in fact, personality traits may be considered to be derived from mixtures of emotions. This idea of derivatives of emotion is elaborated later in the chapter.

The Sequential Model

Ever since the writings of William James on the question of which comes first—the feelings of an emotion or the physiological changes—psychologists have been concerned with the sequence of events in emotion. Despite considerable interest in the question, no definitive answers have been found.

A major reason for this lack of closure is that emotions are not simply linear events; that is, A does not always precede B, and D does not always

TABLE 4.1
Angular Placements for a Population of Emotion Terms

Emotion	Angular placement (degrees)	Emotion	Angular placement (degrees)	Emotion	Angular placement (degrees)
Accepting	0.0	Rejected	136.0	Impatient	230.3
Agreeable	5.0	Bored	136.0	Grouchy	230.0
Serene	12.3	Disappointed	136.7	Defiant	230.7
Cheerful	25.7	Vacillating	137.3	Aggressive	232.0
Receptive	32.3	Discouraged	138.0	Sarcastic	235.3
Calm	37.0	Puzzled	138.3	Rebellious	237.0
Patient	39.7	Uncertain	139.3	Exasperated	239.7
Obliging	43.3	Bewildered	140.3	Disobedient	242.7
Affectionate	52.3	Confused	141.3	Demanding	244.0
Obedient	57.7	Perplexed	142.3	Possessive	247.7
Timid	65.0	Ambivalent	144.7	Greedy	249.0
Scared	66.7	Surprised	146.7	Wondering	249.7
Panicky	67.7	Astonished	148.0	Impulsive	255.0
Afraid	70.3	Amazed	152.0	Anticipatory	257.0
Shy	72.0	Awed	156.7	Boastful	257.3
Submissive	73.0	Envious	160.3	Expectant	257.3
Bashful	74.7	Disgusted	161.3	Daring	260.1
Embarrassed	75.3	Unsympathetic	165.6	Curious	261.0
Terrified	75.7	Unreceptive	170.0	Reckless	261.0
Pensive	76.7	Indignant	175.0	Proud	262.0
Cautious	77.7	Disagreeable	176.4	Inquisitive	267.7
Anxious	78.3	Resentful	176.7	Planful	269.7
Helpless	80.0	Revolted	181.3	Adventurous	270.7
Apprehensive	83.3	Displeased	181.5	Ecstatic	286.0
Self-conscious	83.3	Suspicious	182.7	Sociable	296.7
Ashamed	83.3	Dissatisfied	183.0	Hopeful	298.0
Humiliated	84.0	Contrary	184.3	Gleeful	307.0
Forlorn	85.0	Jealous	184.7	Elated	311.0
Nervous	86.0	Intolerant	185.0	Eager	311.0
Lonely	88.3	Distrustful	185.0	Enthusiastic	313.7
Apathetic	90.0	Vengeful	186.0	Interested	315.7
Meek	91.0	Bitter	186.0	Delighted	318.6
Guilty	102.3	Unfriendly	188.0	Amused	321.0
Sad	108.5	Stubborn	190.4	Attentive	322.4
Sorrowful	112.7	Uncooperative	191.7	Joyful	323.4
Empty	120.3	Contemptuous	192.0	Happy	323.7
Remorseful	123.3	Loathful	193.0	Self-controlled	326.3
Hopeless	124.7	Critical	193.7	Satisfied	326.7
Depressed	125.3	Annoyed	200.6	Pleased	328.0
Worried	126.0	Irritated	202.3	Generous	328.0
Disinterested	127.3	Angry	212.0	Ready	329.3
Grief-stricken	127.3	Antagonistic	220.0	Sympathetic	331.3
Unhappy	129.0	Furious	221.3	Content	338.3
Gloomy	132.7	Hostile	222.0	Cooperative	340.7
Despairing	133.0	Outraged	225.3	Trusting	345.3
Watchful	133.3	Scornful	227.0	Tolerant	350.7
Hesitant	134.0	Unaffectionate	227.3		
Indecisive	134.0	Quarrelsome	229.7		

Note. From *Emotion: A Psychoevolutionary Synthesis* (p. 170), by R. Plutchik, 1980, New York: Harper & Row. Copyright 1980 by Harper & Row. Reprinted by permission.

TABLE 4.2
Judges' Attributions of Words Appropriate to the Description of Mixed Emotions

Primary emotion components		Labels for the equivalent mixed emotions
Joy + acceptance	=	Love, friendliness
Fear + surprise	=	Alarm, awe
Sadness + disgust	=	Remorse
Disgust + anger	=	Contempt, hatred, hostility
Joy + fear	=	Guilt
Anger + joy	=	Pride
Fear + disgust	=	Shame, prudishness
Anticipation + fear	=	Anxiety, caution

Note. From *Emotion: A Psychoevolutionary Synthesis* (p. 162), by R. Plutchik, 1980, New York: Harper & Row. Copyright 1980 by Harper & Row. Reprinted by permission.

follow C. In contrast, clinicians have stated that emotions are circular or feedback processes. For example, Weisman (1965) stated that the function of affect is to restore the individual to a state of equilibrium, or, in other words, that the acts associated with emotions tend to reduce the emotions that produced them. Another psychoanalyst (Spezzano, 1993) proposed that affects trigger responses that tend to control the affect or eliminate it:

> The argument over whether thought precedes affect or affect precedes thought seems to be evolving into the concept of a circle of human experience.... There are many possible variations on the elements of the circle and how they should best be named, but in my view, all psychoanalytic theories talk of this circle when they talk about how people function. (p. 52)

In a related statement, Karasu (1992) observed that each person tries to maintain a certain level of affective equilibrium in everyday life with only moderate fluctuations. Unexpected or unusual events (external or internal) change this affect level, and the resulting behaviors represent an individual's attempt to re-establish the pre-existing state. Greenberg and Paivio (1997) argued that emotions provide us with feedback about our own reactions to events and basically function to promote survival. In an emotional reaction, once the goal of, for example, aggression or escape has been achieved and the individual's relation to the environment has changed, the emotional response declines. Another way this idea has been put is that "All relationships require constant interplay and feedback in order for positive affect to be maximized and negative affect minimized" (Kelly, 1996, p. 84).

The psychoevolutionary theory posits that emotions are part of complex, circular, feedback systems and that stimulus events, either external or internal (as in dreams), act as the primary triggers that start the emotion process going. However, events need to be interpreted for them to have an effect on the individual. For an American, a picture of an American flag may elicit feelings of pride and enthusiasm, but for an Iraqi it may arouse feelings of hate and vengeance. Sometimes the interpretation is obvious; occasionally it is less so. For example, individuals sometimes take an instant dislike to someone they have just met. The reason may not be obvious either to an observer or even to the individual. In such a case, one may assume that an unconscious interpretation or a cognition has occurred, and so one makes an inference about the cognition on the basis of the behavior shown. This is clearly what happens in cases of transference, where the therapist makes inferences about the patient's thoughts on the basis of certain behaviors shown by the patient.

A philosopher has argued that reasonably correct interpretations of other people are crucial to successful adaptations (Bogdan, 1997). This is because social interactions affect the fertility of the actors, and thus their inclusive fitness. The goals and behaviors of one individual have to be recognized and related to the goals and behaviors of others.

The psychoevolutionary theory assumes that following the cognition or interpretation, a feeling state occurs as well as a physiological state of arousal, if appropriate. Cannon (1929) and many others (e.g., Young, 1961) have pointed out that arousal states are generally preparations for action or self-protective changes that may be functionally useful in situations of danger. No one has satisfactorily resolved the question of whether feeling states precede or follow states of physiological arousal; it is just as feasible to argue that they occur together.

Feeling states tend to be followed by impulses to action. Such impulses may be expressed by tensions in the muscles; by facial expressions; by clenching of the fists; or by preparations for running, attacking, or yelling. Clinicians are well aware that impulses to action are not always followed by action, often for fear of retaliation or embarrassment. However, action often does occur; the individual runs, attacks, criticizes, cries, compliments, kisses, or withdraws.

Such overt behavior is, however, not the end of the emotion process. Such behavior generally has an effect on the stimulus or condition that started the chain of events in the first place. For example, running from a source of threat reduces the threat and tends to re-establish the condition that existed before the threat occurred. Similarly, if a major loss occurs in an individual's life such as the death of a parent, the crying and grieving that results tends to produce supportive and helpful contacts from other members of one's social group and at least in a symbolic way, provides a kind of reintegration with the lost parent. Overall, this process is a kind of homeostatic process, but one that is carried out by behavioral rather than internal changes. I call this process a *behavioral homeostatic, feedback system*. From this point of view an emotion is not simply the feeling state but the entire chain of events, including the feedback loops.

Figure 4.3 depicts this process in general terms. Feedback loops may

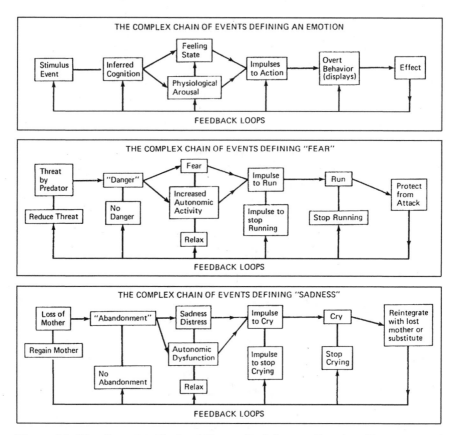

Figure 4.3. The Complex Chain of Events Defining an Emotion. The top panel illustrates feedback loops for emotions in general, and the middle and bottom panel illustrate feedback loops for fear and sadness, respectively.

influence the impulses to action, the feeling states, the cognitions, and the initiating stimulus. This process is what leads to the idea that feelings and behaviors can affect cognitions, just as much as cognitions can influence feelings. Also implied by this model is the idea that the term *feelings* is used to represent subjective, reportable states such as joy, sadness, anger, or disgust, whereas the word *emotion* is used in a much broader sense to refer to the entire chain of events that include feelings, but also cognitions, impulses to action, display behaviors, and the various loops that occur. An individual may not be consciously aware of some of these components.

Table 4.3 summarizes the theory's assumptions about some of the key elements involved in the emotion sequence. For each of the 8 basic emotions a general description of the stimulus event that triggers it is provided, followed by descriptions of the probable cognitions associated with each of the emotions, the subjective feeling states, the overt behaviors, and the effect of the behavior in reducing the disequilibrium.

At the heart of all these descriptions is the idea that emotions have

TABLE 4.3
Key Elements in the Emotion Sequence

Stimulus event	Cognition	Feeling state	Overt behavior	Effect
Threat	"Danger"	Fear	Escape	Safety
Obstacle	"Enemy"	Anger	Attack	Destroy obstacle
Gain of valued object	"Possess"	Joy	Retain or repeat	Gain resources
Loss of valued object	"Abandonment"	Sadness	Cry	Reintegrate with lost object
Member of one's group	"Friend"	Acceptance	Groom	Mutual support
Unpalatable object	"Poison"	Disgust	Vomit	Eject poison
New territory	"Examine"	Expectation	Map	Knowledge of territory
Unexpected event	"What is it?"	Surprise	Stop	Gain time to orient

a purpose in the lives of individuals. This idea stems from the evolutionary perspective, is consistent with psychodynamic thinking, and is becoming more and more accepted in the writings of contemporary clinicians. For example, Hauser (1996) wrote that the primary care that young organisms require is for food, protection, and transportation and that crying is a major method for getting such care. Spezzano (1993) suggested that individuals use love or intimidation to keep others invested in their personal agendas. Vaillant (1997) has discussed the adaptive functions of a number of emotions. Sorrow, for example, increases one's feelings of closeness to others, and listeners often feel compassion and wish to be helpful. Interest, or anticipation, is often energizing and increases one's involvement with others. Fear protects the self, initiates withdrawal, and allows general functioning to continue. Shame leads to remorse and a decrease in the probability of repetition of the shameful act. All these examples imply that emotions are part of an adaptive circular or feedback process.

The Derivatives Model

One of the most important ideas of the psychoevolutionary theory is the concept of *derivatives*. This term is used in three senses. It can mean that certain human behaviors are seen in lower animals; for example, the sneer of the human may be said to be derived from the snarl of the wolf. It can also mean that certain behaviors seen in adults are derivatives of certain behaviors seen in infants. An example might be the feeding and babyish behaviors sometimes seen between adult lovers. A third meaning of the concept is the idea that certain concepts are derived from other, more primitive events or concepts. This is the sense in which the term is used here. It means that a number of conceptual domains are systematically related to one another.

Take, for example, the domain of personality. The subject is usually taught in universities as if it had little or nothing to do with emotions. Yet the language of emotions and the language of personality are remarkably similar. An individual can feel depressed or be a depressed person, can feel nervous or be a nervous person, or can feel joyful or be a joyful person.

In addition to the overlap in the language of the domains of emotion and personality, both domains can be represented by means of a circumplex model. This has been illustrated by Conte and Plutchik (1981), who used two independent methods to establish a circumplex structure for personality traits: a direct similarity scaling method and a semantic differential followed by factor analysis of the data. Angular locations of a sample of 40 personality traits obtained by the two methods were highly correlated (+.98). These locations are shown in Figure 4.4.

This diagram shows that the personality traits are fairly evenly distributed around the circumference of a circle and that opposite traits are

Figure 4.4. Similarity and Polarity Structure of a Sample of 40 Personality Traits.

consistent with ordinary uses of the terms. For example, *quarrelsome* is opposite *peaceful, affectionate* is opposite *pessimistic, bold* is opposite *timid,* and *submissive* is opposite *aggressive.* As noted earlier, these terms can be used to describe both persistent traits and transient emotions, depending on the context. This circumplex for personality traits, using a different method, has been very closely replicated (Fisher, 1997; Fisher, Heise, Bohrnstedt, & Lucke, 1985). Circumplex models have also been used to describe other interpersonal domains including facial expressions (Myllyniemi, 1997), vocational interests (Tracey & Rounds, 1997), parent–child relations (Schaefer, 1997), social acuity or empathy (Gurtman, 1997), and social support (Wiggins & Trobst, 1997).

The psychoevolutionary theory of emotions assumes that emotions, because of their fundamental adaptive role in all organisms, are the precursors of the ways in which emotions become expressed in other but related domains such as personality. It is in this sense that personality traits are derivatives of the more fundamental emotional states, just as most colors in nature are derived from mixtures of a few primary ones. When emotions occur in persistent or repeated form in an individual over long periods of time, we tend to consider them as more or less permanent (dispositional) characteristics of the individual. We then tend to use the language of personality traits to describe the person rather than the language of emotional states. The idea of derivatives is shown in Table 4.4.

This table describes a number of conceptual languages that the psychoevolutionary theory assumes are systematically related to one another. For example, proceeding from left to right across the table, the term *fear* is part of the subjective language of emotions, as are terms like *anger, joy,* and *surprise*. The second column describes the function of each emotion from an evolutionary point of view. The function of fear is *protection*; of anger, the *destruction of a barrier* to the satisfaction of one's needs; of sadness, symbolic reintegration with a lost object in the form of *nurturance*; and for disgust, the *rejection* of a toxic substance or experience.

When an individual's emotional states persist over time or are frequently repeated, we tend to describe the individual as having a particular personality trait. Thus, repeated expressions of fear lead to the designation of someone as *timid*. Repeated expressions of anger or irritability lead to the description of someone as quarrelsome, and repeated expressions of rejection of others leads to such trait designations as *hostile* or *cruel*.

When personality traits exist in fairly extreme form, we use a new language to describe the situation: the language of personality disorders. Thus, a person who has an extreme form of quarrelsomeness (plus some other characteristics) may be diagnosed as having an antisocial personality disorder, and a person who shows an extreme form of timidity might be diagnosed as a dependent personality type. Similar parallels may be drawn for each of the major clusters of personality traits, which are in turn derived from the basic emotions.

The ego-defense language and coping style language are theorized to be ways of dealing with particular emotions. Ego defenses are unconscious, for the most part, whereas coping styles are conscious methods people use to deal with problems that generate emotions. These ideas are further elaborated in chapters 5 and 6.

In an examination of this issue (Plutchik, 1997), I gave three reasons that support the existence of a relationship among emotions, personality, and interpersonal relations: (a) there is extensive overlap of the language describing emotions and personality, (b) the circumplex model describes the interrelationship of emotions and those of personality traits very well, and (c) there is considerable overlap of functions of both emotions and traits.

TABLE 4.4
Emotions and Their Derivatives

Subjective language	Functional language	Trait language	Diagnostic language	Ego-defense language	Coping-style language
Fear	Protection	Timid	Dependent, avoidant	Repression	Suppression
Anger	Destruction	Quarrelsome	Antisocial	Displacement	Substitution
Joy	Reproduction	Sociable	Hypomanic	Reaction-formation	Reversal
Sadness	Reintegration	Gloomy	Dysthymic	Compensation	Replacement
Acceptance	Incorporation	Trusting	Histrionic	Denial	Minimization
Disgust	Rejection	Hostile	Paranoid	Projection	Fault finding
Expectation	Exploration	Controlling	Obsessive compulsive	Intellectualization	Mapping
Surprise	Orientation	Indecisive	Borderline	Regression	Help seeking

Note. From *The Psychology and Biology of Emotion*, by R. Plutchik (p. 102), 1994, New York: Harper Collins. Reprinted by permission.

FUNCTIONAL SIGNIFICANCE OF EMOTIONS AND TRAITS

The Function of Emotions

Although Darwin presented a functional view of emotions in his book, *The Expression of the Emotions in Man and Animals*, published in 1872, his ideas were largely ignored by psychologists until a decade after World War II. Since that time an evolutionary, ethological approach to emotions has become increasingly recognized, and many investigators have contributed ideas to this viewpoint (Plutchik, 1980b).

Evolutionary theory as applied to emotions posits that the natural environment creates survival problems for all organisms that must be successfully dealt with if they are to survive. Problems include appropriate responses to prey and predators, to caregivers and care solicitors, and to potential mates. From this point of view emotions may be conceptualized as basic adaptive patterns that can be identified at all phylogenetic levels. These adaptive patterns (e.g., agonistic behavior, sexual behavior, and investigative behavior) are adaptations that have been maintained in functionally equivalent form through all phylogenetic levels. Emotions are fundamentally communication and action processes in the service of individual and genetic survival. Emotional displays act as signals of intentions of future action that function to influence the interpersonal relations of the interacting individuals. By appropriate reactions to emergency events in the environment (e.g., by flight or fight), the chances of individual survival are increased (Plutchik, 1994).

Nesse (1991) described *emotions* as strategies for negotiating interpersonal relationships: "Friendship and love maintain good relationships, even through rough periods. Anger prevents exploitation. . . . Anxiety and guilt . . . motivate people to fulfill their commitments, to abide by the social contract, and to stay loyal to their friends" (p. 33).

An important illustration of the functional significance of emotions may be seen from the study of infants. From an evolutionary point of view, the newborn is most vulnerable to the dangers of the environment. This reality is the basic reason behind the various signals, displays, communication patterns, and behaviors found in immature organisms that are present at or shortly after birth. These various behaviors have effects that increase the chances of survival in the newborn by influencing the behavior of the caretakers. Because the problems of survival exist from the moment of birth, certain mechanisms must exist both in the child and the caretaker to help ensure survival. If young infants had to wait until they learned how to attract their parents' attention and support, and if the parents had to learn how to provide it, the chances of species survival would be small. Communication patterns have to work the first time they are used. From this viewpoint, emotions may be thought of in part as communication signals emitted by the infant to caretakers that help increase the chances of survival. Emotions are not disruptive, maladaptive states, but rather act to stabilize the internal state of the organism. They represent transitory adjustment reactions that function to return the organism to a stable, effective relationship with its environment when that relationship is disrupted.

A similar point is made by Dix (1991) in a discussion of parenting. Emotions, he argued, are

> barometers for relationships because they reflect parents' assessments of how well interactions . . . with children are proceeding . . . negative emotions are perturbations that realign a system . . . positive emotions motivate attunement to children, facilitate responsiveness to the children's wants and needs, and enable parents and children to coordinate their interactions to the benefit of both. (p. 19)

A final example of the functional significance of emotions may be taken from the work of ethologists who have studied primate vocalizations. For example, Seyforth, Cheney, and Marler (1980) have shown that vervet monkey alarm calls function to designate different classes of external danger related to specific types of predators: Animals on the ground respond to leopard alarms by running into trees, to eagle alarms by looking up, and to snake alarms by looking down.

These examples (see Plutchik, 1994, for an elaboration) indicate that emotional signals or displays are related to important events in the life of each animal: events such as threats, attacks, alarms, courtship, mating, social contact, isolation or separation, greetings, appeasement, dominance, submission, and play. They influence a large variety of interpersonal relations. Emotions may be conceptualized as homeostatic devices designed to maintain a relatively steady (or "normal") state in the face of interpersonal challenges.

The Function of Personality Traits

Psychoanalysts have had the most to say about the functional significance of personality traits. For example, Fenichel (1946), a major synthesizer of psychoanalytic ideas, has described character (personality) as the precipitates of instinctual conflict. In his view, the conflict of emotions leads to fixations and a "freezing" of emotional tendencies. Such a process transforms transient emotional reactions into persistent personality traits. Rapaport (1950) noted that children show their emotions in transient ways but that in later life anxiety is continuous in the anxious person, the pessimist is permanently melancholy, and the cheerful person consistently buoyant.

Another psychoanalyst, Spezzano (1993), has argued that an explicit theory of affects is embedded in psychoanalytic writing and that psychoanalysis is in fact primarily a theory of affect. Among the points he made is the idea that psychopathology is always an attempt at affect regulation. This implies that psychopathology, which generally means in this context character neuroses or personality disorders, has a function: to regulate interpersonal relations. We use love to keep others invested in our personal agendas. We use intimidation to inhibit interactions that would be painful or threatening or to gain power over others. Psychoanalytic interpretation is concerned with the patient's affects, particularly with how patients deceive themselves about their own affects. Self-deception has an obvious function, that is, to mitigate the pain of recognizing our own limitations and our own anxieties.

Nonpsychoanalytic writers also have contributed to the concept of the functional value of personality traits. Millon (1994), for example, has argued that *personality* refers to an individual's lifelong style of relating to others, to coping with problems, and to expressing emotions. These relatively stable patterns of thinking and interacting have the overall function of using, controlling, or adapting to external forces. The expression of personality traits tends to evoke reciprocal and often predictable responses from others that influence whether an individual's problems decrease or stabilize.

Millon (1994) has implied that chronic emotional patterns (i.e., personality traits) such as anxiousness, depression, or self-criticism serve a variety of goals: they produce such secondary gains as eliciting nurturance from others; they excuse the avoidance of responsibilities; they rationalize poor performance; or they justify the expression of anger toward others. He raised the question of what turns a transient emotion into a chronic personality trait and suggested that this occurs because "the range of experiences to which people are exposed throughout their lives is both limited and repetitive" (p. 287).

When this analysis is applied to chronic sadness or melancholy as a trait, it is generally recognized that the most common precipitating event for sadness is a loss of something or someone important to the individual. This loss often results in characteristic facial expressions and vocalizations (such as crying or distress signals). Such distress signals typically produce an empathic response in adults who are exposed to them, a feeling often followed by some attempt at helpful actions. Chronic depression as a trait thus may be considered to be an extreme and persistent distress signal that continually functions to solicit help from others. This may be true regardless of whether the individual is aware of this function.

Cantor and Harlow (1994) suggested that the function of the trait of social anxiety is to solve the problem of insecurity by allowing an individual to accept the lead of other people in social situations. People with social anxiety use their anxiety to avoid attention from others, which in turn removes performance pressure.

An alternative analysis of the function of anxiousness as a trait is given by Trower and Gilbert (1989). They pointed out that most mammals and especially primates live in social groups that are organized and stabilized by means of dominance hierarchies. The fact that each individual in a group enacts a role that defines his or her position within the hierarchy functions to maintain cohesiveness of the group. If someone else of higher dominance status threatens another group member, escape from the group is rarely possible because survival generally depends on the group's support. The result is usually some form of submissive ritual or gesture that allows the threatened individual to remain in the group. Social anxiety may have evolved as a method for maintaining group cohesion. According to this hypothesis, the socially anxious person has an appraisal and coping style that is particularly sensitive to threats and loss of status in a hostile and competitive world.

To take one final example of the function of a personality trait, we may consider the trait of aggressiveness. Novaco (1976) has listed a number of useful functions of aggressiveness in humans. First, it increases the intensity with which we act to accomplish our goals. Aggressiveness is associated with a sense of power that may facilitate the attainment of personal goals. Second, aggressive individuals tend to intimidate others and give the impression of a strong, threatening presence. Aggressive expressions often increase a person's ability to gain resources and survive in the face of threat. Third, aggressiveness reduces feelings of vulnerability and may even prevent feelings of helplessness from reaching levels of conscious awareness. Fourth, aggressive individuals are often central in establishing a dominance or hierarchical structure within a group. Such a social structure acts to stabilize relations among members of a group and thus maintains group cohesion, a property that contributes to the survival of group members. These various ideas suggest that both emotions and personality traits have a similar function, that is, to regulate social relations. Traits are fundamentally persistent expressions of emotional tendencies and are in essence derived from them.

In the following two chapters several other conceptual domains are described that are related to emotions. The first of these is the domain of personality disorders, and the second is the domain of ego defenses.

A DEFINITION OF EMOTION

Given that emotions are complex, feedback systems, a simple definition of the concept of emotion can hardly be adequate. The kind of definition that is frequently seen in textbooks stating that emotions have three components (subjective feelings, overt behavior, and physiological changes) is hardly an adequate description of the complexities described in this and the previous chapters.

Another way to define emotions is to list their major properties.

1. Emotions are communication and survival mechanisms based on evolutionary adaptations. This is simply a recognition that emotions increase the chances of individual survival through appropriate reactions to adversities in the environment (e.g., by fight or flight). Emotional displays also act as signals of intentions of future actions.

2. Emotions have a genetic base. This is a recognition that neither humans nor animals teach their infants and children how to express emotion, although it is possible for individuals to learn how to inhibit the expression of emotions. Considerable evidence now indicates that genetic predispositions underlie emotional expressions.

3. Emotions are complex chains of events with stabilizing negative feedback loops that attempt to produce some level of behavioral homeostasis. The chain of events includes the cognitive elements in emotion, as well as the impulses to action and the inhibiting forces that operate.

4. There is a small number of basic, primary, or prototype emotions, and all others are mixtures, compounds, or blends of the primary emotions. This fact leads to the recognition of the basic interrelations between emotions and personality traits. Personality traits are seen as compromise formations based on conflicts and the repeated mixing of basic emotions.

5. The relations among emotions can be represented by a three-dimensional structural model. In this model, the vertical dimension represents the intensity of emotions, the circle or circumplex defines the degree of similarity of the primary emotion dimensions, and polarity is represented by opposite emotions on the emotion circle.

6. Emotions are hypothetical constructs whose existence and properties are determined by various indirect lines of evidence. We are never certain of exactly what emotion someone else has because of the complex nature of emotions and because more than one emotion may occur at the same time. Any given display of emotion may reflect such complex states as approach and avoidance, attack and flight, sex and aggression, or fear and pleasure. We are often not even certain of our own emotions.

7. Emotions are related to a number of derivative conceptual

domains, such as personality traits, personality disorders, ego defenses, and coping styles.

Another way of simply stating the characteristics of emotions is as follows: Emotions are *universal* (in the sense of being part of the repertoire of all living things). Emotions are *useful* in the sense that they communicate possibilities of danger, threat, or pleasure and therefore influence the behavior of others. Emotions are usually *mixed*, simply because lots of important things are usually going on at the same time. Certain emotions are *primary* or basic (just as there are primary colors), and all other emotions are secondary mixtures or blends. Emotions are expressed in many *indirect* ways, for example, through sports, chess, parachute jumping, music, dance, poetry, art, or migraine headaches, to name a few. Emotions act as *amplifiers* or energizers of behavior. When emotions become involved, an insult becomes the basis for revenge, and a flirtation the basis for a rape. Finally, emotions are not always readily accessible to the individual who is experiencing the emotion. Defenses are self-protective mental mechanisms that *hide* emotions from the person experiencing them. Finally, it is possible to describe emotions within a broad, evolutionary context.

AN EVOLUTIONARY DEFINITION OF EMOTIONS

From an evolutionary point of view, one can conceptualize emotions as certain types of adaptive behaviors that can be identified in lower animals as well as in humans. These adaptive patterns have evolved to deal with basic survival issues in all organisms, such as dealing with prey and predator, potential mate and stranger, nourishing objects and toxins. Such patterns involve approach or avoidance reactions, fight and flight reactions, attachment and loss reactions, and riddance or ejection reactions. The evolutionary perspective suggests that these patterns are the prototypes of what are called emotions in higher animals and in humans. These interactional patterns of adaptation may be thought of as the prototypes of fear and anger, acceptance and disgust, and joy and sadness. The subjective feelings usually identified as emotions are a relatively late evolutionary development and should not be used as the only or major criterion of the presence of an emotional state. Emotions are complex, interactional adaptations and must therefore have a variety of expressive forms, each of which can be used to infer properties of the underlying state. Even though the details of the adaptive processes vary among different animals, species, and phyla, depending on the nature of the environment and genetics, the function of each pattern of adaptation has remained unchanged throughout all phylogenetic levels. From the evolutionary point of view emotions are patterns of adaptation that increase the chances of individual and genetic survival.

5

EMOTIONS AND PERSONALITY DISORDERS

The pain of acute or chronic negative affect lies at the heart of those patterns of emotionality now termed the affective and personality disorders.

—M. J. Mahoney

According to the psychoevolutionary theory of emotion, and particularly the derivatives model, personality disorders are extreme expressions of certain personality traits. The eight primary emotions are associated conceptually with certain families of personality traits (such as shyness, quarrelsomeness, and gloominess). When a trait is expressed in an extreme form, we tend to label the individual possessing that trait by a diagnostic term (e.g., *dependent*, *antisocial*, or *dysthymic*). Other characteristics are also included in a diagnosis of personality disorder, but extreme forms of emotions and traits are the basic elements. The theory provides a series of hypotheses about the connections among these three domains.

If these hypotheses are plausible, then one might expect personality disorders to have a circumplex structure similar to those that apply to personality and emotions. This chapter provides a review of the empirical literature on the comorbidity of personality disorders, which suggests that a circumplex is an appropriate description of the similarity relations of such disorders. Research shows the applicability of the circumplex to personality disorders, and some of the implications of this view are explored.

The psychoevolutionary theory of emotion makes a number of predictions and generates a number of hypotheses. For example, the theory predicts a circumplex or circular ordering of similarity of emotion concepts. This has been demonstrated empirically by Plutchik (1980a), Russell (1989), G. A. Fisher et al. (1985), and others.

One of the hypotheses generated by the theory is that personality traits should also have a circumplex structure, and there is much supporting evidence for this idea (see Plutchik & Conte, 1997). Another derivative hypothesis is that personality disorders are extreme forms of certain personality traits and should therefore have a similar circumplex structure. This hypothesis applies only to the personality disorders and not to psychiatric diagnoses in general.

A number of studies have examined the degree to which personality disorder diagnoses can be related to one another by means of a circumplex structure. In this chapter I review some of those studies.

THE RELATION BETWEEN EMOTIONS AND
PERSONALITY DISORDERS

The 4th edition of the *Diagnostic and Statistical Manual of Mental Disorders (DSM–IV)* identifies a *personality disorder* as

> an enduring pattern of inner experience and behavior that deviates markedly from the expectations of the individual's culture, is pervasive and inflexible, has an onset in adolescence or early adulthood, is stable over time, and leads to distress or impairment. (American Psychiatric Association, 1994, p. 629)

I hypothesize that the personality disorders that have been identified by psychiatrists are extreme forms of personality traits, which are in turn related to the basic emotions. An examination of several personality disorders illustrates these ideas.

The emotion of *fear* is a highly adaptive state that functions to protect an individual from danger by stimulating withdrawal and escape. When states of fear are persistent in an individual, such patterns of behavior are recognized as personality traits and are described with the labels *shy*, *timid*, *withdrawn*, or *submissive*. Labels of this sort do not necessarily imply abnormality, but they are usually considered to be part of the broad spectrum of personality traits seen in any large population. If, however, such personality traits become extreme and function as a dominant aspect of a person's way of relating to other people, clinicians may be inclined to use a diagnostic term taken from the system of personality disorders to describe the trait. Such an individual might be diagnosed as *dependent*, *avoidant*, or *passive*.

Similarly, the emotion of *anger* is a highly adaptive state that functions to stimulate attacks on barriers to the satisfaction of an individual's

TABLE 5.1
Hypotheses About the Connections Between Emotional Feelings, Personality Traits, and Personality Disorder Diagnosis

Emotion	Personality trait	Personality disorder
Fear	Shy, timid, nervous	Dependent, avoidant
Anger	Quarrelsome, grouchy, critical, sarcastic	Antisocial, narcissistic
Sadness	Gloomy, apathetic, lonely	Dysthymia
Joy	Sociable, generous, sympathetic	Hypomania, mania
Disgust	Hostile, scornful, rebellious, critical	Paranoid
Acceptance	Trustful, tolerant, contented	Histrionic
Expectation	Curious, orderly, controlling	Obsessive–compulsive
Surprise	Indecisive, impulsive	Borderline

needs. When states of anger occur frequently in an individual, such patterns of behavior are recognized as personality traits and are described by such labels as *quarrelsome, grouchy, critical,* or *sarcastic.* Labels of this sort do not necessarily imply abnormality, but they are considered to be part of the broad spectrum of personality traits seen in any large population. If, however, such personality traits become extreme and function as a dominant aspect of a person's way of relating to other people, clinicians tend to describe the state using a diagnostic term taken from the system of personality disorders; in this case, such terms as *antisocial* or *narcissistic* might seem appropriate.

The same reasoning may be applied to each of the eight basic emotions. *Sadness* becomes associated with the traits of *gloominess, apathy,* or *loneliness* and in an extreme form with *dysthymia. Joy* is related to *sociability, generosity,* or *sympathy* and in an extreme form to *hypomania* or *mania. Disgust* is connected to the traits of *hostility, scornfulness,* or *defiance* and in an extreme form to the diagnosis of *paranoia. Acceptance* is associated with the traits of *trustfulness, tolerance,* and *gullibility,* and in extreme forms it is related to the diagnosis of *histrionic.* The emotion of *expectation* or *interest* is related to the traits of *curiosity, orderliness,* and *control,* but in extreme form it may be diagnosed as *obsessive–compulsive.* Finally, the emotion of *surprise* may be related to the personality traits of *indecisiveness* or *impulsivity* and to the diagnosis of *borderline personality disorder.* It should be noted that these suggestions are in the nature of hypotheses, and the reader may disagree with one or more of the proposed connections. One justification for these suggestions is that they form part of a large nomological network, which taken together has good explanatory power and has implications for research and clinical theory. These hypotheses are summarized in Table 5.1.

Similar ideas have been proposed by others. For example, Leary and Coffey (1955) have suggested that the traits of being cooperative and overly agreeable are associated with the hysterical personality disorder; that being trustful and dependent are associated with the phobic personality disorder; that modest, self-punishing traits are associated with the obsessive personality disorder; that skeptical, distrustful traits are connected with the schizoid personality disorder; and that critical, aggressive traits are part of the psychopathic personality disorder. In 1982, Wiggins suggested a similar set of relations between personality traits and personality disorders, and these ideas were further elaborated by Kiesler (1986) and Benjamin (1993). Table 5.2 summarizes these ideas.

There is only limited agreement among these writers, but this may be because our conceptions of personality disorders have changed considerably over the past 40 years. The key idea is that all schemas recognize a connection between personality traits and personality disorders.

THE PROBLEM OF COMORBIDITY

Many psychiatric patients appear to experience a number of psychiatric disorders simultaneously. The term *comorbidity* was introduced to characterize this situation.

Empirical Studies

Many researchers have found evidence of such comorbidity. For example, in a study of 231 consecutive patient admissions, Herpertz, Steinmeyer, and Sass (1994) found that 41% had more than one personality disorder diagnosis according to *DSM–III–R* (American Psychiatric Association, 1987). Labouvie, Miller, Langenbucher, and Morgenstern (1997) reported extensive overlap between Axis I and personality disorder diagnoses in a sample of 366 substance abusers. Marshall (1996) provided a summary of the literature showing comorbidity between panic disorder, social phobia, depression, and dependent and avoidant personality disorders.

In a study of 40 patients with obsessive–compulsive disorder, most were also found to have another Axis II diagnosis, but with an interesting variation in the frequency of each personality disorder. The comorbidity figures reported were as follows: avoidant (52%), dependent (40%), histrionic (20%), paranoid (20%), narcissistic (8%), schizotypal (5%), and passive–aggressive (5%). In addition, almost 6 out of 10 of the patients had two or more personality disorder diagnoses (Rodriguez Torres & Del Porto, 1995). These observations suggest that comorbidity is not an all-or-nothing phenomenon but can exist in degrees. The same point was made by Corruble, Ginestet, and Guelfi (1996), who reported on the basis of an extensive review of the literature that 20–50% of inpatients and 50–85% of outpatients with a current major depressive disorder have an associated personality disorder. Those with such personality disorders are likely to be

TABLE 5.2
Hypothesized Relations Between Personality Traits and Personality Disorders

Traits	Personality Disorder
Leary and Coffey (1955)	
Cooperative, overly agreeable	Hysterical
Trustful, dependent	Phobic
Modest, self-punishing	Obsessive
Skeptical, distrustful	Schizoid
Critical, aggressive	Psychopathic
Wiggins (1982)	
Ambitious, dominant	Compulsive
Warm, agreeable	Histrionic
Unassuming, ingenious	Dependent
Lazy, submissive	Passive–aggressive
Aloof, introverted	Schizoid
Cold, quarrelsome	Paranoid
Arrogant, calculating	Narcissistic
Kiesler (1986)	
Dominant, assured	Narcissistic
Exhibitionistic, sociable	Histrionic, narcissistic
Friendly, warm	Borderline
Trusting, deferent	Borderline
Submissive, unassured	Avoidant, dependent
Inhibited, detached	Schizoid, schizotypal
Hostile, cold	Paranoid, antisocial
Mistrusting, competitive	Paranoid, schizotypal
Benjamin (1993)	
Wall off, ignore, self-neglect	Schizoid
Separate, protect, blame, attack	Paranoid
Recoil, self-neglect	Schizotypal
Separate, blame, ignore	Antisocial
Trust, affirm, protect, blame, attack, self-attack, self-neglect	Borderline
Trust, wall off, protect, blame, self-attack	Histrionic
Separate, protect, blame, attack, ignore, self-blame, self-neglect	Narcissistic
Sulk, recoil, wall off, blame, self-control, self-blame	Avoidant
Trust, submit, sulk, self-blame, ignore, self-control, self-blame, self-neglect	Obsessive–compulsive

Note. From "Personality Disorders and the Interpersonal Circumplex," by T. A. Widiger and S. Hagemoser, in *Circumplex Models of Personality and Emotions*, edited by R. Plutchik and H. R. Conte, 1997, pp. 301, 303, 305, 310, Washington, DC: American Psychological Association. Copyright 1997 by American Psychological Association. Reprinted by permission.

called borderline in about 30% of the cases, histrionic in about 20% of the cases, antisocial in about 10% of the cases, and narcissistic in less than 5%. Again, comorbidity is a matter of degree.

In a study of 404 adult outpatients with major depression, Fava et al. (1996) found that most had one or more comorbid diagnoses of avoidant, histrionic, narcissistic, and borderline disorders. Klein, Lewinsohn, and

Seeley (1996) studied a sample of 1,709 adolescents and found that those with hypomanic traits were also more likely to attempt suicide, have recurrent major depression, and show disruptive behavior. Spalletta, Troisi, Saracco, Ciani, and Pasini (1996) found that almost half of the patients who had dysthymia also had a personality disorder.

Grilo, Becker, Fehon, Edell, and McGlashan (1996) reported that adolescent patients with co-existing conduct and substance use disorders were likely to have a comorbid borderline personality disorder as well. Okasha et al. (1996) reported comorbidity between borderline personality disorder and somatoform disorder, as well as between generalized anxiety disorder and avoidant personality disorder.

In a large group of outpatients, those with dependent personality disorder were likely to have comorbid social phobia and borderline as well as histrionic traits (Reich, 1996). Similarly, Loranger (1996) reported that dependent patients were more likely than those with other personality disorders to have major depression and bipolar disorder. In a sample of 200 patients, Skodal et al. (1995) found that panic disorder was associated with dependent, borderline, and avoidant personality disorders and that social phobia was associated with avoidant personality disorder.

Implications

How should comorbidities be interpreted? Plutchik and Van Praag (1998) have pointed out that anxiety, depression, aggression, impulsivity, and suicidality are not distinct and unrelated entities; there is considerable comorbidity among these and other states. Of interest is that such comorbidity shows a special pattern, one that might be called a *similarity structure*. For example, anxiety and depression, whether considered as emotions or as diagnoses, are often found together in the same individuals. When medications reduce one of these symptoms in a patient, there is a high probability that the other will also be reduced. Such high comorbidity is less likely to be found between anxiety and aggression or between depression and impulsivity. The evidence suggests the existence of degrees of comorbidity and even the possibility of negative comorbidity. This would mean that having one particular personality disorder decreases the likelihood of having a different specific one.

If the above conclusions are valid, then the idea of degrees of comorbidity can be represented by a *circumplex*—a circular order of elements that expresses certain types of relations. These include the relations of similarity and polarity. If the elements being considered vary in degree of similarity to one another (as do emotions, personality traits, and diagnoses) and show polarities (such as joy vs. sorrow, dominance vs. submission, antisocial vs. avoidant behavior), then a circle as an analog model may be used to represent these relations. Statistically, a set of correlations among these elements should show systematic increases and decreases in the degree of correlation between the elements, depending on their degree of conceptual closeness (Plutchik, 1997).

Carson (1996) proposed a similar view of the circumplex as a seamless set of elements in a circle whose borders blend and interpenetrate. He questioned the persistent tendency to reify the DSM taxonomic system in categorical terms and suggested that the categories reflect a desire for "a precision we do not have and cannot get" (p. 243).

Carson cited the chairperson and research coordinator of the DSM–IV Task Force (Frances, Widiger, & Fyer, 1990), who have noted that the occurrence of comorbidities is largely a function of the number of diagnostic categories that are assumed to exist. A large number of diagnostic categories leads to a large number of comorbidities, many of which are artifacts of the system. An example that Carson cited is the proposed diagnosis of "double depression," which refers to the co-occurrence of mild chronic plus major depressive features (Keller & Shapiro, 1982). He concluded that clinical practice is not helped by placing patients into arbitrary and overlapping diagnostic categories.

Beginning in the 1970s, researchers have attempted to apply the circumplex concept to a variety of domains including emotions, personality traits, and personality disorders. Much of this work is reviewed in the book *Circumplex Models of Personality and Emotions* (Plutchik & Conte, 1997).

AN EMPIRICAL CIRCUMPLEX OF PERSONALITY DISORDERS

Diagnostic Clusters

Over the years a number of attempts have been made to describe the relations among the personality disorders by means of a circumplex. One of the problems has been the lack of a consistent terminology for personality disorders as described in the DSM series. For example, DSM–II (1968) listed 10 personality disorders; 3 of them (*explosive*, *asthenic*, and *inadequate*) were later dropped. Plutchik and Platman (1977) studied the remaining 7 —*compulsive, cyclothymic, hysterical, paranoid, passive–aggressive, schizoid*, and *sociopathic*—for degree of similarity. To these they added one more term: *well-adjusted*.

Twenty psychiatrists were asked to think of patients who had been diagnosed with each of the labels and to select emotion words (such as *gloomy, sociable*, or *impulsive*) that described each patient. The psychiatrists' choices were scored in terms of the eight basic affect dimensions of the *Emotions Profile Index* (Plutchik & Kellerman, 1974). This procedure provided an emotion profile for each diagnosis.

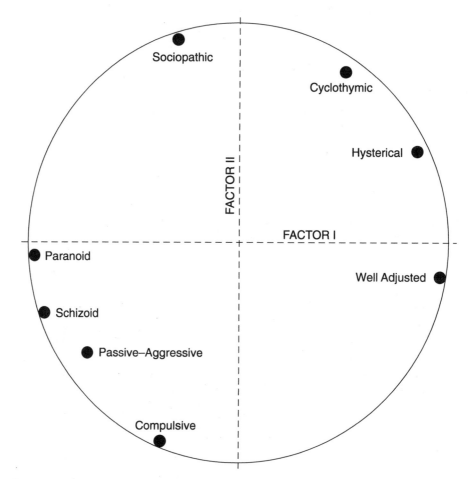

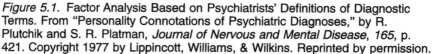

Figure 5.1. Factor Analysis Based on Psychiatrists' Definitions of Diagnostic Terms. From "Personality Connotations of Psychiatric Diagnoses," by R. Plutchik and S. R. Platman, *Journal of Nervous and Mental Disease, 165,* p. 421. Copyright 1977 by Lippincott, Williams, & Wilkins. Reprinted by permission.

These profiles were then intercorrelated for all possible pairs of diagnoses. The matrix of intercorrelations was then factor analyzed using the principal-components method, and it was found that the first two factors accounted for 91% of the variance. The factor loadings for each diagnosis were plotted using the first two axes, which resulted in the circumplex shown in Figure 5.1.

This figure indicates that personality disorders fit into a circumplex structure, with *cyclothymic* opposite *compulsive, hysterical* opposite *schizoid,* and *well-adjusted* opposite *paranoid.* Some spaces are found that could represent other personality disorders, not defined in *DSM–II* but which appear in the third edition of the *DSM (DSM–III;* American Psychiatric Association, 1980) and *DSM–IV.* It is important to emphasize that this circular

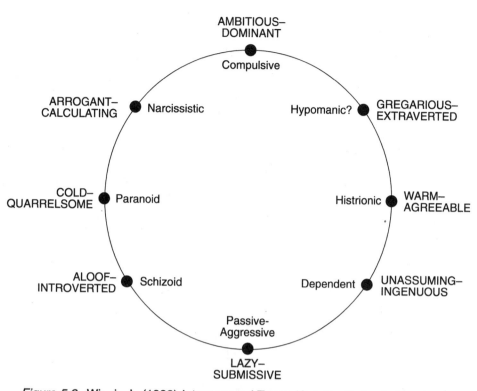

Figure 5.2. Wiggins's (1982) Interpersonal Types (Outside Perimeter) and Corresponding Diagnoses (Inside Perimeter). From "Structural Approaches to Classification," by R. K. Blashfield, in *Contemporary Directions in Psychopathology: Toward the* DSM–IV (p. 334), edited by T. Millon and G. L. Klerman, New York: Guilford Press. Copyright 1986 by the Guilford Press. Adapted with permission.

configuration of diagnostic labels is not a sign of psychiatrists' fuzzy ideas about diagnoses; it reflects instead the clear recognition of the overlap of traits associated with each diagnosis. Another way to conceptualize this idea is that diagnostic labels represent implicit probability estimates of the likelihood of observing certain clusters of traits.

Another early attempt to provide a circumplex structure for the personality disorders was made by Blashfield (1986) and was based on Wiggins's (1982) interpersonal types. This is shown in Figure 5.2. Wiggins listed eight personality disorders and arranged them at equal distances around the perimeter of a circle on theoretical (rather than empirical) grounds. In this circumplex, *histrionic* is opposite *paranoid*, *narcissistic* is opposite *dependent*, and *schizoid* is opposite *hypomanic*. The term *hypomanic* was not listed in *DSM–II* or *DSM–III*, but Wiggins believed that the *gregarious–extraverted* personality dimension in its extreme form should lead to the hypomanic personality disorder.

As stated earlier, one of the problems involved in studying personality disorders is the changing terminology from one *DSM* edition to another. In addition, children have been labeled with somewhat different terms than have adults. In *DSM–III*, for example, children are said to have *schizoid, avoidant, conduct, oppositional,* or *identity* disorders, whereas adults may have any one or more of the 11 personality disorders: *paranoid, schizoid, schizotypal, histrionic, narcissistic, antisocial, borderline, avoidant, dependent, compulsive,* or *passive–aggressive.*

A study carried out with one of my colleagues provided data that could be used to establish an initial approximation to a circumplex order for diagnoses in preadolescent psychiatric patients (Pfeffer & Plutchik, 1989). We obtained *DSM–III–R* diagnoses for 106 preadolescent psychiatric inpatients, 101 preadolescent psychiatric outpatients, and 101 nonpatient preadolescents. We found that children with a diagnosis such as conduct disorder were also given other diagnoses with varying frequencies. For example, of those 66 children who were diagnosed as having a conduct disorder, 51% were also diagnosed as having a borderline personality disorder, 39% as having a specific development disorder, 23% as having an attention deficit disorder, and 21% as having a dysthymic disorder. The same type of overlap analyses was done for each disorder. The approximation to a circumplex structure is shown in Figure 5.3. This model is meant to represent the relative, not absolute, positions on a similarity scale of the different diagnoses. Such a circumplex reveals which diagnoses are most difficult to differentiate from one another, as well as those that are easy to distinguish.

In another study designed to apply the circumplex idea to personality disorders, Plutchik and Conte (1997) used a modified paired comparison procedure. We asked 16 experienced clinicians to rate the degree of similarity or dissimilarity of the 11 *DSM–III–R* Axis II personality disorders. To this list we added three other categories: sadistic, self-defeating, and dysthymic personality disorders. (This latter disorder simply represents an expression of the idea that many patients have pervasive patterns of depressive cognitions and behaviors that are, in fact, personality traits. Benjamin, 1993, agreed with this idea and has described the characteristics of a new category, which she called *depressive personality disorder.*)

When the clinicians made their similarity–dissimilarity judgments, they were not given single diagnostic labels (e.g., *histrionic, paranoid,* or *narcissistic*) because of the ambiguities associated with such labels. Instead a brief descriptive paragraph was written for each personality diagnosis based explicitly on the criteria given in *DSM–III–R.* A separate group of clinicians rated the adequacy of the descriptions, and a few changes were made to increase the validity of the descriptions. The judges were asked to compare the written descriptions of the personality disorders for similarity on a scale ranging from +3 (the two descriptions are identical in meaning) to −3 (the two descriptions are opposite in meaning), with 0

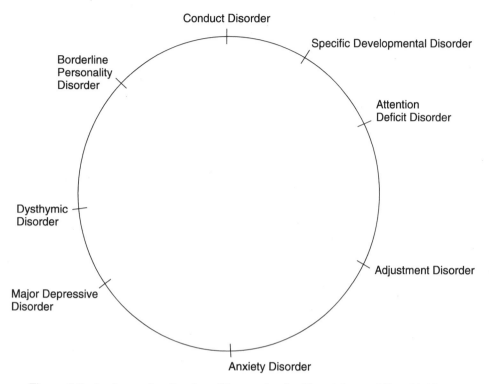

Figure 5.3. An Approximation to a Circumplex for Preadolescent Psychiatric Disorders Based on a Confusion Matrix. From "Co-Occurrence of Psychiatric Disorders in Child Psychiatric Patients and Nonpatients: A Circumplex Model," by C. R. Pfeffer and R. Plutchik, 1989, *Comprehensive Psychiatry, 30,* p. 280. Copyright 1989 by W. B. Saunders Company. Reprinted with permission.

indicating that there is no relation between the descriptions. The ratings were transformed into angular placements on a circle, with results as shown in Figure 5.4 (the method of transformation is described in detail in Conte & Plutchik, 1981).

The locations of the diagnoses around the circumplex may be compared to the traditional but arbitrary clusters that have been proposed in *DSM–III.* The first cluster includes *paranoid, schizoid,* and *schizotypical* diagnoses, applied to individuals who often appear "odd" or eccentric. The second cluster includes *borderline, narcissistic, histrionic,* and *antisocial* diagnoses. Individuals with such diagnoses are said to appear dramatic or erratic. The third cluster includes *dependent, compulsive, avoidant,* and *passive–aggressive* diagnoses. Individuals with these disorders often appear anxious. As a convenient shorthand, these clusters have been referred to as the *eccentric,* the *erratic,* and the *anxious* groups.

Examination of Figure 5.4 shows that *paranoid, schizotypical,* and *schizoid* are sequential and clearly form the eccentric cluster, although *compulsive–obsessive* appears to be also part of the eccentric cluster and has features

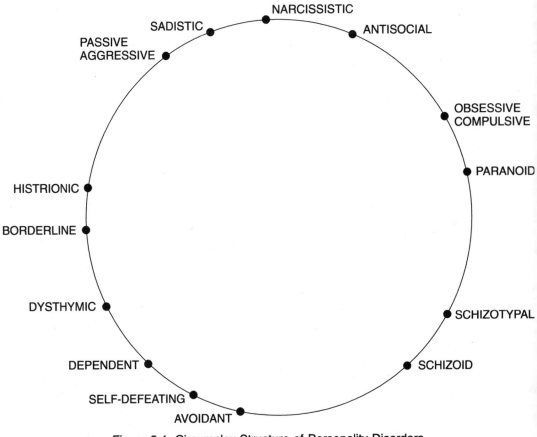

Figure 5.4. Circumplex Structure of Personality Disorders.

that are similar to those of the *paranoid* diagnoses. The second cluster, the dramatic grouping, is not confirmed empirically. *Narcissistic* and *antisocial* are found to be similar and are related to the proposed *sadistic* diagnosis. *Passive–aggressive* is also found to be part of this grouping. This cluster seems to be centered around aspects of aggression and might properly be labeled the *aggressive* cluster.

The traditional anxious cluster purportedly consisting of *avoidant, dependent, obsessive–compulsive,* and *passive–aggressive* is not confirmed. The empirical locations suggest that the *avoidant* and *dependent* diagnoses are highly similar to one another and are similar to the *self-defeating* and *dysthymic* disorders. This modified version of the anxious cluster should be called the *anxious–depressed cluster* instead.

Of some interest is that the *histrionic* and *borderline* diagnoses are near each other on the circumplex and are also near the dysthymic diagnosis. They probably could be fit into the *anxious–depressed* cluster. The presence of strong features of both anxiety and depression in these two diagnoses supports this placement.

One may think of these findings shown in Figure 5.4 as providing a measure of the degree of overlap of personality disorders. Diagnoses that are close on the circumplex are likely to be confused, whereas those that are further apart are rarely confused.

The modified method of paired comparisons used in this study has revealed an empirical circumplex for the personality disorders. It shows the traditional clusters to some degree but with some important differences. The so-called *erratic cluster* seems clearly to be related to problems of handling aggression. The *anxious cluster* includes self-defeating personality and dysthymic personality, even though dysthymic is not included in Axis II. This cluster might be called the *anxious–depressed cluster*. Emotions appear to be related to all of the personality disorders.

These findings help demonstrate that some degree of comorbidity exists for all personality disorders and that there is a gradual transition from one personality disorder to another in terms of similarity. Strictly speaking, this implies that clusters are somewhat arbitrary and are based on arbitrary selection of boundaries. The circumplex concept implies that all personality disorders, those that are now recognized and those that may be clinically labeled in the future, can be represented by placements on a circle varying in degree of closeness.

Table 5.3 helps explain the partially arbitrary nature of the personality disorders; it compares the labels given for personality disorders in the different *DSM* editions, as well as in a recent psychoanalytically oriented listing. A number of the diagnostic labels have changed over time, and the definitions themselves have been modified as well. There is no reason to believe that this process of addition and subtraction of terms and redefinitions will not continue into the future. It is likely that this process is a

TABLE 5.3
Different Proposed Lists of Personality Disorders

DSM–II (1967)	DSM–III (1980)	DSM–III–R (1987)	DSM–IV (1994)	Psycho-analytic (Akhtar, 1992)
Paranoid	Paranoid	Paranoid	Paranoid	Paranoid
Schizoid	Schizoid	Schizoid	Schizoid	Schizoid
Passive–aggressive	Schizotypal	Schizotypal	Schizotypal	Schizotypal
Compulsive	Compulsive	Obsessive–compulsive	Obsessive–compulsive	Obsessive
Hysterical	Histrionic	Histrionic	Histrionic	Hysterical
Cyclothymic	Narcissistic	Narcissistic	Narcissistic	Narcissistic
Sociopathic	Antisocial	Antisocial	Antisocial	Antisocial
Explosive	Avoidant	Avoidant	Avoidant	Phobic
Asthenic	Dependent	Dependent	Dependent	Masochistic
Inadequate	Borderline	Borderline	Borderline	Borderline
	Passive–aggressive	Passive–aggressive		Hypomanic
		Sadistic		Infantile
		Self-defeating		As-if

reflection of the circumplex structure of personality disorders and the inevitable overlaps of meaning that occur. Some version of a "depressive" or "dysthymic" personality disorder as well as a "hypomanic" disorder is likely to be incorporated into the personality disorder circumplex.

Table 5.4 represents a summary of nine circumplex models that have been applied to personality disorders. In each case, different methods of data acquisition and different analyses, judges, and patient samples were used. The table lists the relative sequence of personality disorders around the circumplex. The estimate of the exact angular location of each diagnosis was based on the actual published figures.

Despite the differences in method, many commonalities may be seen. Starting with paranoid as an arbitrary reference point, almost all studies have found that narcissistic and antisocial diagnoses are close to it on the circumplex; borderline is usually found somewhere in the middle of the list, whereas dependent, self-defeating, and avoidant are generally found near the schizoid or schizotypal diagnoses. For example, narcissistic has a mean location of 45°; histrionic has a mean location of 117°; and schizoid has a mean location of 295°. Despite some differences among studies, there appears to be good agreement on the sector of the circumplex in which each diagnosis is located. These findings support the value of a circumplex analysis of personality disorder diagnoses and demonstrate both the similarity and polarity structure of such diagnoses.

Implications

The following list summarizes some of the ideas that have been presented thus far concerning the circumplex for personality disorders:

1. There is now considerable evidence based on different methods and patient populations that personality disorders vary in degree of similarity to one another and show polarities as well. These facts can be best described by means of a circumplex.
2. The exact number of personality disorders as well as the most appropriate ways of labeling and defining them are still a matter of controversy. The controversies are largely a function of how one chooses to group the elements of overlapping categories. Changes will probably continue to be made in the future.
3. The existence of overlapping categories is one of the reasons that most patients are given several personality disorder diagnoses. This is also the reason for the relatively low reliability of diagnoses in the personality disorder domain.
4. It is evident that degree of conflict within the individual is

TABLE 5.4
A Summary of Angular Circumplex Locations of Personality Disorders

Plutchik and Platman (1977)	Angle (degrees)	Wiggins (1982)	Angle (degrees)
Paranoid	0	Paranoid	0
Sociopathic	82	Narcissistic	45
Cyclothymic	130	Compulsive	90
Histrionic	156	Hypomanic	140
Well-adjusted	187	Histrionic	180
Compulsive	283	Dependent	220
Passive–aggressive	320	Passive–aggressive	270
Schizoid	340	Schizoid	315

Plutchik and Conte (1985)	Angle (degrees)	Millon (1987)	Angle (degrees)
Paranoid	0	Paranoid	0
Antisocial	40	Narcissistic	27
Narcissistic	53	Histrionic	58
Borderline	65	Passive–aggressive	81
Histrionic	115	Borderline	103
Well-adjusted	180	Self-defeating	128
Dependent	216	Dependent	153
Compulsive	300	Avoidant	193
Avoidant	327	Schizotypal	221
Passive–aggressive	330	Schizoid	245
Schizotypal	333	Compulsive	275
Schizoid	335	Aggressive	305
Antisocial	335		

Romney and Bynner (1989)	Angle (degrees)	Pincus and Wiggins (1990)	Angle (degrees)
Paranoid	0	Paranoid	0
Narcissistic	32	Antisocial	22
Compulsive	90	Narcissistic	78
Hypomanic	147	Histrionic	106
Histrionic	180	Dependent	236
Dependent	203	Avoidant	274
Passive–aggressive	270	Schizoid	310
Schizoid	330		

Sim and Romney (1990)	Angle (degrees)	Strack, Lorr, and Campbell (1990)	Angle (degrees)
Paranoid	0	Paranoid	0
Narcissistic	12	Narcissistic	30
Histrionic	40	Aggressive	40
Hypomanic	54	Histrionic	60
Compulsive	112	Antisocial	70
Dependent	172	Passive–aggressive	104
Borderline	185	Borderline	150
Schizotypal	202	Self-defeating	190
Avoidant	233	Avoidant	210
Schizoid	254	Schizotypal	211
Passive–aggressive	281	Schizoid	232
Antisocial	350	Dependent	240
Compulsive	306		

TABLE 5.4 (Continued)

Plutchik and Conte (1994)	Angle (degrees)
Paranoid	0
Obsessive–compulsive	20
Antisocial	60
Narcissistic	85
Sadistic	102
Passive–aggressive	117
Histrionic	160
Borderline	170
Dysthymic	192
Dependent	210
Self-defeating	225
Avoidant	240
Schizoid	292
Schizotypal	312

From "The Circumplex as a General Model of the Structure of Emotions and Personality," by R. Plutchik, in *Circumplex Models of Personality and Emotions*, edited by R. Plutchik and H. R. Conte, 1997, p. 36, Washington, DC: American Psychological Association. Copyright 1997 by American Psychological Association. Reprinted by permission.

a function of how diverse or opposed his personality diagnoses are. This may, in fact, be an indirect way of measuring conflict.

5. It is apparent that emotions are intimately involved in personality disorders. Anger and aggression are central to such disorders as antisocial and paranoid personality disorders, whereas anxiety and depression are central to avoidant, dependent, and dysthymic disorders. It is thus not surprising that a circular order of similarity applies to both emotions and personality disorder diagnoses. Both these domains are essentially concerned with interpersonal relations.

A CIRCUMPLEX FOR IMPULSES TO ACTION

Most theories of emotion acknowledge the complex nature of the emotional response. However, although considerable attention has been paid to the autonomic arousal aspect of emotion, relatively little attention has been paid to the issue of impulses to action that are implied by emotions. In other words, although feelings of fear and anger are often associated with the behaviors of flight or fight, such feelings need not necessarily result in such behaviors. This is simply because the situation may prevent the carrying out in action of the feelings. The existence of a gate, a stockade, a rope, or a predator may prevent the behaviors of flight or fight from occurring. However, the impulse to run or the impulse to attack may still be present. The combination of such impulses is what is usually referred to as *conflict*.

One of the few attempts to incorporate the concept of impulse into a theory of emotion was made by Nina Bull almost 50 years ago. She proposed her attitude theory of emotion, which she described (1952) in the following terms:

> Emotion is conceived of as a sequence of neuromuscular events in which a postural set or preparatory motor attitude is the initial step. This preparatory attitude is both involuntary and instinctive and is the end result of a slight, tentative movement which gives a new orientation to the individual, but does not immediately go into the consummatory stage of action. (p. 217)

In two ingenious studies using hypnotized participants, Bull and her collaborators (Bull & Gidro-Frank, 1950; Pasquarelli & Bull, 1951) found consistent bodily postures reported when certain emotion words (e.g., *fear, anger, disgust, triumph, depression*) were suggested. When other hypnotized participants were asked to "lock" their bodies into these defined postures, they could not change their emotional feelings even when suggested by the hypnotist unless they were allowed to change their postures. On the basis of these results, Bull drew two important conclusions: (a) Both skeletal muscle activity and visceral activity are involved in emotional feelings and (b) different emotions have different postures or impulses to action associated with them.

Action impulses associated with emotions can be studied in several ways. One preliminary attempt to identify such impulses was described by Plutchik (1980b). A summary of this study is presented below.

A list of 142 emotion words was arranged in random order and presented to 15 judges. The judges were given the following instructions:

> On the following pages there is a list of emotions. When we think about each one, we can usually recognize that it implies an urge to act in some particular way. For example, when we think of anger, we usually recognize an urge to attack or hurt someone. When we think of sadness, we usually recognize an urge to cry or mourn for someone.
>
> Please read the list, and give your opinion about what urges or impulses to action are implied by each emotion. Please make a first choice and a second choice from the list of eight types of impulses presented below. Place the numbers of your choices in the appropriate spaces. The Eight Impulses to Action
> (1) to attack or hurt
> (2) to cry or mourn
> (3) to embrace or mate
> (4) to explore or search
> (5) to stop activity

(6) to reject or get rid of

(7) to welcome or be with

(8) to withdraw or get away (p. 355)

Table 5.5 (see p. 104) presents a summary of the judgments based on the relative frequencies of first and second choices for each emotion. In some cases there was almost complete agreement on these choices. In other cases there was much less agreement. The table presents first and second choices for each emotion term, although in many cases a third choice helped to distinguish among the emotions. Emotions printed in bold letters express the primary emotions most clearly.

In Table 5.5 the emotion words have been listed in the circumplex order obtained on the basis of a direct similarity scaling method. The angular location of each emotion on a circle is listed alongside the emotion term and the impulse to action that the judges have identified.

Examination of the table reveals clusters of emotions that show a systematic progression around the circle. The first cluster consists of a series of terms such as *accepting, agreeable, calm*, and *obliging*, all of which have "to welcome or be with" as a major component impulse. All these terms and impulses imply an act of affiliation or incorporation. In most cases the second impulse consists of an urge to embrace or mate; other impulses may also be present.

The second group of emotions has as a primary impulse the urge "to withdraw or get away" and includes such terms as *timid, panicky, embarrassed, self-conscious*, and *nervous*. The second impulse, in most cases, is an urge "to stop activity." The differences between the different emotions are related in part to the relative magnitude of the primary and secondary impulses and in part to the presence of additional impulses, such as an urge to cry or to reject.

The third group of emotions consists of terms such as *sad, depressed, unhappy*, and *despairing*. Most of these terms have as a primary impulse "to cry or mourn" and as a secondary impulse "to withdraw or get away."

The fourth group of emotions, the orientation emotions, includes such terms as *vacillating, puzzled, confused*, and *surprised*. The primary impulse in most of these emotions is "to stop activity," and the secondary one is "to explore or search." A third impulse judged to exist in several of these emotions is "to withdraw or get away."

The fifth grouping of emotions consists of those that have the feeling of rejection as a major component. Emotions such as *disgusted, resentful, revolted*, and *displeased* all have as their primary impulse "to reject or get rid of," and all have either withdrawal or attack as a secondary impulse.

The sixth group of emotions consists of those that have as their primary impulse the urge "to attack or hurt." Examples of such emotions are *furious, quarrelsome, aggressive*, and *sarcastic*. The secondary impulse in most cases is "to reject or get rid of."

The seventh group of emotions contains such terms as *impulsive, expectant, curious,* and *planful.* Most have as a primary emotion the urge "to explore or search." The secondary emotion in most cases is the urge "to welcome or be with."

Finally, the eighth major cluster of emotions that completes the circle is mostly concerned with sociability and includes such terms as *eager, delighted, happy,* and *cooperative.* The secondary impulse in almost all cases is the urge "to embrace or mate," and in many cases a third impulse is also present. It should be mentioned that the first grouping and the last contain most of the same component impulses. This suggests that there is no sharp line of distinction between the emotions of joy and acceptance and their derivatives, at least as measured by these impulses.

Of great interest is that the judgments of impulses associated with emotions tend to cluster emotions in very much the same way as do the direct judgments of similarity. The results support the concept that emotions are complex sequences of events that include impulses to action as an important part of the sequences. They also provide still another language to describe an important aspect of emotions, a language that is likely to have particular value in the clinical context. Although patients may not always be able to describe the emotions they feel in clear, subjective terms, they are likely to be able to describe the impulses to action that are mixed up in their internal conflicts.

THE QUESTION OF AXES

A question that sometimes arises when considering circumplex models involves the underlying dimensions that give rise to the circumplex. It has been assumed by many investigators that in a two-dimensional surface (as is the case with the circumplex), there are two independent axes that are basic and that their interaction accounts for all the terms of the circumplex. Using factor analytic studies of personality, different investigators have proposed such axes as dominance–submission, love–hate, emotional stability–neuroticism, extroverted–introverted, or conservative–radical. The identification of such axes is somewhat arbitrary and depends on the initial choices and sampling of items and on the assumptions and preferences of the investigators.

There is, however, another way to consider the question of axes. In any circular configuration it is unnecessary to consider any particular pair of axes as more basic than any other pair. The axes are arbitrary reference points that simply enable one to plot the positions of variables relative to one another. The axes may be removed or ignored, and all relationships among the variables remain unchanged.

An important feature of a circular structure is that it may reveal empty sectors that might be filled systematically in subsequent research. In theory, adding variables (e.g., traits, diagnoses) should not change the relative configuration of the original ones but would result in a more complete mapping of the universe being studied. The goal of a circumplex analysis is to sample all sectors of an interpersonal domain equally.

An alternative way of saying this is that in any true or nearly true circle, the positions of all points (or elements) on the circle relative to one another are invariant irrespective of the coordinates used to locate them. Assumed underlying dimensions cannot explain the circumplex because any particular set of axes is arbitrary and no more basic than any other. In a relatively seamless circle of elements, any rotation of axes does not change the relations among the elements. From a descriptive point of view, it is inappropriate to reify certain axes as more fundamental than others.

THE APPLICATION OF CIRCUMPLEX MODELS TO CLINICAL PRACTICE

Three brief examples demonstrate the application of circumplex ideas to clinical practice.

In 1983, Kiesler described what he called the *interpersonal circle*, which is a circumplex of interpersonal behaviors. These include such behaviors as dominant, submissive, hostile, and friendly. One of the offshoots of this model is the theory of complementarity. This theory hypothesizes that dominant behaviors tend to elicit friendly ones, and hostile behaviors tend to elicit hostile ones.

In a further development of these ideas, Kiesler, Schmidt, and Wagner (1997) have used the theory to develop an Impact Message Inventory designed to measure the typical automatic, relatively preconscious sets of emotional reactions each person has to others. Such reactions include feelings, action tendencies, and fantasies. The impact messages imply claims of one person on another that relate to issues of control and affiliation. Factor analysis of the Impact Message Inventory reveals that the Inventory has a circumplex structure. The authors concluded that impact messages are best understood in terms of emotions.

Horowitz and his colleagues (Horowitz, Rosenberg, Baer, Ureno, & Villasenor, 1988) have developed an Inventory of Interpersonal Problems (IIP) based on a large sample of initial interviews of people starting psychotherapy. The IIP contains 127 statements of problems (e.g., "It is hard for me to say 'no' to other people") and has been factor analyzed to examine the relationships among the items. Results of this analysis reveals that the items, which essentially refer to different aspects of interpersonal relations, form a circumplex. The eight sectors of the circumplex have been called by Horowitz et al. (in order) *domineering, intrusive, overly nurturant, exploitable, nonassertive, socially avoidant, cold,* and *vindictive,* and the test has been widely used in clinical research.

In a follow-up to this work, Horowitz, Dryer, and Krasnoperova (1997) presented a model of interpersonal behavior that contains four principal postulates: (a) interpersonal behaviors can be described in terms of the two dimensions of affiliation, ranging from hostile to friendly behavior, and dominance, ranging from yielding to dominating behaviors; (b) an interpersonal behavior invites a complementary reaction, and the relationship between the two is also characterized in terms of the circumplex; (c) noncomplementarity creates an interpersonal tension between partners; and (d) people learn complete interpersonal sequences rather than isolated, individual responses to particular stimuli. Empirical evidence is provided to illustrate each of these postulates.

In the final section of their chapter, the authors examined the nature of interpersonal goals. They emphasized that interpersonal problems are a function of frustrated interpersonal goals. To understand a person's interpersonal problems, they maintained, it is necessary first to assess that person's interpersonal goals and wishes and to determine whether his or her partner's behavior is in accordance with them. The IIP fulfills this function. The authors discussed its construction, development, and application and provide evidence to show that like interpersonal behaviors and problems, interpersonal goals can be described in terms of a two-dimensional circumplex.

The third example is taken from the work of Henry (1997). His clinical research is based on Benjamin's (1993) Structural Analysis of Social Behavior, which is a kind of tripartite circumplex system. One circumplex measures interpersonal actions toward another person, a second circumplex measures interpersonal actions that are received *from* another person, and the third measures behavior by the self toward the self.

Henry described a method for using the Structural Analysis of Social Behavior model in the description of the dynamics of a patient's interpersonal problems and in the subsequent measurement of the outcome of treatment. He went on to show how the use of this model has enabled him, along with Benjamin, to generate a theoretical model of abnormal personality that proposes a qualitative definition for differentiating abnormal from normal personality. This is in contrast to earlier definitions in which pathology was seen quantitatively as a matter of degree of the expression of certain traits. Further uses of this circumplex model are described. These include the development of new instruments to test the underlying theory and to assess current interpersonal wishes, fears, and power tactics. That all these instruments yield data in the same metric facilitates the integration of diverse clinical information and provides for congruence of problem, treatment, and outcome data. Henry concluded by demonstrating ways in which he believed the circumplex provides a basis for the integration of theories of psychopathology and psychotherapy that are as diverse as the cognitive, behavioral, and psychodynamic theories.

These examples suggest the potential power of the circumplex models of emotions, personality, and personality disorders to stimulate research, to guide the development of measuring instruments, and to help explain clinical problems.

TABLE 5.5
Impulses to Action Associated With a Large Sample of Emotions Arranged in a Circumplex

Angle (degrees)	Emotion	First choice	Second choice
0	**Accepting**	**To welcome or be with**	**To embrace or mate**
5	Agreeable	To welcome or be with	To embrace or mate
12	Serene	To welcome or be with	To embrace or mate
26	Cheerful	To welcome or be with	To embrace or mate
32	Receptive	To welcome or be with	To embrace or mate
37	Calm	To welcome or be with	To embrace or mate
40	Patient	To welcome or be with	To embrace or mate
43	Obliging	To welcome or be with	To embrace or mate
52	**Affectionate**	**To embrace or mate**	**To welcome or be with**
58	Obedient	To welcome or be with	To stop activity
65	Timid	To withdraw or get away	To stop activity
67	Scared	To withdraw or get away	To cry or mourn
68	Panicky	To withdraw or get away	To stop activity
70	**Afraid**	**To withdraw or get away**	**To stop activity**
72	Shy	To withdraw or get away	To stop activity
73	Submissive	To welcome or be with	To stop activity
75	Bashful	To withdraw or get away	To stop activity
75	Embarrassed	To withdraw or get away	To stop activity
76	Terrified	To withdraw or get away	To stop activity
77	Pensive	To explore or search	To welcome or be with
78	**Cautious**	**To explore or search**	**To withdraw or get away**
78	Anxious	To explore or search	To withdraw or get away
80	Helpless	To cry or mourn	To withdraw or get away
83	Apprehensive	To explore or search	To withdraw or get away
83	Self-conscious	To withdraw or get away	To stop activity
83	Ashamed	To withdraw or get away	To reject or get rid of
84	Humiliated	To withdraw or get away	To reject or get rid of
85	Forlorn	To cry or mourn	To withdraw or get away
86	Nervous	To withdraw or get away	To stop activity
88	Lonely	To cry or mourn	To withdraw or get away
90	Apathetic	To withdraw or get away	To stop activity
91	Meek	To withdraw or get away	To stop activity
102	Guilty	To withdraw or get away	To cry or mourn
108	**Sad**	**To cry or mourn**	**To withdraw or get away**
113	Sorrowful	To cry or mourn	To withdraw or get away
120	Empty	To cry or mourn	To stop activity
123	Remorseful	To cry or mourn	To withdraw or get away
125	**Hopeless**	**To cry or mourn**	**To stop activity**
125	Depressed	To cry or mourn	To withdraw or get away
126	Worried	To explore or search	To withdraw or get away
127	Disinterested	To reject or get rid of	To withdraw or get away
127	Grief-stricken	To cry or mourn	To withdraw or get away
129	Unhappy	To cry or mourn	To withdraw or get away
133	Gloomy	To cry or mourn	To withdraw or get away
133	Despairing	To cry or mourn	To withdraw or get away
133	Watchful	To explore or search	To stop activity
134	Hesitant	To stop activity	To explore or search
134	Indecisive	To stop activity	To withdraw or get away
136	Rejected	To cry or mourn	To withdraw or get away
136	Bored	To stop activity	To reject or get rid of

TABLE 5.5 (*Continued*)

Angle (degrees)	Emotion	First choice	Second choice
137	Disappointed	To cry or mourn	To withdraw or get away
137	Vacillating	To stop activity	To explore or search
138	Discouraged	To stop activity	To withdraw or get away
138	Puzzled	To explore or search	To stop activity
139	Uncertain	To explore or search	To stop activity
140	Bewildered	To explore or search	To withdraw or get away
141	Confused	To stop activity	To explore or search
142	**Perplexed**	**To explore or search**	**To stop activity**
145	Ambivalent	To stop activity	To explore or search
147	**Surprised**	**To stop activity**	**To explore or search**
148	Astonished	To stop activity	To explore or search
152	Amazed	To stop activity	To explore or search
157	Awed	To stop activity	To explore or search
160	Envious	To attack or hurt	To reject or get rid of
161	**Disgusted**	**To reject or get rid of**	**To withdraw or get away**
166	Unsympathetic	To reject or get rid of	To withdraw or get away
170	Unreceptive	To reject or get rid of	To withdraw or get away
175	Indignant	To reject or get rid of	To attack or hurt
176	Disagreeable	To reject or get rid of	To attack or hurt
177	**Resentful**	**To reject or get rid of**	**To attack or hurt**
181	Revolted	To reject or get rid of	To withdraw or get away
182	Displeased	To reject or get rid of	To withdraw or get away
183	Suspicious	To explore or search	To reject or get rid of
183	Dissatisfied	To reject or get rid of	To withdraw or get away
184	Contrary	To reject or get rid of	To attack or hurt
185	Jealous	To attack or hurt	To reject or get rid of
185	Intolerant	To reject or get rid of	To reject or get rid of
185	Distrustful	To withdraw or get away	To reject or get rid of
186	Vengeful	To attack or hurt	To reject or get rid of
186	Bitter	To attack or hurt	To reject or get rid of
188	Unfriendly	To reject or get rid of	To attack or hurt
190	Stubborn	To reject or get rid of	To stop activity
192	Uncooperative	To reject or get rid of	To stop activity
192	Contemptuous	To attack or hurt	To reject or get rid of
193	Loathful	To attack or hurt	To reject or get rid of
194	Critical	To reject or get rid of	To attack or hurt
201	Annoyed	To reject or get rid of	To attack or hurt
202	Irritated	To reject or get rid of	To attack or hurt
212	**Angry**	**To attack or hurt**	**To reject or get rid of**
220	Antagonistic	To attack or hurt	To reject or get rid of
221	Furious	To attack or hurt	To reject or get rid of
222	Hostile	To attack or hurt	To reject or get rid of
225	Outraged	To attack or hurt	To reject or get rid of
227	Scornful	To reject or get rid of	To withdraw or get away
227	Unaffectionate	To reject or get rid of	To withdraw or get away
230	Quarrelsome	To attack or hurt	To reject or get rid of
230	Impatient	To explore or search	To attack or hurt
230	Grouchy	To reject or get rid of	To withdraw or get away
231	Defiant	To attack or hurt	To reject or get rid of
232	Aggressive	To attack or hurt	To reject or get rid of
235	Sarcastic	To attack or hurt	To reject or get rid of

TABLE 5.5 (*Continued*)

Angle (degrees)	Emotion	First choice	Second choice
237	**Rebellious**	**To attack or hurt**	**To reject or get rid of**
240	Exasperated	To reject or get rid of	To stop activity
243	Disobedient	To reject or get rid of	To withdraw or get away
244	Demanding	To attack or hurt	To welcome or be with
248	Possessive	To embrace or mate	To welcome or be with
249	Greedy	To attack or hurt	To reject or get rid of
250	Wondering	To explore or search	To welcome or be with
255	**Impulsive**	**To explore or search**	**To welcome or be with**
257	Anticipatory	To welcome or be with	To explore or search
257	Boastful	To welcome or be with	To reject or get rid of
257	Expectant	To welcome or be with	To explore or search
260	Daring	To explore or search	To welcome or be with
261	Curious	To explore or search	To welcome or be with
261	Reckless	To attack or hurt	To reject or get rid of
262	Proud	To welcome or be with	To embrace or mate
268	Inquisitive	To explore or search	To welcome or be with
270	Planful	To explore or search	To welcome or be with
271	**Adventurous**	**To explore or search**	**To welcome or be with**
286	Ecstatic	To embrace or mate	To welcome or be with
297	**Sociable**	**To welcome or be with**	**To embrace or mate**
298	Hopeful	To welcome or be with	To explore or search
307	Gleeful	To welcome or be with	To embrace or mate
311	Elated	To embrace or mate	To welcome or be with
311	Eager	To welcome or be with	To embrace or mate
314	Interested	To explore or search	To welcome or be with
315	Enthusiastic	To welcome or be with	To embrace or mate
319	Delighted	To welcome or be with	To embrace or mate
321	Amused	To welcome or be with	To embrace or mate
322	Attentive	To explore or search	To welcome or be with
323	**Joyful**	**To embrace or mate**	**To welcome or be with**
324	Happy	To welcome or be with	To embrace or mate
326	Self-controlled	To stop activity	To welcome or be with
327	Satisfied	To welcome or be with	To embrace or mate
328	Pleased	To welcome or be with	To embrace or mate
329	Ready	To welcome or be with	To embrace or mate
331	Sympathetic	To welcome or be with	To embrace or mate
338	Content	To welcome or be with	To embrace or mate
341	Cooperative	To welcome or be with	To embrace or mate
345	Trusting	To welcome or be with	To embrace or mate
351	Tolerant	To welcome or be with	To embrace or mate

Note. From *Emotions: A Psychoevolutionary Synthesis* (pp. 356–358), by R. Plutchik, 1980, New York: Harper & Row. Copyright 1980 by Harper & Row. Reprinted by permission.

6

EMOTIONS, DECEPTION, EGO DEFENSES, AND COPING STYLES

Self-deception and self-alienation are for many patients the very essence of what troubles them.

— Paul L. Wachtel

One important way to gain insights into clients' problems and lifestyles is to identify the kinds of defenses that they use in their interpersonal relations. This can be difficult to do, however, because the concept of defenses is confused and controversial.

In the present chapter I attempt to clarify these issues by reviewing the nature and role of defenses in human life and by proposing a theoretical model that relates defenses to personality and emotions. Knowledge of the model may enable clinicians to recognize and uncover emotional preoccupations in their patients. I also distinguish between defenses and coping styles in terms of levels of consciousness and adaptive value.

The previous chapter focussed on the relationship between personality disorders and emotions. Here I examine another set of hypotheses derived from the psychoevolutionary theory. These hypotheses relate to the ubiquitous nature of deception and its expression in psychotherapy. I also examine the concept of ego defenses in detail and propose that ego defenses function to control the expression of emotions and that particular ego defenses act to control particular emotions. I conclude the chapter with an analysis of the distinctions between ego defenses and coping styles and their implications for therapy.

DECEPTION

We are all aware that normal social interactions are not entirely truthful. We censor what we tell other people and hide many of our feelings. When someone asks how we feel, we are unlikely to give a complete rundown on all the aches, pains, problems, and emotions we are currently experiencing; in most cases we simply give a socially expected response. Such responses are, in fact, deceptions, but deceptions that are acceptable within the broad purview of social interaction and are generally designed to help interactions run smoothly or to avoid embarrassment. Most clinicians see such inhibitions of expression from their patients particularly in the early stages of therapy.

Of much greater clinical significance are patient self-deceptions. Clinicians recognize that respectable codes of "oughts and shoulds," duties and obligations, may conceal self-deceptions. "Even when a patient volunteers an appraisal of how he feels it is usually so saturated with a wish to make his feelings appropriate that the report is hardly trustworthy" (Weisman, 1965, p. 226). Psychoanalysts believe that most people are faulty observers of their own affective states (Spezzano, 1993) and that the perception of other people is also inaccurate. Facial expressions are not necessarily a readout of inner emotional states but are usually designed to influence the emotional states and behaviors of other people. For example, smiles are often seen when adults greet one another, but they do not necessarily reflect feelings of pleasure or happiness. Smiles are usually a way of telling a speaker that one is listening, that one understands what is being said, or that one agrees with what is being said. The smile acts to maintain a relationship between a speaker and a listener without necessarily expressing any emotional state at all.

Similarly, a crying face is a signal that one needs or wishes to receive help. A threat face indicates that one is ready to fight or that one has the ability to fight. In most situations, people use facial expressions to try to influence others so they may get what they want. Although this might be called *deception*, it does not imply some kind of evildoing. Deception, as a form of protection, is found widely throughout the plant and animal kingdom. Camouflage markings are forms of deception, as are eyespots on the wings of butterflies. Like human facial displays, these are survival-related adaptations.

Deception and Evolutionary Psychology

An aspect of evolutionary thinking that has implications for understanding psychopathology and psychotherapy concerns the role of deception. One consequence of intergroup aggression is the development of threat features that act to dramatize and exaggerate an individual's capabilities. These features include facial hair patterns such as tufts, ruffs, or manes in lower animals and beards and eyebrows in humans. In species in which biting is a part of aggression (as is the case with primates), tooth displays are often used to intimidate an adversary. In many such species, jaw muscles are exaggerated with a face ruff or beard. These displays and threat patterns are used by animals to gain advantage through deception.

Other examples of deception concern the odors that people have that are normally increased at sexual maturity and tend to become stronger with age. Most mammals, including humans, exude a strong odor during times of conflict. Despite these normal patterns, humans mimic prepubertal juveniles as much as possible by shaving their faces, underarms, and legs and by deodorizing and powdering their skin. The probable aim of these actions is to reduce conflict within a crowded society of strangers. This suggests that society can never be a completely truthful organization.

Another side to deception occurs in organized groups. From an evolutionary viewpoint, in a situation of sexual competition, an individual without resources should mimic someone who has resources, status, and power. In an effort to serve one's own individual interests, there is some advantage in keeping some of those interests secret as well as in suggesting that one has more power than the competitor thinks. When two individuals compete for mates or territory, expressive behaviors are used as tricks to promote success.

A surprising implication of this view, developed extensively by Alexander (1987), is that deception of others tends to be associated with deception of self. Deception enables individuals to get other people to see them as they wish to be seen, so that the individual's interests can be better served. It is important to emphasize that self-deception is not necessarily a pathological trait. Self-deception may have evolved as a way to deceive others. An individual who erroneously describes himself as "generous" may be using this self-image to achieve benefits from others. The ability to present oneself in socially desirable ways and to believe in the self-image has powerful reinforcing value, related both to popularity and reproductive success.

Alexander noted, however, that it may not always be in our own interest to make unconscious deceptions conscious simply because conscious deception is socially more unacceptable than unconscious deception. An individual who is perceived by others to be unconsciously deceptive may be forgiven; one who is perceived as a conscious deceiver may be thought of as a liar and a cheat. Moreover, if deception is in fact an offshoot of natural selection, then there must be continual selection for individuals becoming both better at fooling others and better at perceiving deception in others.

Some of the conclusions that Alexander (1987) reached concerning the implications of evolutionary biology are as follows: (a) Evolution (natural selection) prepares individuals to live in a world that has existed over countless generations. However, individuals can live contrary to what their evolutionary background has prepared them to do; (b) evolutionary knowledge can only provide information about the ultimate causes of current conditions and what average expectable behavior might be in certain environments; and (c) humans "have an evolved tendency to favor relatives, invest in reciprocators, and portray themselves favorably to potential reciprocators" (p. 194). There is an evolutionary basis for altruism, sympathy, loyalty, and cooperation as well as an evolutionary basis for competition, fear, and aggression.

Deception as a Clinical Issue

Everyone has secrets. According to Yalom (1995), the two most common secrets relate to one's feelings of inadequacy or incompetence and one's lack of caring or love for someone close. That such secrets are not revealed is a form of deception. However, many deceptions are not conscious. For example, the descriptions of a marriage by the two partners are often disparate and also different from that of an interested friend. Such differences may be deliberate or may be unconscious efforts to avoid shame or humiliation. In a therapeutic context, a patient who wants the respect and esteem of the therapist has difficulty in exposing what he or she believes to be weaknesses.

There are many reasons for inaccurate self-descriptions. First, there is a barrier between experience and language. The attempt to change a diffuse, chaotic emotional experience into a coherent organized narrative distorts the experience. Second, there is always a process of selection, often unconscious, about what one chooses to disclose; something is always left out. Third, experiences of emotion may be too painful to verbalize but may be partially expressed in nonverbal forms, that is, changes in facial expression, posture, tone, and skin color. The sheer complexity of a life makes accurate communication extremely difficult.

Deception—and I am not using the term in a pejorative sense—is a normal part of life and an integral experience in psychotherapy. Sigmund Freud recognized this a long time ago; he described deception as an aspect of ego defenses and developed a theory about how defenses function in therapy and in life (Freud, 1915/1957). Although Freud's theories have been criticized during the past 100 years, his concept of ego defenses has been accepted and incorporated into textbooks, clinical practice, and daily life. In the next sections I examine in detail the origins of the concept of ego defenses and relate these ideas to emotions and clinical practice.

EGO DEFENSES

The Classical Psychoanalytic View of Ego Defenses

Freud assumed that anxiety occupies a unique position in the econ-omy of the mind; it is, he believed, the cause of both repression and symp-tom formation. He also believed that anxiety triggers defensive functioning in a weak or immature ego (Freud, 1926/1959). "Defense mechanisms are fixations on a small and rigid repertoire of attempts, primitive and inade-quate, to solve the ego's task of adapting the claims of the instinctual drives to reality's conditions for their 'gratification'" (Sjoback, 1973, p. 115).

The first situation of danger faced by an infant is helplessness. Freud (1915/1957) assumed that defensive processes emerge during this very early stage of mental development and that they have one or more of three functions: (a) blocking or inhibition of mental contents, (b) distorting mental contents, or (c) screening and covering mental contents by use of opposite contents.

This concept of defense is at the core of Freud's theory of neurosis. Defenses invariably lead to self-deception. Freud (1937/1957) put this idea in the following way:

> Repression is fundamentally an attempt at flight. . . . But we cannot flee from oneself; flight is no help against internal dangers. And for that reason the defensive mechanisms of the ego are condemned to falsify one's internal perception and to give only an imperfect and distorted picture of one's id. (p. 237)

By implication, Freud's theory of neurosis is in essence a theory of the effects of self-deception and self-concealment resulting from the operation of defensive processes.

How do clinicians recognize a defensive process? Because defenses by definition are theoretical constructs that can only be inferred from indirect evidence, what is the nature of the evidence used to infer them? Defenses are inferred from overt behavior and from the contents of communications. Such behavior and communications have certain characteristics:

1. The behaviors are rigid.
2. There is the sense of little control over them.
3. Anxiety occurs when defense-related behavior is blocked.
4. Incongruities exist between verbal communications and facial expressions or posture.

These are complex criteria. A great deal of observation is needed to make such inferences, and they are, at best, uncertain because they involve a complex inferential process based on an integration of theory and obser-vations.

Questions Related to Ego Defenses

Three questions frequently arise in discussions of ego defenses; each is discussed in turn.

How Many Ego Defenses Are There?

In 1936, Anna Freud listed nine defenses: regression, repression, reaction formation, isolation, undoing, projection, introjection, turning against the self, and reversal. Ten years later (A. Freud, 1936/1946), she added intellectualization and identification. To this list, Sigmund Freud, in various subsequent writings, added denial, displacement, rationalization, and derealization. At various times, clinicians have proposed a number of other concepts as defenses: compensation, fantasy, idealization, substitution, somatization, acting out, sublimation, magical thinking, asceticism, avoidance, negation, and splitting (Bibring, Dwyer, Huntington, & Valenstein, 1961; Kaplan & Sadock, 1989; Moore & Fine, 1990; Sjoback, 1973). Bond, Gardner, Christian, and Sigal (1983) described 24 defenses including inhibition, pseudoaltruism, as-if behavior, and clinging. Perry (1990) listed and defined 28 defenses including affiliation, anticipation, self-observation, and hypochondriasis. The *Diagnostic and Statistical Manual of Mental Disorders* (DSM–III–R; American Psychiatric Association, 1987) added the following defenses: autistic fantasy, devaluation, dissociation, passive-aggression, and suppression. Given this diversity, Schafer (1954) proved to be prescient: "There cannot be any 'correct' or 'complete' list of defenses, but only lists of varying exhaustiveness, internal theoretical consistency, and helpfulness in ordering clinical observation and research findings" (p. 161). In this connection, it is also worth quoting Sperling (1958):

> Many psychoanalysts use the term "mechanism of defense" in so many and ill-defined senses, and often in a sense which seem in various ways to deviate from Freud's conceptions of defense mechanisms, that to list everything that has been labeled a "defense" would entail a grave dilution . . . of the essence of the theory of defensive processes as constructed by Freud and the more prominent theorists among his followers. (p. 25)

This issue is examined in a different context in a following section.

Can Defenses Be Ordered in Terms of Levels of Primitiveness?

Although the question of the degree of primitiveness of ego defenses has occupied many psychoanalysts over the years, Sigmund Freud did not write much about defense mechanisms other than repression. Moreover, Anna Freud (1936/1946) wrote, "the chronology of psychic processes is still one of the most obscure fields of analytic theory" (p. 56). The British psychoanalyst Edward Glover (1949) agreed: "Practically all reconstructions of early phases of development are in the nature of guesses and are strongly influenced by the prejudices and preconceptions of the observer" (p. 27).

Despite these cautions, various proposals have been made concerning the chronology of the appearance of ego defenses. Fenichel (1946) suggested the following order (from more to less primitive): denial, projection, introjection, repression, reaction formation, undoing, isolation, and regression. Consistent with this proposal is the statement by English and Finch (1964) that projection is primitive and by Arieti (1974) that denial is primitive. Inconsistent with the chronology is the statement by Ewalt and Farnsworth (1963) that regression is a primitive defense.

The most detailed attempt to order ego defenses in terms of levels of maturity has been made by G. E. Vaillant (1971, 1976). According to him, the most primitive ("narcissistic") defenses are denial, projection, and distortion. The "immature" defenses typical of character disorders include fantasy, hypochondriasis, acting out, and passive–aggressive behavior. "Neurotic" defenses include intellectualization, repression, displacement, reaction formation, and dissociation. At the top of this theoretical hierarchy are the "mature" defenses of sublimation, suppression, altruism, anticipation, and humor. It is worth noting that Vaillant considered certain concepts to be defenses (particularly the so-called mature defenses) that are not on the lists of other psychoanalysts and at the same time ignored the defenses of regression and rationalization.

Perry (1990) has suggested another classification system for defenses. He proposed seven classes of defenses: (a) action defenses (e.g., passive aggression), (b) borderline defenses (e.g., splitting), (c) disavowal defenses (e.g., denial), (d) narcissistic defenses (e.g., omnipotence), (e) other neurotic defenses (e.g., repression), (f) obsessional defenses (e.g., undoing), and (g) mature defenses (e.g., sublimation). It is worth noting that the language of personality disorders is used to describe some of these types of defenses, an important point to which I return later.

In addition to Vaillant's attempt to group defenses in terms of levels of maturity, several other groupings not involving the concept of maturity have been proposed. For example, Verwoerdt (1972) has suggested that three classes of defense mechanisms deal with threats and influence the development of pathophysiological reactions. The first type of defense is a form of retreat from the threat. It implies regression and is revealed by hypochondriasis, dependency, and self-centeredness. The second class of defense is an attempt to exclude the threat from awareness. This includes denial, suppression, rationalization, projection, and introjection. The third way to deal with threat is to overcome it. According to Verwoerdt, this is done by intellectualization, isolation, counterphobic reactions, obsessive–

compulsive styles, and sublimation. This model also provides for various combinations of these defensive maneuvers.

lhilevich and Gleser (1991) have proposed yet another classification system. They suggested that all defenses can be classified in terms of five general defensive styles. The first class is *turning against an object;* it refers to managing internal conflicts or threats by attacks on the presumed source of danger. *Projection* is a style that handles threat by attributing negative intent to others on the basis of distorted evidence. *Principalization* is a defense style that involves platitudes and rationalizations to deal with threat. *Turning against self* manages threat by disapproval of self, and *reversal* handles threat by minimizing the threat or blocking it from awareness. Each style presumably reduces anxiety in a different way.

Are Defenses Adaptive?

Most psychotherapists assume that "normality" is an ideal fiction and that the difference between neurosis and normalcy is only a matter of degree. This implies that defensive processes occur to some degree in everyone. However, that defenses can be recognized at some levels in all individuals does not mean that they are desirable or useful. Sigmund Freud (1916/1963) concluded that repression is always a pathogenic process and cannot be considered "the watchman of our mental health" (p. 294). Years later, he wrote, "The work of analysis aims at inducing the patient to give up the repressions (using the word in the widest sense) belonging to his early development and to replace them by reactions of a sort that would correspond to a psychically mature condition" (1937/1964, p. 257).

Similarly, Fenichel (1946) argued that defenses have unfavorable effects on mental functioning and do not promote mental health. Loewenstein (1967) described defenses as rigid, inappropriate, stereotyped, and oriented toward substitute gratifications inconsistent with the reality principle. Freud (1937/1964) concluded

> The mechanisms of defense serve the purpose of keeping off dangers ... and it is doubtful whether the ego could do without them during its development. But it is also certain that they may become dangers themselves. ... These mechanisms are not relinquished after they have assisted the ego during the difficult years of its development. ... This turns them into infantilisms. ... Thus ... the defense mechanisms, by bringing about an ever more extensive alienation from the external world and a permanent weakening of the ego, pave the way for, and encourage, the outbreaks of neurosis. (p. 237)

Thus, it is evident that classical psychoanalysts interpreted ego defenses as unfavorable and undesirable modes of mental functioning. They believed that defenses should be abandoned when they have fulfilled their task of protecting the young and immature ego from disruptions caused by anxiety and possibly other painful affects. They should then be replaced by nondefensive means of controlling and modulating emotions.

In more recent years, several clinicians have attempted to expand the classical notion of defenses as infantile, rigid, and stereotyped and have suggested that some ego defenses are "good," flexible, and adaptive. This is illustrated by Vaillant (1971, 1975, 1976), who proposed a fourfold classification of ego defenses described earlier ranging from the most "primitive," to those that are "immature," to those that are "neurotic," and finally to those that represent good adaptation or "maturity." Mature defenses include sublimation, altruism, and humor. The concept of mature defenses is inconsistent with the thinking of most classical analysts.

Haan (1977) proposed an alternative way to think about this issue. She proposed that ego processes may be divided into at least two broad categories: (a) defense processes and (b) coping processes. Defenses are characterized by rigidity, distortion of present reality, pressure from the past, undifferentiated thinking, magical thinking, and gratification by subterfuge. In contrast, coping processes are flexible, open to choice, oriented to present reality as well as the future, and focused on realistic compromises between wishes and affects. Defenses are forms of negation (of logic, of causality, of self-evaluation, of present reality), whereas coping styles are modes of problem solving of general problems of living.

To illustrate some differences between ego defenses and coping styles, Haan (1977) briefly described the results of various studies. For example, defenses have been found to be negatively related to IQ and socioeconomic status and positively related to psychopathological functioning, low ego strength, extremist political attitudes, adverse drug reactions, and problem drinking. In contrast, coping styles have been reported to be positively correlated with IQ, socioeconomic status, measures of nonpathological functioning, and moral development. Negative correlations have been found between coping styles and adverse drug reactions, obesity, and problem drinking. These findings suggest that coping styles have a different relation to reality issues than do defenses and support the value of such a dichotomy. Other studies have shown that measures of defensiveness correlate positively with anxiety and jealousy (Lougeay, 1986; Plutchik, Kellerman, & Conte, 1979).

Given these observations, what can be concluded about the question of whether defenses are adaptive? The view suggested here is that defenses are of limited adaptive value. They are relatively primitive, unconscious methods used initially by children to deal with threats, anxiety, and conflicts. When they are used by adults they represent unconscious, often inflexible, methods for dealing with anxieties. Ego defenses should be contrasted with coping styles, which are methods adults consciously use to solve problems. From this perspective, what Vaillant called *mature defenses* are adaptive adult coping styles. They are conscious, flexible, and often creative means for handling conflicts, anxiety, anger, and other emotions.

In examining these and related ideas concerning the meaning of defenses, it becomes evident that they relate to many important clinical issues. The following section describes some of the properties of defenses in more detail, from which the outlines of a general theory of defenses will emerge.

General Characteristics of Ego Defenses

A careful reading of the literature on ego defenses leads to the conclusion that there is considerable overlap of meaning among many of the defenses. For example, English and Finch (1964) pointed out that it is not always easy to distinguish between the various mechanisms of defense and that there are no distinct boundaries delimiting one from the other. They noted that some defenses are related closely to each other, such as reaction formation and undoing, or denial and projection. Noyes and Kolb (1963) observed that projection is, in many respects, a form of identification. Arieti (1974) stated that isolation and splitting are two names for the same concept. Bellak, Hurvich, and Gediman (1973) maintained that the psychoanalytic literature uses the terms *internalization*, *identification*, *introjection*, and *incorporation* interchangeably and inconsistently. Vaillant (1971) stated that the term *intellectualization* includes the concepts of isolation, rationalization, ritual, undoing, and magical thinking.

Freud did not distinguish between *identification* and *introjection* and used them occasionally as synonyms (White, 1963). *Repression* and *isolation* have sometimes been used to refer to the same ideas, and *repression* has not always been clearly separated from *denial* (Fenichel, 1946). Both *isolation* and *denial* produce partial expulsion of ideas from consciousness. In the sense that *isolation* tends to separate ideas from affects, it is like *splitting*. *Undoing* has been described as being related to *reaction formation* (Fenichel, 1946). Humor and wit have been described as forms of *denial* (Sjoback, 1973).

In addition to demonstrating the similarity of meaning of many defenses, the literature also hints at the idea of polarity in relation to ego defenses. For example, Arieti (1974) considered reaction formation as the replacement of an unacceptable drive derivative by its opposite. Both Chapman (1967) and English and Finch (1964) considered introjection and incorporation to be the opposite of projection. Acting out may be seen as the opposite of repression, just as identification may be considered the opposite of projection.

The literature thus implies at least two concepts in relation to defenses. One is that defenses overlap and vary in their degree of similarity to one another. The second is that some defenses may be seen as polar opposites. From an analogue point of view, the concepts of similarity and polarity can be represented schematically by means of a circle. These observations have important implications for theory.

Toward a Theory of Ego Defenses

The definitions of the different ego defenses each seem to have a theme. For example, *displacement* is generally defined as the discharge of anger toward individuals who are less dangerous than the "real" object of the anger. *Projection* is associated with the hostile rejection of other individuals because they are believed to possess the person's own unacceptable or dangerous traits or feelings. *Compensation* refers to the attempt to find substitutes for real or imagined losses or inadequacies.

What is implied by each of these examples is that the defense is a reaction to a complex, mixed emotional state that involves a particular emotion plus anxiety. Thus, for example, displacement involves anger mixed with anxiety over the expression of the anger. Projection involves disgust with (or rejection of) self mixed with anxiety over the self-hatred. Compensation involves sadness about a loss and anxiety over whether the lost object can be regained. Denial involves a person's uncritical acceptance or falsification of his or her perception of a potentially dangerous or unpleasant object mixed with anxiety over the possible consequences. Reaction formation involves the desire for lustful experiences mixed with anxiety over the expression of such feelings. Regression involves the desire for help with dangerous events mixed with anxiety over the need for help. All these events are unconscious. These observations suggest that emotions are intimately involved with ego defenses.

Defenses as Derivatives of Emotions

From a psychoevolutionary point of view, emotions are complex psychobiological processes that have evolved to deal with adversities in an individual's life. Emotions have two purposes: (a) to communicate intentions from one individual to another and (b) to support behavior that increases long-term chances of survival. Fundamentally, emotions are basic adaptive processes, identifiable in all organisms.

Most people tend to think of emotions in terms of feeling states, but feelings are too idiosyncratic, ambiguous, and unreliable to serve as the basis for a general theory of emotion. It is well known, for example, that verbal reports of emotions may be deliberate attempts to deceive another person or may simply be conventional responses. In some cases, because of repression or denial, individuals do not report emotion even though other types of evidence suggest that emotions are present. Emotions are also believed to occur in animals from whom verbal reports are not available.

These observations do not mean that a person's report of an emotional feeling is necessarily incorrect or meaningless. It implies only that subjective reports are not "gold standards" or the ultimate definers of emotion; they are subject to error, as are all forms of measurement.

A Theory of Ego Defenses

The psychoevolutionary theory postulates that the many terms that have been described as ego defenses are in fact synonyms or closely related concepts reflecting a small number of "basic" defenses. The theory posits eight basic defenses: repression, displacement, reaction formation, compensation, denial, projection, intellectualization, and regression. These terms were selected because of the overlap of meanings in published articles plus factor-analytic work described in Plutchik et al. (1979). One of the reasons for the complexity associated with ego defense concepts is that emotions frequently are mixed and that the basic defenses are also combined in subtle ways, perhaps sufficiently so to sometimes justify the use of special terms. It is assumed that each ego defense developed in infancy or childhood to help the individual deal with a particular emotional state in conflict with anxiety, as described previously.

From the point of view of the present theory, all ego defenses have a basic underlying structure. For each defense, there are (a) associated personality traits, (b) a social need, (c) a characteristic method, and (d) a purpose or function. This idea is shown in detail in Table 6.1 and is elaborated in part from the description provided by Kellerman (1979).

Several examples of these hypotheses may be considered. People who use displacement a great deal tend to be aggressive, provocative, critical, or cynical. Their need is to find scapegoats to whom hostility can be safely directed. The method used is to attack a substitute for the source of the frustration, and the function of displacement is to express anger without fear of retaliation.

To take another example, people who frequently use denial are likely to be suggestible, trustful, and gullible. Their need is to avoid conflict with others in social relationships. The method they use, in contrast to the individual who uses repression, is to interpret social problems as benign, trivial, or even desirable. The function of this unconscious strategy is to maintain the feeling of being liked or loved. From this description, it is evident that denial and repression have certain similarities. Both imply a need to avoid pain or conflict in social relationships. The differences between them are in the methods used and in the ultimate purpose of the behavior. That there are various degrees of overlap between the different ego defenses helps explain why so many overlapping names have been proposed over the years and why an implicit similarity structure exists among all the defenses. The theory I describe assumes that this implicit structure is in fact a circumplex.

TABLE 6.1
The Underlying Structure of Ego Defenses

Ego defense	Associated traits	Social needs	Method	Function
Repression	Timid, passive, lethargic, obedient	Need to avoid or withdraw from social relationships	Forget painful events	To maintain passivity and avoid decisions and anxiety
Displacement	Aggressive, provocative, cynical	Need to find a scapegoat who will absorb hostility	Attack a symbol or substitute for source of frustration	To express anger without fear of retaliation
Reaction formation	Altruistic, puritanical, conscientious, moralistic	Need to show good (or correct) behavior	Reverse feelings of interest to their opposite	To hide interest in bad and especially sexual behavior
Compensation	Boastful, daydreamer, worried about inadequacies	Need to be recognized, admired, and applauded	Exaggerate positive aspects of self	To improve a perceived weakness or replace a loss
Denial	Uncritical, trusting, suggestible, gullible, romantic	Need to avoid conflict in social relationships	Interpret threats and problems as benign	To maintain feeling of being liked or loved
Projection	Critical, fault finding, blaming	Need to identify imperfections in others	Blame or be hypercritical	To decrease feelings of inferiority, shame, or personal imperfections
Intellectualization	Obsessional, domineering, possessive	Need to control all social relationships	Find a rational justification for all acts	To prevent the expression of sudden or unacceptable impulses
Regression	Impulsive, restless, undercontrolled	Need to act out all impulses	Express impulsive and immature behaviors	To achieve acceptance of impulsive acts

Note. From Plutchik, R. (1995). A theory of ego defenses (p. 28). In H. R. Conte & R. Plutchik (Eds.), *Ego defenses: Theory and measurement.* New York: Wiley.

DECEPTION, EGO DEFENSES, AND COPING STYLES

The Circumplex Structure of Ego Defenses

If the theory of defenses as derivatives of emotions is correct, then the circumplex structure of emotions should be reflected to some degree in the relations among ego defenses. A study (Plutchik, Kellerman, & Conte, 1979) dealing with the relative similarity of a set of 16 ego defenses was carried out several years ago, the results of which helped determine the eventual set of 8 defenses described in this chapter.

Figure 6.1 shows the results of using similarity scaling on a set of 16 ego defense concepts. Experienced psychiatrists were asked to make paired

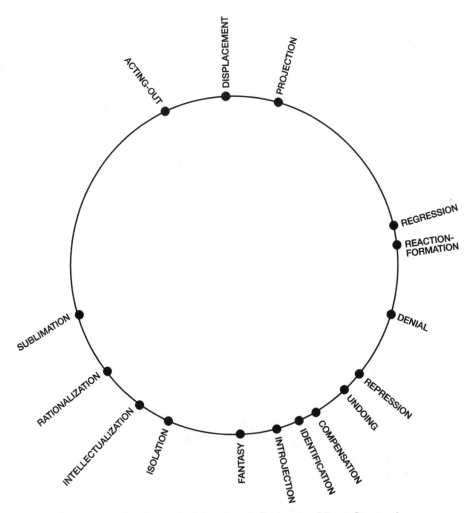

Figure 6.1. Similarity Scaling of 16 Ego Defenses by Direct Comparison Method. From "A Theory of Ego Defenses" (p. 30) by R. Plutchik, in *Ego Defenses: Theory, and Measurement*, edited by H. R. Conte, & R. Plutchik 1995, New York: John Wiley & Sons. Copyright 1995 by John Wiley & Sons. Reprinted by permission.

comparisons of these concepts in terms of degree of similarity. The details of the method have been described by Plutchik et al. (1979). The results of the analysis reveal an approximate circumplex showing the degree of nearness of all defenses and polarities. Thus, for example, denial, repression, and undoing are considered to be relatively similar in meaning, just as intellectualization, rationalization, and isolation are relatively similar in meaning. The cluster of projection, displacement, and acting out are also found near one another and thus represent similar methods by which the ego defends itself.

Polarities may also be seen in Figure 6.1. The displacement ego defense is opposite the defenses of fantasy and introjection, sublimation is opposite regression and reaction formation, and acting out is opposite repression. These relations make clinical sense.

COPING STYLES

The theory makes a distinction between ego defenses and coping styles. As described previously, ego defenses are unconscious, rigid, and of limited adaptive value to an immature ego. In contrast, coping styles are conscious methods of solving problems, are flexible, and generally are adaptive. For each defense, a corresponding conscious coping style is postulated. Thus, for repression, there is conscious avoidance; for displacement, there is conscious substitution; and for denial, there is conscious minimization. Exhibit 6.1 provides brief definitions of the 8 basic defenses and the corresponding coping styles.

The defenses cover all the classical ones. The terms used to describe the coping styles were created to emphasize the key aspect of each coping method. In each case, the defense refers to an unconscious process designed to hide, avoid, or modify some threat, conflict, or danger. The coping styles refer to methods of problem solving. These methods of problem solving, although conceptually related to the defenses, are not equivalent to them; they are conscious strategies each of which can be applied to a wide variety of problems.

Eight basic coping styles are related to the basic emotions and have applicability to life problems. They are described below.

Mapping

One way that individuals deal with problems is by using their innate curiosity and intelligence to get more information about the problem. If a person goes to a physician and describes headaches, a rash, and a slight fever, the physician will probably ask for more information about feelings and symptoms and perform blood tests, take X rays, and make other eval-

EXHIBIT 6.1
The Eight Basic Defenses and Coping Styles

1. **Defense:** *Repression, isolation, introjection.* Exclusion from consciousness of an idea and/or its associated emotions to avoid painful conflicts or threats.
   Coping: *Avoidance.* An attempt to solve a problem by avoiding the person or situation believed to have created the problem, or by "thought-stopping" or turning attention away from the problem.
2. **Defense:** *Denial.* Lack of awareness of certain events, experiences, or feelings that would be painful to acknowledge.
   Coping: *Minimization.* An attempt to solve a problem by assuming that the problem is not as important as other people think it is.
3. **Defense:** *Displacement.* Discharge of pent-up emotions, usually of anger, on objects, animals, or people perceived as less dangerous to the individual than those that originally aroused the emotions.
   Coping: *Substitution.* An attempt to solve a problem by doing unrelated pleasurable activities; for example, reducing tension-related problems by using meditation, exercise, or alcohol.
4. **Defense:** *Regression, acting-out.* Retreat under stress to earlier or more immature patterns of behavior and gratification.
   Coping: *Help seeking.* Asking assistance from others to help solve a problem.
5. **Defense:** *Compensation, identification, fantasy.* The development of strength in one area to offset real or imagined deficiency in another.
   Coping: *Improving shortcomings.* Solving a problem by improving weaknesses or limitations that exist either in yourself or in the situation you are in.
6. **Defense:** *Intellectualization, sublimation, undoing, rationalization.* Unconscious control of emotions and impulses by excessive dependence on rational interpretations of situations.
   Coping: *Mapping.* Getting as much information about a problem as possible before acting or making a decision.
7. **Defense:** *Projection.* Unconscious rejection of emotionally unacceptable thoughts, traits, or wishes and the attribution of them to other people.
   Coping: *Blaming.* Blaming other people or "the system" for the existence of a problem.
8. **Defense:** *Reaction formation.* Prevention of the expression of unacceptable desires, particularly sexual or aggressive, by developing or exaggerating opposite attitudes and behaviors.
   Coping: *Reversal.* Solving a problem by doing the opposite of what you feel; for example, smiling even when you feel angry.

---

uations. In a sense, the physician expands his or her understanding of an illness by making a map of the territory, by getting to know as much as possible about the situation. Only then is the physician in a position to make an educated judgment designed to diagnose the problem and begin to arrive at the best solution.

In the same sense, people need as much information as possible about a problem before taking actions to deal with it. If a mother were to discover some marijuana in her son's room, mapping would imply that she find out whether (a) it is actually marijuana, (b) it really belongs to her son, and (c) he is actually using it. Only after obtaining such information would she be in a position to act appropriately. *Mapping* means trying to cope with a problem by getting more information about it.

Avoiding

One way to deal with a problem is by avoiding the situation that gives rise to the problem. People do this every day. If someone is difficult to get along with, one may attempt to avoid contact with that person. If someone is very uncomfortable in an airplane, he or she may decide to avoid planes. Many people who hate cold weather relocate to warmer climates. If an individual cannot get along with a supervisor, he or she might request a transfer to another department or resign. People who get a divorce have decided to avoid further marital conflict. Some forms of avoidance are obviously more extreme than others, but all people occasionally use avoidance as a coping style. In summary, avoidance is a way of coping with a problem by removing oneself from the situation that tends to trigger the problem.

Help Seeking

People may solve problems by asking for help. Sometimes help seeking is carried out informally. For example, people call their friends to get opinions and advice about various life problems. Relatives may take turns helping someone who is ill. Neighbors frequently do errands and favors for each other. These are all ways in which people seek help.

Sometimes difficult life problems may require help from an expert. For example, going to a doctor, taking a car to a service station, consulting a therapist or a clergy member, writing to an "advice column," dealing with a financial advisor, or joining a support group are all ways in which people seek help.

Minimizing

Many situations have ambiguous implications, and different people can interpret the same situation in different or even opposite ways. It is possible to see a glass as half full (the optimistic view) or half empty (the pessimistic view). The objective facts are the same, but the emotion an individual feels depends on how he or she interprets the facts. *Minimizing* refers to the idea that one can minimize the importance or seriousness of events in one's life and that one can choose this method of coping as a conscious strategy.

In studies of middle managers in a large national corporation, those managers who tended to minimize problems experienced less stress on the job and were still rated as good managers (Bunker, 1982). It is important to emphasize that minimizing is not the same as denial, but is, in fact, a useful coping style for handling problems.

Reversing

Reversing refers to the coping style that leads individuals to do the opposite of what they feel. Such behavior is not a sign of hypocrisy but is a frequent, and socially effective, way of handling certain problems. If someone asks how an individual is feeling, one does not generally expect a catalog of current aches and pains.

In many ways a large part of acceptable and social behavior depends on people acting in ways opposite to the way they feel. The ideas of politeness, tact, graciousness, and diplomacy all relate to people acting differently than they feel. When politicians are interviewed they generally seem friendly and gracious and tend to suppress the anger and irritation they are likely to feel at some of the questions asked of them. Similarly, many people undertake arduous training programs to lose weight or develop skills or engage in dangerous sports such as hang gliding, sky diving, or mountain climbing. They do this despite feelings of anxiety, or boredom, or insecurity; they act determined, secure, or courageous (i.e., the opposite of what they feel). Nurses or surgeons, who deal with unpleasant or painful life problems, generally act the opposite of what they feel in order to solve problems effectively.

Reversing is an important coping style that nearly everyone uses to a greater or lesser degree. It would be nearly impossible to have successful relationships without it. In fact, many family conflicts arise because when people are at home they act exactly the way they feel.

Blaming

Some people cope with problems by blaming other people. This method works well under certain conditions, at least for a while. It makes the person doing the blaming feel good because he or she does not take responsibility for the problem. If the blamer is in a position of authority, he or she may be able to get away with it. For example, if an error is found in a company's books the manager may say a subordinate made the mistake and thereby absolve himself or herself of any responsibility.

Placing blame on a person or situation helps one feel a little better, but it does not solve the problem. One problem with blaming is that it makes the person being blamed feel bad, and the blamed person is likely to develop resentment. Resentment, in turn, tends to lead to a desire for revenge, thus starting the vicious cycle of blame–resentment–revenge. Therefore, although blaming others helps people cope with a problem in the short run, it has some undesirable consequences in the long run.

Substituting

Sometimes life creates problems for which there are no direct solutions. *Substitution* refers to indirect methods of coping. For example, someone who has an unpleasant job but for various reasons cannot leave it might make an effort to do enjoyable things such as hobbies, travel, or exercise during hours when he or she is not working. Couples who cannot have children frequently adopt or take foster children into their home. Sometimes people turn to alcohol and drugs as a form of substitution for the anger they may feel toward an insensitive supervisor. What all these approaches have in common is that they represent indirect substitute solutions to problems.

Improving Shortcomings

Sometimes a problem is created by a weakness in oneself. When there is a problem, many people tend to look at how others are handling things poorly. However, it is also possible to look at oneself more closely and consider one's own contribution to the problem. Assume for example that someone has been passed over for a promotion and that the advancement has been given to someone else. Clearly, many coping styles may be necessary to handle the disappointment, embarrassment, and resentment that may result from this. One important possibility is to improve one's own shortcomings. The individual might evaluate himself or herself with regard to the qualifications that he or she knows are necessary for advancement (e.g., leadership skills, formal training, speech ability, willingness to travel or work late) and decide to change or modify some of them.

Improving shortcomings may also include changing a situation. For example, a child who does poorly in school may need to have a tutor, change classes or teacher, or transfer to a special school. He or she might have an undetected learning or physical problem that would be improved by exercises, glasses, or special training.

Shortcomings may exist in one's own personality or attitudes. Arguments with a spouse may reflect a lack of tolerance or acceptance of other's idiosyncrasies. Developing an enlarged sense of acceptance may go a long way toward overcoming the friction. It is thus evident that an important way to cope with problems is to identify shortcomings in the situation or in oneself and to take steps to reduce them.

IMPLICATIONS

Ego defenses have been described as one aspect of a more general theory of emotions. All organisms are born with certain genetically determined biobehavioral mechanisms that deal with environmental adversities. There are a limited number of such mechanisms, and they are concerned with such survival-related activities as avoiding predators, finding prey, incorporating food, expelling waste products or toxins, and ensuring genetic survival through sexual behavior.

In humans, particularly during early stages of growth and development, the infant and young child are relatively helpless and have few methods for dealing with dangers. These reactions include calling for help (distress signals), ignoring the danger, and making believe that the danger is not serious. They are the prototypes of the ego defenses that we recognize in adults. As mentioned earlier, the defenses are relatively limited, rigid, unconscious, and primitive methods that both children and adults use to deal with anxiety-provoking situations. They are related not only to the 8 basic emotions postulated by the psychevolutionary theory of emotions but to clusters of personality traits and to diagnoses of personality disorders. As the ego strengthens and matures, dangers and difficulties are seen as problems to be dealt with in relatively more conscious ways. These conscious and therefore flexible problem-solving methods are referred to as *coping styles*, and although they bear some resemblance to defenses, they have emergent properties that make them different.

One interesting characteristic of coping styles is that they are under conscious control. An individual may hear or read about them and decide to use one or another coping style to solve a current problem. Ego defenses have a much stronger emotional investment and are thus more difficult to modify.

One value of the proposed model of ego defenses is that it focuses attention on a small number of "basic" defenses. Rather than having to remember and search for as many as 28 overlapping and obscurely defined defenses, the therapist can attempt to thoroughly understand the key ones. Once defenses are identified, it is then possible to infer the existence of certain personality traits that tend to be associated with each defense. Also of great interest is the likelihood of being able to infer the existence of certain personality disorders as well. The chain of relations works both ways, and a knowledge of traits and diagnoses implies the likely existence of certain defenses. Finally, recognition of defenses may provide insight into the kinds of affects an individual finds conflictful or troublesome.

A knowledge of the relations among emotions, traits, personality disorders, and ego defenses does not exhaust the range of hypotheses derived from the psychoevolutionary theory. In the next chapter I examine some important implications of the theory for the specific conduct of therapy and consider tactics that clinicians may use to understand and uncover emotions.

7

THERAPIST TACTICS FOR UNCOVERING EMOTIONS

Despite increased interest in the role of emotion in the process of psychotherapy, we currently lack a valid gauge of its importance in the change process.

—S. Wiser and M. Goldfried

Psychotherapists deal with emotions all the time simply because maladjustment reflects emotional disorders. One of the many goals of psychotherapy is to uncover emotions and to recognize their significance for the individual. This is true for all forms of psychotherapy, including cognitive–behavioral, psychodynamic, and rational emotive. Despite this common goal, however, not all clinicians are fully aware of the many tactics that are available to help them understand and explore their patients' emotions.

In this chapter I describe tactics that any therapist of any school of therapy might use to uncover emotions. These include such obvious things as identifying precisely the stimuli that trigger the patient's emotions and looking for ambivalence. They also include less obvious tactics such as using metaphors when words fail and looking for the functional significance of the patient's personality traits. Most of these tactics are derived from the psychoevolutionary theory, although clearly anyone may use these tactics regardless of his or her theoretical persuasion. Several additional tactics are described that are taken from the writings of various clinicians.

In previous chapters I examined the importance of emotions in normal social interactions as well as in psychotherapy. I also described several theories of emotion and some of their implications for therapy. In the present chapter I consider various methods and tactics that clinicians may use to encourage the expression of emotions, to change emotions, and to understand them when they appear. Some of them are well-known to clinicians; others may not be. All are derived from, or are consistent with, the psychoevolutionary theory. In each case, the tactic is described and is followed by a very brief clinical illustration.

SIXTEEN TACTICS BASED ON THE PSYCHOEVOLUTIONARY THEORY

Identify the Stimuli That Trigger Emotion

Self-deception or the presence of ego defenses such as denial or repression may prevent individuals from being aware of the stimuli that trigger their emotions, which then affect other aspects of their lives. Therefore, *one task in therapy is to identify precisely the stimuli that trigger emotions and their consequences.*

> A client was particularly concerned about her excessive weight and had already had a stomach stapling operation, with limited success. The therapist explored in detail the many reasons why she ate: to avoid boredom, to be sociable, to reduce hunger, to soothe nervousness, to cope with anger, to reward herself after hard work, and to remind herself of pleasant times in the past. She gradually realized that the most common trigger for eating was her anger at something or someone. As she began to learn to cope appropriately with her anger, over a period of time, her need to eat decreased and her weight stabilized at a considerably lower value.

Redefine the Stimulus That Produces Unpleasant Emotions

All emotion theories recognize that stimuli per se are not the crucial determinants of an emotional reaction; what determines emotions are the interpretations (evaluations or cognitions) that one makes of stimuli and events. People do not automatically become emotional at what others say; they first need to interpret comments as insults or threats before they experience anger or as compliments before they experience pride or joy. This leads to the idea that *one way of dealing with stressful life events—that is, events that produce unpleasant emotions—is by consciously redefining (i.e., reconceptualizing) the stimulus or situation or by putting it into a new context.*

> A woman felt angry, resentful, and depressed because of an abusive relationship with an alcoholic husband. When she began to think of him as "sick" rather than as "cruel," she felt less angry and sad and

more compassionate. (Other examples of reinterpreting the stimulus would be to consider a difficult child as "only going through a stage" or difficult older parents as "senile and unable to help themselves" rather than as "thoughtless" or "selfish.")

A 54-year-old woman came for therapy because of depression. She described a long series of painful experiences with her mother, whom she frequently referred to as "the woman who gave birth to me." She was extremely preoccupied with memories of her unpleasant childhood. She saw her mother as evil and told her own children that her parents were dead. Nevertheless, she constantly wished that her mother had loved her. Her symptoms lessened when she learned to think of her mother as emotionally sick rather than as evil. She came to believe that God did not make her mother capable of being a mother. It also helped to focus on her own self-esteem associated with the raising of three successful and well-functioning children of her own.

Identify the Emotional Components of Conflicts

The psychoevolutionary theory proposes that all emotions are either one of the 8 basic emotions or are mixed states. It further assumes that the basic emotions seldom, if ever, occur in pure form and that when they do, they do so only transiently. Most emotions, therefore, are mixed emotions or blends. A further assumption is that the blending of emotions always produces some level of conflict. *To understand the nature of the conflict, one must identify the emotional components.*

A client said that she felt guilty about leaving her husband and getting her own apartment. Previous research suggests that guilt is a mixture of fear and pleasure, and it was possible to explore these components of her guilt. She was in conflict over her fear of not being able to make it on her own (i.e., continued dependence) and her pleasure at the thought of making it (i.e., being independent). She was fearful about breaking up her family and joyous about remaking her family. She was conflicted over the fear that her husband would interfere and stop her from leaving and her pleasure at the thought of saying "no" to him. Examining these components separately enabled her to evaluate the relative importance of each one and then to make some reasoned decisions.

Examine Impulses to Action

The concept that an emotion is a complex chain of events containing both feeling states and impulses to action does not necessarily mean that each component of the chain is equally distinct or accessible to consciousness. Studies by Davitz (1970), for example, have shown that the feelings of an emotion are often vague, confused, and obscure and that the same emotion can be described by many different words and phrases. For example, depression has been described by college students as feeling "empty, drained, hollow, undercharged, heavy, tired, sleepy, unmotivated, helpless, insignificant, incompetent, self-pitying, sorry, and suffocating" (p. 253). In contrast, the impulse to action in any given emotion is somewhat clearer, probably because there are fewer relevant actions possible. *This implies that the subjective feeling states of emotion (i.e., the labels they are given) are usually more ambiguous and obscure than the impulses to action.*

> A client was talking about a brother who had committed suicide. To the question, "How did you feel about it?" her answer was that she didn't know, but when she was asked what she felt like doing, she immediately replied "I felt like crying, but couldn't because I really felt like killing him myself for what he did to our mother."

Look for Ambivalence

That most emotions that people experience are mixed emotions implies that impulses to action are diverse. This means that life is filled with feelings of ambivalence. When a client describes an emotional situation, the therapist should assume that only part of the story has been told. No one is ever certain what the truth is. Ambivalence is particularly evident if a person reports doing something that he or she does not want to do. *Therefore always look for ambivalence.*

> A relatively young man inherited his father's business after the father died suddenly of a heart attack. The son knew nothing about the business, having been trained to go into one of the professions. He developed anxiety about making decisions and began to rely increasingly on the foreman, who in turn treated him like a child. The young man began to hate the foreman, but in therapy he gradually revealed his respect for the foreman's undoubted skill and decisiveness. Once the ambivalence was recognized and confronted, the new owner of the business began to establish a less conflicted relationship to the foreman.

Explore Client Reluctance to Consider Alternatives and Client Fears

Clients often report that they are reluctant or unable to do something that they want to do (e.g., eat alone in a fancy restaurant, visit a nudist colony for a day, learn parachute jumping). Conversely, they often say that they do things that they really do not want to do (e.g., visit people they do not like, allow themselves to be taken advantage of, buy something they do not need or want). Close examination of such situations invariably reveals that some kind of fear is always present: of rejection, of humiliation, of criticism, or of looking foolish. Fear is the great inhibitor of action.

When a client appears stuck on one theme or is reluctant to examine alternative ideas or actions, look for the fear.

An older woman had recently moved into a new house. After a few weeks she called her son and asked him to come over and move some furniture for her. The son said that he was busy then and would help her some other time. The woman hung up the telephone and shortly thereafter developed a painful constriction in her throat and began to cry. In therapy she became preoccupied with this incident and continued to ruminate about it. The therapist focused on what fears she might have in connection with the incident, and it became evident that her critical feelings about her son were inhibited by fear of rejection. Therapy then explored the origins and nature of this fear.

Explore the Idiosyncratic Meanings Clients Give to Feelings

We take it for granted that everyone is unique; talents differ, educations differ. What we do not appreciate as clearly is that the very words we commonly use have different connotations and meanings for different people. *The labels people give to their own feelings and emotions have idiosyncratic meanings that should be explored.* This is particularly true of words like *upset, frustrated,* and *stressed.*

A patient described himself as *sick.* When he was asked what the opposite of *sick* was, he said *free* (rather than the more obvious word *well*). It turned out that his sickness was his inability to free himself from an unhappy marriage.

A client came into the group bristling with anger. She had been brooding for a week that someone in the group had described her as *stubborn.* It appeared that *stubborn* meant to her *bad* and *mean* and that the opposite of stubborn was *nice* and *friendly.*

Explore Client Capacity to Experience and Express a Range of Emotions

One thing meant by the term *emotional maladjustment* is that there is a kind of emotional skewness in an individual; that is, one or two emotions may be strong, or troublesome, or at the center of that individual's existence. Depression, for example, implies that feelings of sadness are the dominant theme and the major way of relating to other people. Someone who is hostile uses anger as the major emotion that becomes expressed in a large number of situations.

The psychoevolutionary theory implies that all emotions have survival value for the individual. Joy is an expression of pleasurable contact that may be associated with the propagation of one's genes. However, fear is just as adaptive as joy in that it mobilizes the individual to avoid threat or conflict. So too is anger, in the sense that it mobilizes the individual to cope with a barrier to the satisfaction of his or her needs. The same general argument can be made for each basic emotion; each is adaptive and serves a survival need. From this point of view, an individual who appears to experience primarily only one emotion is maladjusted, whereas successful adaptation implies the ability to feel and express all emotions in appropriate settings.

> A client described himself as coping with most problems by seeking help. This coping style was an expression of his feeling small, helpless, needy, and sad. Measurement of his emotional proclivities and exploration of this imbalance in his affect states led to his awareness of his limited range of feeling. Over time, one measure of improvement was a gradual expansion in his range of expressed affect.

Reduce the Influence of the Environment, and Disconnect From the Past

When something goes wrong many people have a strong urge to find an explanation or a scapegoat. They try to account for their unhappiness, depression, anxiety, or anger by relating it to a dull job, a demanding boss, or an unfaithful spouse. Sometimes they may blame their neighborhood, their parents, or their siblings.

Such attitudes are expressions of the individual's feeling of loss of some degree of control over his or her life. They are also expressions of the belief that events directly determine our emotions, when in fact, it is our interpretation of events that determines our emotions. Cognitive evaluations of life events determine what we feel, and to that extent, our world of emotions is created by our cognitions.

This is true also of our past. Everyone's past is complex, ambiguous, and impossible to define precisely. Recognizing that our cognitions determine our emotional world implies that our cognitions also determine our conception of our own past. So-called "bad" pasts can be reinterpreted in more benign ways just as our conceptions of an unsatisfactory job can be reinterpreted to make it less stressful or boring. These changes can be brought about by the use of various coping styles described in a previous chapter.

> One member of a therapy group was 70 years old. She was married to a former alcoholic who was insensitive, withdrawn, and sometimes demanding. After several years in group therapy in which coping styles were actively taught, she changed her coping styles so that she handled problems differently. She began to accept things she could not change; she became less angry, she stopped ruminating about her unhappy childhood; and she began to do more things that pleased her (like travel). She used the coping styles of minimization, suppression, and

substitution much more than she had previously. She began to feel that she was largely responsible for her life and was not controlled by her past, nor her immediate environment. As a result, she reported being happier than she had been most of her life.

Recognize That Emotions Are in the Details

Patients in therapy often avoid talking about important emotion-producing events in their lives because of embarrassment, denial, or other sources of inhibition. Often, patients talk around a topic and avoid details of important encounters. In such situations, the therapist should encourage the patient to examine the details as specifically as possible.

A 40-year-old man described a divorce he had about 10 years ago. He told of a nice relationship, a good sales job, and excellent job performance. He had difficulty describing the reasons for the breakup of the marriage and kept drifting off to other topics. When encouraged to go into the details, it became evident that he felt humiliated by a downturn in business, which resulted in escape behavior of drinking and drug use along with increased and exhausting efforts to improve the business situation. His arrogance followed by humiliation led to feelings of panic and paranoid thoughts. Without being fully conscious of the inner turmoil, he finally escaped from all his responsibilities by having a nervous breakdown.

Use Metaphors When Words Fail

Emotions are complex chains of events that include many nonverbal events, such as physiological changes, muscle tensions, preparations for action, unconscious interpretations of events, and defenses that inhibit the recognition of one's own feelings. Even subjective feelings are often not easily specifiable, and individuals may have confused ideas about the proper words to apply to their own feelings. For example, most people have difficulty distinguishing between fear and anxiety, jealousy and envy, and guilt and shame. When the therapist recognizes that ambiguities exist about what emotions exist or about what triggers them, it is sometimes possible to use metaphors to help elicit emotions and their sources.

A young woman entered therapy because of feelings of depression but was unable to say why she felt depressed. An art therapist offered her oil pastels and a large sheet of paper and asked her simply to make lines in any colors she wished. In a few minutes the lines became longer, bolder, and darker, and the patient began to verbalize feelings of anger toward her father from whom she felt estranged. The use of art as a metaphor helped her find words to express her emotions.

Generate Hope

Typical of most individuals who seek psychotherapy is a sense of frustration with life's problems, a sense of hopelessness, and a sense of unresolvable conflicts. Psychotherapy cannot solve all problems or resolve all conflicts, but it can contribute to an individual's sense of hope for the future. A sense of hope is critical to the continuation of therapy and to the development of motivation to begin to deal with the issues that fog one's mind.

> A 52-year-old man on medications for chronic depression described a history of sexual abuse, drug addiction, alcoholism, addiction to pornographic films, and increasing debt. Tactful exploration revealed that there were a few periods in his life when he was happy: when he shared a room with his brother at home; in high school, as a reasonably good athlete on the running team; and when he performed in a college musical. Focusing on these positive experiences and setting some realistic goals for handling his debts greatly increased his feelings of hopefulness.

Balance Undesirable Emotions With Desirable Ones

Emotions interact with one another in complex ways. For example, two different experiences of loss may each produce feelings of sadness that add up to create an intense feeling of depression. Conversely, a happy emotion following a sad one may counteract the sad feeling, to create some kind of mixed emotion that is not as troublesome as the unpleasant one.

> A woman in her late 20s came to a medical clinic for treatment of a host of problems: diabetes, bleeding ovary, gall bladder dysfunction, and premenstrual syndrome. She was also depressed and friendless. In exploring her background and life history it was learned that she had done well at a community college and liked to write stories. The therapist then gave her an assignment to write a short story. In a relatively short time she had begun to develop a portfolio, which she called "Memories of a Cat Lady." The pleasures generated by writing reduced the feeling of depression.

Relieve the Pressure of Multiple Stresses

Emotions are reactions to life events and are attempts to deal with them in some ways. For example, both depression and suicidal thinking can be cries for help, even when the patient is not fully aware of what kind of help is needed. When multiple, troublesome, and difficult life events occur to an individual at the same time, the pressures may become overwhelming and produce depression and an urge to escape it by means of suicide. The therapist should consider such a situation to be an emergency and try to help the patient find ways to reduce the pressures.

A 28-year-old woman came to a clinic because she was severely depressed and suicidal. She spoke in a low voice and slowly described her divorce, a brief period in Alcoholics Anonymous, hospital and credit card bills, work at a day job as a secretary, night school several nights a week, problems of arranging care for her 3-year-old son, and feelings of intimidation by her current boyfriend. She described herself as "overwhelmed" and "tired" and as having nightmares and thoughts of suicide. The therapist encouraged her to identify several examples of her competence related to her work, her school performance, and her musical talents. Such recognitions increased her sense of hopefulness. She was then encouraged to borrow money from her mother to help pay off her debts. She took a leave from school for one semester to earn money. In therapy, she began to learn ways to communicate her feelings more effectively when she felt intimidated. Her depression and suicidal feelings began to decrease, and she was more able to face her other problems.

Identify Emotions From Core Conflicts

In any of the versions of short-term or long-term dynamically oriented psychotherapy, there is a need to identify and deal with core conflicts. Such conflicts are usually said to include opposing motivations (e.g., the urge to be both independent and dependent) and opposing wishes (e.g., the wish both to control other people and to be told what to do).

A woman in her late 20s had been raised in a small Midwestern community and in a church where the sexes were kept separated until the elders decided it was time for marriage. After meeting her future husband twice, she was married. The marriage was unhappy, and she separated from her husband. However, her parents, friends, siblings, and church elders kept putting pressure on her to return to the marriage. For a long time she was inhibited from acting because of her core conflict: a wish to be independent and a wish to be dependent on others. After a period of therapy, she recognized that her wish for independence, associated with her feelings of rebelliousness and sociability, were stronger than her dependent feelings of passivity and sadness. She eventually came to a decision to end the marriage, find a new church, end parental control, and start a new relationship. She decided to try to take responsibility for her own life. Recognizing the core conflict led to a fuller understanding of her emotions.

Look for the Functional Significance of the Patient's Personality Traits

As stated in an earlier chapter, both emotions and personality traits have functional significance for the individual. For example, love helps to maintain good relations, whereas guilt increases the likelihood that people fulfill their commitments. Emotional signals are related to important events in the life of each person such as threats, dominance, submission, and play. Aggressiveness as a personality trait also serves various functions. Aggressive individuals tend to intimidate others and thereby increase their ability to gain what they want. Aggressiveness also reduces one's feelings of helplessness. Aggressive individuals are often central in establishing a dominance hierarchy within a group. Such a hierarchy acts to stabilize relations among members of a group and thus maintain group cohesion.

> A client was asked to describe her good qualities. She said that she was caring, polite, intelligent, resourceful, kind, and able to laugh at her own problems. When asked to describe qualities with which she was not satisfied, she said that she was short-tempered, stubborn, insecure, a spendthrift, and inclined to walk away from a disagreement. The therapist selected one of these traits and asked her how she developed her stubborn streak and what value it had for her currently. In responding to this question she explored feelings of resentment toward her brother, who was her father's "pet." Being stubborn was the only way that she could get what she wanted. Currently, her stubbornness was a way that she used to avoid feelings of being controlled by other people.

L. M. VAILLANT'S INTERVENTIONS FOR UNCOVERING EMOTIONS

The tactics described in the preceding section are useful for dealing with emotions but do not exhaust the range of possibilities. Vaillant (1994) has described interventions that may assist in the experiencing of affects. These are discussed below.

Share Feelings With the Client

"As you speak, it brings up sadness in me as well, but my sadness must be only a small representation of what you must feel" (p. 200).

Desensitize Conflicted Feelings

"You just pulled away from the joy (or sadness or anger or tenderness) that you were feeling as you described (that situation) with (that specific person). Can you sense that?" (p. 201).

Verbally Label Emotions

"You have made two fists with your hands. What do you think you might be feeling?" (p. 202).

Use Past Feelings to Identify Current Feelings

"So you don't feel angry at all now? Have you *ever* had an incident in your life when you were really furious at someone?" (p. 204).

Explore the Client's Physiological Experience of the Emotion

Patient: My throat is tight.

Therapist: What would happen if you didn't tighten your throat?

Patient: I'd cry . . . (p. 205).

Assess Affect Through Fantasy and Guided Imagery

"Are there any thoughts or images that come with that sorrow? Say whatever comes to mind . . . What would you want to say to him if he was here right now?" (p. 206).

Integrate Opposing Feelings

"You seem much more comfortable with angry feelings now. But are there more positive sides of the relationship that need to be remembered as well, to put the anger in perspective? What touches you most about your husband?" (p. 209).

Vaillant's Conclusion

Vaillant (1994) concluded with the following admonition:

In any exposure to feeling, care always must be taken to ensure *the containment of feeling in fantasy* so that acting out does not occur. The practicing of experiencing emotions in fantasy, in graded steps, builds the capacity to reflect on feelings without having to act on them. This teaches the patient a new way to handle emotional experience. (p. 214)

OTHER TACTICS

Other therapists have also suggested tactics for uncovering emotions. For example, Karasu (1992) recommended that clinicians use as a guideline "affect first, content afterward" (p. 53).

> *Patient*: Maybe my reaction is coming out too strong. Maybe I am responding to the wrong people, but that is how I feel.
>
> *Therapist*: Coming out too strong, to the wrong people? [The therapist narrows the affect and the target.] (p. 53)

Yalom (1995) suggested that the therapist inquire about some critical incident in the course of therapy, by which he means a particularly helpful single event in therapy. The most important critical incidents he has found are the following:

1. The patient expresses strong negative or positive affect.
2. After expressing anger or love or other strong emotion, no catastrophe resulted.

Greenberg and Paivio (1997) argued that our emotions provide us with information about our own reactions to situations. Emotions are messages from ourselves to ourselves. For example, if someone feels submissive with salespeople and is inclined to buy things that he or she does not really want, this reveals an important area that needs to be explored in psychotherapy. Greenberg and Paivio also believed in the value of role playing (particularly in the form of the "empty-chair" technique) to provide a language for describing emotions and for intensifying emotions when it is thought to be desirable.

CONCLUSION

Clinicians are aware of the need to recognize and understand the emotions of their clients because emotional maladjustment is the major reason clients seek psychotherapy. Knowledge of the client's emotions reveals major life issues, core conflicts, and significant stresses. From the client's point of view, recognizing his or her emotions provides insight, releases tension, and helps establish goals.

Despite the importance of emotions in the psychotherapy enterprise, there are few writings that deal explicitly with helping the therapist uncover and interpret the patient's emotions. In this chapter, I have described a number of tactics that therapists of any school may use to accomplish these aims.

8

PSYCHOTHERAPY AND
EXISTENTIAL ISSUES

Clinical paradigms always emerge intuitively and are justified and
validated by their clinical usefulness.

—Irvin D. Yalom

From an evolutionary point of view, organisms must deal with a
number of universal existential issues if they are to survive and re-
produce. One is the issue of *hierarchy*, that is, where one fits in the
vertical dimension of social life. A second issue is concerned with
territoriality, that is, learning what parts of the environment and of the
body belong to the core of the self. Clinical problems associated with
boundary issues and control issues are related to territorial conflicts.
The third universal existential issue is concerned with *identity*, which
from a clinically oriented view deals with the question of who we are.
Crises of identity are common in therapeutic practice particularly
among adolescents and those going through a midlife crisis. The
fourth issue, *temporality*, is related to the universality of death and
with the need to cope with the anxieties connected with it. This chapter deals with the relevance of these and other existential issues for
psychotherapy.

All humans must deal with certain fundamental problems related to
their survival. They must find their place in a hierarchy or rank-ordered
world and deal with threats to the positions obtained. They must handle
territorial conflicts over what part of the environment belongs to them.
They must identify the group members with whom they feel safe so they

can interact with them, and they must somehow come to terms with the limited length of an individual life. These four areas of concern are fundamental in the sense that they all relate in some way to issues of inclusive fitness and the likelihood of sexual reproduction and maintenance of one's genes in future generations. I refer to those issues as the problems of *hierarchy, territoriality, identity,* and *temporality* (Plutchik, 1980a).

An understanding of these existential problems is relevant to clinical practice. The general principle is this: *Knowledge of an existential crisis reveals the underlying emotions involved.*

HIERARCHY

The concept of *hierarchy* refers to the vertical dimension of social life. This is seen almost universally as dominance hierarchies both in lower animals and in humans. In general, the major expressions of high hierarchical positions are first access to food, to shelter, to comforts, and to sex, that is, the resources needed for both personal and genetic survival.

The vertical organization of social life is reflected in the age relations among people, in asymmetric power relations between the sexes, in economic and military organizations, and in social classes. Generally speaking, hierarchical organizations reflect the fact that some people know more than other people, that some people are stronger or more skillful than others, and that all people vary in affective dispositions. All individuals must face these realities and come to terms with them whether or not they want to and whether or not they are aware of them.

Of great importance is that an individual's attempt to cope with hierarchical issues implies competition, status conflict, and power struggles. People near the top of a hierarchy tend to feel dominant, self-confident, and assertive, whereas those near the bottom feel submissive and anxious (Buirski, Plutchik, & Kellerman, 1978). Depression appears to be related, in part, to perceived downward mobility within a particular hierarchy (Plutchik & Landau, 1973).

Haley (1980) has demonstrated the importance of understanding hierarchical relations in the context of family therapy. He explained that all organizations, including the family, are hierarchical in form, with some members having more authority, power, and status than others. His clinical experience with adolescents suggested that psychopathology was usually the result of a malfunctioning organization, and it implied that the task of the therapist is to help change the organization so that the parents, rather than their offspring, are in charge.

In clinical practice hierarchical issues are expressed by strong preoccupations with aggressive pursuit of dominance, or its opposite, the acceptance of submissive roles. Struggles along the ladder of life are typically concerned with the emotions of anger and fear.

TERRITORIALITY

In every species, each organism must learn what aspects of the environment and of the self "belong" to it, that is, it develops a sense of *territoriality*. From an evolutionary point of view, territories define an area or space of potential nourishment necessary for survival or an area that is safe from attack or predation. Territories may be defined explicitly by scent markings, tree scratches, or boundary lines or implicitly by the distance one organism allows another to approach before aggression is initiated. Crowding usually generates territorial crises.

Individuals attempting to cope with territorial issues are concerned with feelings of possessiveness, jealousy, and envy. Those who are in possession of some aspect of the environment (including other people) feel in control. In contrast, individuals whose boundaries have been penetrated (or whose possessions have been taken) feel despair and lack of control. Control issues and preoccupations are commonly seen in patients who enter treatment.

IDENTITY

In simplest terms, *identity* refers to the basic question of who we are, or alternately, what group or groups we belong to. The issue of identity is a fundamental existential crisis for all organisms because isolated individuals neither propagate nor survive long.

In lower organisms, genetic coding mechanisms enable an individual to recognize other individuals of the same species. In humans, however, group memberships are very complex because of the variety of categories that one can use to define an identity. The most important criteria of group membership are undoubtedly sex, race, age, religion, occupation, and geography. That these often conflict with one another is one reason for the identity crisis. Adolescents are particularly prone to a crisis of sexual identity, whereas older people are more likely to have to confront religious or occupational crises of identity. Hogan (1983) has emphasized the survival value of status and popularity. These concepts are basically synonyms for the ideas of hierarchy and identity.

Certain emotions are closely tied to the sense of identity. For those who are part of our group and who share our identity, we feel a sense of belonging, of acceptance. We share language, customs, rituals, jokes, and play. We allow hugging, kissing, and, under certain conditions, sexual behavior. The emotion associated with a lack of identity is rejection or disgust. Prejudice against strangers is universal and reflects the sense of danger to survival connected with individuals who are not members of our group. To feel comfortable about rejecting someone, we often try to disconnect that person from our group (e.g., to dehumanize by certain critical labels). Acceptance and liking versus rejection and hate are the emotional poles connected with the struggle to identify.

TEMPORALITY

Temporality refers to the limited span of life, part of which is spent in infancy, childhood, and adolescence learning fundamental skills about social living. From an evolutionary point of view, the purpose of the acquisition of skills is to enable the individual to survive as long as possible and to become a successful reproducing adult member of a group.

The reality of death creates the inevitability of loss and separation for those who are living. There is a need for social solutions to the problem of loss, because individuals without support from other members of their social group do not survive well or long. During the course of evolution several solutions have evolved for the problem of loss or separation. One solution is the development of distress signals, which serve as the functional equivalent of cries for help. The second evolutionary solution for the problem of loss is the evolution of sympathetic or nurturing responses in other members of the social group. It might even be argued that altruism is an extreme form of the nurturing response.

In humans, the problem of the limited span of existence has affected the evolution of a series of social institutions that function to deal with death and loss. These include mourning rituals; birth, death, and reunion myths; preparation for an afterlife; and certain aspects of religion.

Emotions are an integral part of these basic experiences of loss and separation. Sadness is a cry for help that functions as an attempt to reintegrate the individual with a lost person or a substitute. If the signal of a need for help and nurturance works only partly, it may produce a persistent, long-term distress signal of depression. If the cry for help actually works and brings help, it produces an opposite emotion, joy, which stems from the experience of rejoining or of possession. In clinical practice, depression is commonly seen. However, it is possible to distinguish between grief as a normal reaction to a loss, and depression, which usually appears as a chronic, mixed state of several emotions. Viederman and Perry (1980) described grief as a transient reaction to illness or loss unaccompanied by a decrease in self-esteem or the feeling that one is unlovable. Depression is associated with a decrease in one's sense of worth and self-esteem and is usually accompanied with irrational feelings of guilt, helplessness, and hopelessness.

Yalom's Concept of Existential Issues

Yalom (1995) maintained that one of the curative factors in psychotherapy is the confronting of existential issues. By *existential* he meant the fear of death, loss and isolation, the problem of meaninglessness, and the question of how much freedom we have and what we can do with it. In his interesting detailed discussion of these issues, Yalom (1980) described a number of clinical implications of these universal existential issues. To illustrate this, I examine his discussion of the universal fear of death. (This idea is similar to my notion of the crisis of temporality.)

Yalom believed that anxiety is the basic fuel of psychopathology and that the various defenses against coming to terms with this existential fear (the fear of annihilation) are the sources of psychopathology and character formation.

Death anxiety is handled in a number of ways. The first and most common way is by *denial.* A second method for coping with death anxiety is by developing an irrational belief in one's *specialness.* At a deep level people with this belief are convinced of their personal invulnerability from harm or death. They may also develop a daredevil approach to life; they taunt death by reckless behavior or by compulsive heroism. They believe in their own immortality. The third way of dealing with that anxiety is through a belief in an *ultimate rescuer.* The ultimate rescuers are (first) parents and then (as life unfolds) God.

When these methods of dealing with death anxiety do not work well, because of such experiences as the death of a parent during childhood; severe childhood abuse; or traumatic experiences of death through sickness, accidents, or war, then the likelihood of psychopathological symptoms increases. One example of such a symptom is the development of hypochondriacal preoccupations. A person with such concerns is continually worried about the well-being of his body. A related syndrome is the obsessional concern of some patients with controlling their world and preventing the unexpected. An obsessive patient who fears dirt, germs, and illness is fundamentally troubled about his or her own fear of personal annihilation. According to Yalom (1995), many people who reach middle age develop hypochondriacal concerns over health and appearance, and some engage in sexual promiscuity to prove their youthfulness.

Other examples of the indirect expressions of death anxiety are the individual who is a workaholic who appears to need to get as much done as possible before the grim reaper strikes and the person with the narcissistic personality who has an exaggerated belief in his or her own specialness along with a diminished recognition of or belief in the specialness of others. If an individual is successful in the drive for power and control, he or she may gain a sense of specialness. An excessive dependent attachment to a great leader may be an expression of one's belief in an ultimate rescuer.

The other side to the issue of death anxiety is this: An awareness of the closeness of death may promote a shift in perspective, as was seen in Ebeneezer Scrooge in Dickens' *A Christmas Carol*. Such a shift represents a transcendence over the anxiety state.

However, one does not necessarily have to place oneself in danger to learn to cope with death anxiety. Yalom (1980) suggested that a "disidentification" process is therapeutically helpful. This process is based on asking a patient to identify who he or she is. Answers are usually given in terms of roles and identifications (e.g., female, White, college graduate, American, ambitious, businesswoman). The patient is then asked to imagine shedding these various roles by disidentifications. When most of these are shed the core of the individual is still present. This idea is consistent with various ascetic traditions and is one way to establish a constructive reassessment of the priorities in an individual's life.

Drawing on his work with cancer patients, Yalom concluded that continued discussions of death and the anxieties surrounding it often leads to a kind of "desensitization." The exposure to the dreaded fear in attenuated doses in a supportive setting leads gradually to a decrease in anxiety. Finally, examination in detail of each of the components or derivatives of death anxiety such as fear of pain, worries about an afterlife, fear of the unknown, fear for one's body, loneliness, and sadness about one's sense of failure leads to some degree of anxiety management. General curative factors listed by Yalom include the instillation of hope; the recognition of the universality of problems, misery, and unacceptable impulses; expression and release of affect; and the development of empathy and assertiveness.

THE STRATEGY OF CHANGE: FIVE BASIC QUESTIONS

Psychotherapy implicitly or explicitly deals with one or more of five fundamental questions that imply certain therapeutic activities (Plutchik, 1990).

1. Who Am I?

The question "Who am I?" implies a need for *assessment*. In traditional hospital psychiatry, assessment means making a diagnosis; doing a mental status; and determining family background, medical history, and current conflicts. In psychoanalytic outpatient practice, assessment is more likely to mean a set of judgments about personality styles, ego functions, ego defenses, and probable fixations in childhood.

Other important areas of assessment include an individual's social supports, interpersonal conflicts, sense of personal control, willingness to take risks, skills or competencies, and close and loving attachments. Irrespective of the explicit goal of assessment, all assessments are basically ways of determining how well an individual is functioning at present in terms of survival of self and in terms of inclusive fitness. Assessments are important because individuals have a strong tendency to deceive others as well as themselves.

2. How Did I Get to Be Me?

The question "How did I get to be me?" implies *historical reconstruction*, that is, the recognition of early experiences, traumas, identifications, and fantasies that presumably have a bearing on an individual's present lifestyle. Therapists with a psychoanalytic orientation are especially likely to focus considerable attention on the past. The assumption is that if a patient can discover the supposed historical roots of a particular problem and the current transferential relationship is identified, then the problem is likely to disappear.

However, the assumption of a limited, identifiable set of environmental events that are the source of a later problem is likely to be incorrect. In light of the evolutionary considerations described earlier, there must surely be genetic potentials of many kinds that play a role in the development of an individual's personality and life problems. To the extent that this is true, no historical reconstruction can be complete. In a complex, open system such as a human being, none but the most limited of causal connections are possible between the events of childhood and adult behavior.

3. What Rewards Do I Get Out of Being Me?

The question "What rewards do I get out of being me?" implies a *functional analysis* and has bearing on the second question. There is considerable experience to suggest that individuals maintain their traits over time because of current experiences or events that serve to reinforce them. For example, some individuals are aggressive because it intimidates others and results in the intimidator getting his way. Some people sulk because sulking gets them something they want; those who develop agoraphobia may be intent on keeping a spouse or parent in close attendance.

4. What Do I Want to Become (or Change To)?

The question "What do I want to become?" implies *goal setting*. To get somewhere, we need to know where we want to go. One of the special qualities of human beings is their great capacity to fantasize about the future and about events that have not yet happened. This process is like setting the goal of a self-correcting instrument. When the goal is clear, appropriate mechanisms often "kick in" to accomplish it. One problem, however, is that one's goals are often not clear and individuals are blinded by self-deception or by the need to get approval for goals considered desirable by others. A second problem is that people have multiple and conflicting goals. For example, the desire of a married woman to lead a free and unrestrained life may conflict with her desire to be a good mother and devoted wife. Psychotherapy must therefore explore the patient's goals in some detail.

5. How Can I Reach This Goal?

The question "How can I reach this goal?" is concerned with *skill acquisition and competence*. If you know where you want to go, do you have the skills to enable you to get there? In recent years, a considerable literature has developed that suggests that social-skills training is very efficacious in producing therapeutic changes (Liberman, Mueser, & Wallace, 1986). Social-skills training is concerned with such fundamental skills as having a conversation, making friends, sizing people up, courting, conducting a sexual relationship, negotiating, and parenting. From a broad psychoevolutionary point of view, the development of such skills is essential to accomplishing most life goals and increasing inclusive fitness (i.e., the likelihood of one's genes being represented in future generations).

Clinical Implications

It is evident that different psychotherapeutic schools may be partly distinguished in terms of the basic questions with which they are most concerned. Almost all therapies begin with some level of assessment, sometimes through the use of formal tests and often by means of detailed interviews. The schools differ in terms of the questions they consider most important. Often, the focus during an interview is on an individual's problems, difficulties, life stresses, and troubled history. There is usually less attention paid to an individual's skills, talents, social supports, and resources.

Many people grow up in troubled homes with many life problems, yet become competent mature adults, which suggests that many countervailing forces probably exist. This idea has been most explored in the area of suicide research, where it is now recognized that risk factors for suicide interact with protective factors to produce a vectorial sum of influences on outcome. In my own research on suicide I have identified more than 62 risk factors for suicide and more than 17 protective factors (Plutchik, 2000).

I have attempted to relate these by means of a two-stage model of countervailing forces that helps explain why some combinations of varia-bles lead to suicide attempts, whereas others lead to violence against others (Plutchik & Van Praag, 1990). The total context that leads individuals to seek psychotherapy is as complex as that seen in cases of suicide attempts. Thus it seems evident that research should explore the risk and protective factors that are associated with dysfunction. "All human beings are in a quandary, but some are unable to cope with it: psychopathology depends not merely on the presence or absence of stress but on the interaction between ubiquitous stress and the individual's mechanisms of defense" (Ya-lom, 1980, p. 13).

The question of historical reconstruction is evidently of great interest to psychodynamic clinicians and of relatively less interest to cognitive–behavioral therapists. "The past . . . is not the most rewarding area for therapeutic exploration. The future-becoming-present is the primary tense of existential therapy" (Yalom, 1980, p. 11). The issue of causality is of concern here. Identification of traumatic events of childhood such as sexual abuse is sometimes seen as being of major causative significance for later problems of adequate functioning. This may or may not be true in view of the fact that many individuals with such a history lead productive, satis-fying adult lives. Many patients appear to develop their problems in ado-lescence or later life, and some clinicians believe that problems and dys-functional behavior are maintained by current rewards obtained from their interpersonal relations.

This point is related to the third question regarding the benefits an individual gets out of his or her particular set of behaviors or traits. This issue should be of relevance to every therapeutic school although it is often not explored in as much depth as it could be. As mentioned in an earlier chapter, social anxiety and passive behavior may help an individual avoid decision making and may help to stabilize the power relations within a family or other group. One patient described his passivity as a way of avoiding the stress of competing with other men. A similar analysis may be made for every interpersonal characteristic of an individual.

A common therapeutic aim is to help patients find out what they really want in their lives. This is often difficult because they have conflict-ing goals, they are sometimes not aware of what they want, or they may not be able to verbalize clearly their aims for the future. Goal setting is an important therapeutic activity because clear goals may motivate an indi-vidual to try to accomplish them, even in the face of adversity. Horney (1948) has discussed the important role of future goals as an influence on behavior. Individuals are motivated by purposes and ideals and are not merely shaped by past events. Goals focus energy, increase will, and establish directions.

The fifth question asks whether individuals have the skills to accomplish their goals. Many therapeutic approaches do not seem to be much concerned with this issue. The belief seems to be that if an individual lacks certain social or technical skills there are schools and programs available in the general community to help provide them. However, getting the technical skills that one needs (e.g., those needed to become a computer expert) is not necessarily comparable to getting the social skills one needs. Quite often, patients learn some of these kinds of skills by observing the therapist's tact, sensitivity, and interactional style. There is a potential role for explicit social skills training in the therapeutic encounter.

In summary, these five basic questions represent principles that help explain the highly variable day-to-day interactions that take place in the course of psychotherapy, and responding to these questions may serve as the underlying strategy guiding psychotherapeutic interaction.

Existential issues are also of considerable significance in psychotherapy. Although patients do not often enter therapy with an explicit statement of hierarchical struggles or identity confusion, such issues often become evident as therapy progresses. If the therapist recognizes the presence of these issues (or the various disguises in which they can be cloaked), then this knowledge arms him or her with additional tools for understanding the patient's anxieties, emotions, and conflicts and may facilitate the progress of treatment.

9

THERAPEUTIC COMMUNICATION

Cognitive meanings are fused with affectivity.
—Paul T. Young

Psychotherapy is fundamentally about a special kind of communication between a therapist and one or more patients with the objective of producing desired changes in the patients. Although therapy is a verbal interaction, it differs from social conversations in its goals, roles, settings, topics, and focus.

I present a theoretical model of patient–therapist communications that includes patient verbalization, translation, transformation, theory, and therapist response as elements of a complex feedback process. This sequence of events influences the subsequent patient verbalizations in a continuing, behavioral, homeostatic system. Related studies provide empirical information on appropriate and inappropriate therapist responses to patient input. A number of suggestions are made about the nature of desirable and undesirable interventions. I also examine some of the questions of concern to psychotherapists about therapeutic dialogue and suggest some ways in which emotions are essential aspects of such a dialogue.

THE NATURE OF COMMUNICATION

In *The Evolution of Communication*, Hauser (1996) listed seven definitions of the word *communication*. All are similar; the simplest is that given

149

by Krebs, Davies, and Parr (1993): "communication is the process in which actors use specially designed signals or displays to modify the behavior of reactors" (p. 349). Linguists recognize that human language is different from nonhuman language. Pinker (1994), a psycholinguist, observed that

> nonhuman communication systems are based on one [or more] of three designs: a finite repertory of calls (one for predators, one for claims to territory, and so on), a continuous analog signal that registers the magnitude of some state (the livelier the dance of the bee, the richer the food source that it is telling its hive mates about), a series of random variations on a theme (a bird song repeated with a new twist each time). . . . (p. 334)

The human vocal tract provides a selective advantage over other configurations because (a) non-nasalization allows sounds to be more easily identified; (b) it produces sounds with distinct spectral peaks, resulting in fewer listening errors; and (c) it provides a greater rate of data transmission than other communication systems (Hauser, 1996).

At least two other important aspects of speech are relevant to psychotherapy. The content and the form of speech provide information about the emotional and motivational states of a speaker. Speech provides both digital and analog coding. *Digital coding* (the use of discrete words to convey information) is believed to be a late phylogenetic development. *Analog coding* refers to the graded signals varying in intensity, frequency, or tempo that convey information about emotional states. Humans use graded vocal signals just as lower animals do to convey emotional states.

The second aspect of speech relevant to psychotherapy is based on communicative displays, which are usually the result of more than one behavioral impulse in conflict (Hahn & Simmel, 1976; Wilson, 1975). Attack and retreat, affinity and sexuality, caregiving and exploration all interact to produce the graded facial, vocal, and postural signals that determine appropriate social interactions. Evidence from studies of animals, children born deaf and blind, and preliterate and isolated groups of humans demonstrates that facial expressions of rage, surprise, fear, and happiness are universal and probably have an innate basis. However, human beings have highly developed facial musculature, and a large number of facial expressions can be voluntarily created and given arbitrary meanings akin to those of a language. In ordinary interactions between humans, there is a subtle interplay between innate display signals that are characteristic of humans and those conventional expressions that people learn. Anthropologists have also suggested that language activities have been selected during evolution as a means of social manipulation in the context of subsistence activities (Parker, 1985). A similar view has been presented by Fridlund (1994), who has provided evidence that facial expressions function primarily to manipulate the emotional states of other people. The overall conclusion is that communication reflects ideas, emotions, and conflicts.

However, neither emotions nor conflicts are immediately evident to a listener when exposed to a particular communication. A complex process of inference, based on knowledge, theory, and personal sensitivities, occurs in order to identify both emotions and conflicts. This is why the process of becoming a competent clinician is a long and complex one. The clinician "must attend to the antecedents and consequences of understated needs, unlabeled motivations, and metaphorical meanings of behavior in order to change them" (Vaillant, 1994, p. 151). The idiosyncratic use of language by patients is another complicating factor (A. A. Lazarus, 1997), as is the fact that communications often have meanings that are not necessarily understood by the patient (Szajnberg, 1992).

The complexity of the translation process from overt communication content to associated emotions, motivations, and conflicts means that interpretations are not only inexact, but, to a greater or lesser degree, incorrect as well (Karasu, 1992). From the point of view of psychodynamic thinking, interpretations, whether correct or not, have the role of regulating the patient's emotions. Interpretations ideally provide information about the patient's unconscious mental processes in relation to other people and may, in time, lead to a sense of competence in recognizing and controlling one's own affects (Spezzano, 1993).

SOCIAL CONVERSATION VERSUS THERAPEUTIC COMMUNICATION: TWENTY DIFFERENCES

Psychotherapy is clearly a verbal interaction between someone who is a therapist and one or more people designated as patients or clients. This verbal interaction has some resemblance to typical social conversations, but there are, in fact, many important distinctions that one can draw. These distinctions, although sometimes a matter of degree, are usually fairly clear cut; they are described below.

1. *Goals (short term)*: The purpose of social conversation is to socialize, to exchange ideas, and to have fun. The goal of therapeutic communication is typically to uncover the meanings of symptoms, to explore feelings, to change faulty cognitions, or to rehearse behavior changes.
2. *Emotions*: Social conversation usually focuses on emotions that are thought of as pleasant, such as attachment, curiosity, controlled competitiveness, and pleasure. In contrast, therapeutic communication is usually concerned with painful emotions such as depression, anxiety, resentment, revenge, shame, hate, and guilt.

3. *Roles*: Most social conversation is carried out in the context of two or more friends or associates talking together. Therapeutic communication usually implies different roles for each participant, for example, professional to client, expert to novice, parent to child, or teacher to student.
4. *Purpose (long term)*: Social conversation is usually directed at maintaining a relationship that may continue indefinitely. Therapeutic communication tries to produce a desired change (e.g., decrease in symptoms or increase in self-esteem), so that the relationship can end.
5. *Power*: In a social conversation, there is no inherent assumption that one person has more power than the other (although this may sometimes be true). Both participants try to influence one another's ideas or behavior. In therapeutic communication, the therapist is generally seen as having a higher power than the client, and the aim is for the therapist to influence the client in a desired way, but not vice versa.
6. *Modeling*: Although people in social settings do sometimes try to hide some of their personality traits from others, there is no compelling reason for them to be anyone other than themselves. In contrast, therapists are trained to express, through their therapeutic communication, a model of themselves as accepting, concerned, and professional.
7. *Setting*: Social conversations are held anywhere. They are usually informal and open ended. Therapeutic communication is formal, structured, purposeful, and generally conducted only in the therapist's office.
8. *Structure*: Social conversation has no time limits and usually no financial arrangements are made, except in dating situations. Therapeutic communication always involves a limited time of contact and almost always involves a fee for service.
9. *Topics*: Social conversation may deal with any topic (e.g., work, family, gossip, politics, sports). Therapeutic communication primarily deals with personal life experiences.
10. *Intimacy*: Although social conversation may involve deep and moving contents, it is more likely to involve superficial communications. The aim of therapeutic communication is to create a deep intimate bond between therapist and patient so that the patient may feel willing to talk about highly personal material.
11. *Self-disclosure*: In social conversation, there is often relatively little self-disclosure except of a superficial kind (e.g., "I also

EMOTIONS IN THE PRACTICE OF PSYCHOTHERAPY

visited Alaska last year"). When self-disclosure occurs, usually both parties contribute. In psychotherapy, self-disclosure is usually limited to the patient. Therapists are typically taught not to reveal much about themselves.

12. *Direction of interaction*: In social conversation, interactions are mostly bidirectional, with both parties contributing ideas and stories. Most therapists encourage the patient or client to do most of the talking, so that the content is usually initiated by the patients.

13. *Focus*: In social conversation, each person takes a turn being the focus of attention. Often, there is a certain amount of competition concerning to whom the most attention is directed. In psychotherapy, the focus of attention is almost exclusively on the patient and his or her life, emotions, and experiences.

14. *Amount of communication*: Although people vary greatly in their tendencies to talk a lot or a little, on the average the amount of contribution to the social conversation is roughly equal. In most types of therapies, the client talks considerably more than the therapist.

15. *Nature of reality*: Most social conversation is concerned with things that go on in the world outside of the client (e.g., sports, current news, family events). A good deal of therapeutic communication is concerned with the inner subjective world of the client.

16. *Revelation*: In social conversation, all participants generally feel free to reveal many aspects of their lives outside of the particular setting and conversation. In therapeutic communication, patients are expected to reveal aspects of their lives outside of the therapeutic setting, whereas therapists are not expected to describe their lifestyles.

17. *Values*: Each participant in a social conversation is free to express values, opinions, and attitudes about any and all topics. In contrast, therapists usually avoid expressing their personal values on issues brought out by the clients.

18. *Meaning*: For the most part, social conversation tends to deal with the surface aspects of events, what psychoanalysts would call the *manifest content* (however, this term is not intended to imply that the conversation is unimportant or uninteresting). In therapeutic communication, the therapist is often concerned with the hidden meanings of client communications.

19. *Theory*: Social conversation is generally unplanned, and topics may change and drift in random ways. In psychotherapy,

the therapist has a theory of therapy and of the human mind and uses such theory to guide the nature of the interactions.

20. *Sexuality*: Social conversation has a multitude of functions: It exchanges information, it enhances feelings of affiliation, it can attempt to manipulate the relationship between the people who are talking, and it can be a prelude to sexual or aggressive encounters. In therapeutic communication, the therapist is generally able to control his or her reactions to sexual or aggressive provocations.

Additional distinctions may be made between social conversation and therapeutic communication, but the list above is sufficient to demonstrate that significant differences exist between them.

THE NATURE OF THERAPEUTIC DIALOGUE

In an interesting book titled *Therapeutic Communication*, Wachtel (1993) observed that relatively little has been written on the words therapists use and when they should use them. The focus of his book is on distinguishing between comments that are helpful to patients in contrast to comments that tend to maintain the problems that brought the patient to treatment. He gave the following example: A therapist may tell a patient that he seems hostile or that he appears to be grouchy. The first comment tends to create resistance and anger at the therapist because of its negative connotation, whereas the second is more likely to be accepted by the patient as a realistic description of a current mood. In general, labels such as *hostile, passive, seductive, masochistic,* or *manipulative* tend to create feelings in patients that they have been criticized, resulting in further feelings of shame, anger, or anxiety, which are the very kinds of feelings that led them to enter therapy.

Most clinicians who have written about the issue of therapeutic communication have pointed out that therapist comments that create shame, embarrassment, guilt, blame, anger at the therapist, or a decrease in self-esteem are undesirable. Such comments are likely to produce resistance to further engagement rather than cooperation with the therapeutic process. Patients enter therapy with the feeling that they lack something in their relations to important people in their lives and that their personality or self is inadequate. If a therapist then directly or subtly implies that the patient is irresponsible, controlling, narcissistic, or regressed, the sense of inadequacy is increased rather than diminished. Above all, the therapist should not try to argue or preach to the patient in order to convince him or her that the labels and interpretations are accurate.

It has already been noted that insight is seldom a basis of successful therapy. Benjamin (1993) stated that insight is not a goal of therapy, but only a stage. "Insight only tells the patient what needs to be changed" (p. 94); many therapeutic interactions need to take place before therapy can be considered to be successful. Clinicians know that narratives presented by patients are not complete and are not necessarily an objective recounting of events, so that a constant process of evaluation and interpretation takes place in the mind of the therapist. The process of therapy involves a kind of decoding of the bits and pieces of a complex, often disconnected narrative, in order to create a plausible (but not necessarily complete) understanding of an individual's life.

A PROPOSED MODEL OF
PATIENT–THERAPIST COMMUNICATIONS

Anyone who has seen a written transcript of a psychotherapy session is usually surprised by the partial incoherence of segments of the transcript. Here is a brief illustration of this point. It represents part of the 95th session of an analytic treatment (P is the patient and A is the analyst) taken from *Therapeutic Discourse* (Maranhao, 1986).

A: No, I think you're afraid that, you know when we started to talk about this that you—what comes up is how angry you feel at [inaudible] . . .
P: Yes, at you?
A: Men. And you are frightened that you won't be liked. [. . .]
P: I never was. "When you get to college, dear, boys will like you," my mother said. I don't think she said "boys will like you"—that's what I, that's what I felt it really meant. But she said that you'll find boys that you like, that you have more in common with. You see, [inaudible] be based on common interest and good healthy things like that couldn't be based on [raises voice] fucking and sex [inaudible] to be something nice. It had to be a real relationship, not just sex. Shit. [. . .]
P: You know, I feel like I'm going to be released from this room and that I'm going to be raging, in a raging fury, and nobody will know why. [laugh] [inaudible] I just walk along, you know, nice and straight. If I get angry enough all at once, then would I get over it? Primal scream. I can't imagine, you know, feeling really, feeling like there isn't anything wrong with me. I was thinking about that the other day. What would it be like, you know to feel that you really just, you know, you were where you ought to be, and everything is just really full? (p. 43)

Every verbal interaction between two people has elements of ambiguity, incongruity, and vagueness in it. Despite this, conversations usually go on as if the participants are either unaware of the partial incoherences or are able to ignore them.

In psychotherapy, therapist interventions are part of a complex feedback system in which patient statements influence therapist reactions, which in turn influence subsequent patient comments. Because patient comments are often fragmented and partially incoherent, therapists generally fill in the blanks as best they can to create a reasonable narrative in their own minds. This idea is illustrated in Figure 9.1.

Patient communications, even if ambiguously or unclearly presented, are somehow translated by the therapist into meaningful sentences in his or her own mind. Conceptually, the therapist then categorizes some of the ideas presented by the patient, first in simple descriptive terms, and then into more general theoretical categories related to such ideas as resistance, defense, or transference. These ideas are related in the mind of the therapist to broad theoretical issues related to diagnoses and goals of treatment. The therapist then considers what he or she should say in terms of the various categories of response that are potentially available. Should he or she interpret the patient's remarks, or should he or she disclose something about himself or herself or make an empathic comment? When this decision is made (often rapidly and unconsciously), it is translated into meaningful sentences and revealed to the patient. This feedback then starts a new round of patient–therapist interactions.

These ideas may be illustrated in the following way. The patient may begin a session talking about feelings of helplessness or about feelings of discouragement concerning progress in therapy. The therapist may think, "the patient seems to be asking for help," "the patient appears to be criticizing me," or "the patient is talking about his mother and appears to be angry at her." These descriptive categories are then transformed into theoretical categories, which may be of the form "the patient is showing resistance," "the patient is handling his anxiety by displacement," or "the patient is developing a transference attachment to me." The theoretical descriptions of the patient's communications are then related to another broad set of theoretical categories, which may include the diagnoses of the patient, the theoretical conceptions of the form of therapy preferred by the clinician, the goals of treatment, an estimate of the degree of vulnerability of the patient, and other concepts. On the basis of an interaction of the theoretical interpretation of what the patient said and a theoretical conception of what therapy is all about, the clinician then considers a number of possible responses that he or she might make. These responses include such possibilities as interpreting the patient's resistance to change, challenging the patient, disclosing information about oneself, or exploring affects. When a decision is made among these various possibilities, the clinician's theoretical response categories must be translated into a meaningful sentence, which is then spoken aloud. This is the clinician's overt communication. It is evident, however, that the appearance of this communication implies the existence of a complex decision-making process

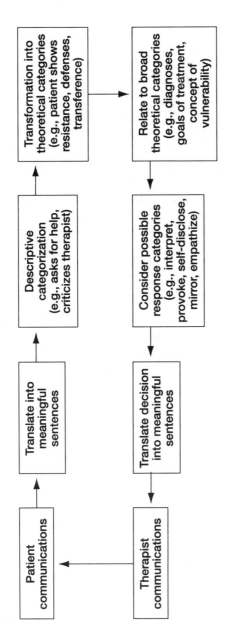

Figure 9.1. Preliminary Statement of the Major Elements Involved in a Therapist's Interventions in Response to Patient Communications. From "Strategies of Therapist Interventions: A Preliminary Empirical Study," by R. Plutchik, H. R. Conte, S. Wilde, and T. B. Karasu, 1994, *Journal of Psychotherapy Practice and Research, 3,* p. 332. Copyright 1994 by American Psychiatric Press. Reprinted with permission.

with various feedback loops. An example of a feedback loop may be the countertransference reaction of the therapist, of which he or she may not be aware, that triggers defensive behaviors or resistances in the patient.

Knowledge of this circular, feedback process may sharpen a clinician's awareness of the role that therapy plays in the shaping of his or her responses to patient communications. This feedback model has also provided the theoretical basis for an empirical study of the various categories of response that clinicians use during the psychotherapeutic encounter.

In a study of the issues raised by this model of patient–therapist interactions, my colleagues and I reviewed a large number of psychotherapy transcripts representing different schools of therapy and different points of view (Plutchik, Conte, Wilde, & Karasu, 1994). The aim of the review was to identify the nature and basis of therapist interventions during psychotherapy. Previous reports had suggested categories such as questioning, advising, interpreting, and reflecting (Stiles, 1979) or categories such as getting information, support, focus, and clarification and providing hope (Hill & O'Grady, 1988). We believed that a review of a large number of transcripts would enable us to identify the implicit categories used by therapists when making interventions. We also hoped to identify, through a survey of experienced clinicians, what kinds of interventions would be considered appropriate and what kinds inappropriate.

To accomplish this latter aim, we identified 41 patient communication categories from the various transcripts. Examples of such communications are: (a) suicidal thoughts, (b) complaints about a lack of progress in therapy, (c) an intention to harm someone, (d) sexual thoughts toward the therapist, and (e) a desire to prolong the session. The 41 communications were then presented to a group of seven experienced clinicians who provided a list of possible responses that a therapist could reasonably make to each communication. This resulted in from 5 to 8 possible therapist responses for each item. Possible therapist responses include (a) asking for associations, (b) ignoring it, (c) pointing out the patient's sarcasm, and (d) looking for historical antecedents.

Patient remarks and possible therapist responses were then compiled in a survey form and were mailed to members of the clinical psychiatry faculty at the Albert Einstein College of Medicine; 141 responses were obtained.

The clinicians were given the list of patient communications and a list of 5–8 possible responses that one might make to each communication. They were asked to rate the extent to which they agreed or disagreed with each possible response to each patient communication. A 5-point scale was used, with responses ranging from *strongly disagree* to *strongly agree*. An additional analysis by a separate group of clinicians attempted to codify all the possible therapist responses into a small number of categories.

Table 9.1 provides examples of clinicians' responses considered to be

TABLE 9.1
Examples of Clinicians' Responses Considered to Be Highly Inappropriate Interventions

Circumstance	Therapist's response
1. If your patient is chronically late . . .	Say nothing.
2. If your patient talks about the contribution of other people to his or her problems . . .	Ally with the patient against others.
3. If your patient appears to become overanxious while talking . . .	Suggest to the patient that it might be better to postpone talking about this topic.
4. If your patient disparages himself or herself . . .	Disagree with him or her.
5. If your patient feels hopeless . . .	Disclose related experiences of your own.
6. If your patient asks you what to do . . .	Give him or her the advice asked for.
7. You begin the session by . . .	Recapitulating the highlights of the last session.
8. If your patient reveals suicidal ideation . . .	Remain silent.
9. If your patient is silent for what appears to be a long time . . .	Introduce a new topic.
10. If your patient expresses sexual feelings toward you . . .	Explicitly discourage discussion of sexual subjects.

Note. Inappropriate items were selected on the basis of the lowest clinician ratings as well as high agreement (low variability of judgment) among clinicians. From "Strategies of Therapist Interventions: A Preliminary Empirical Study," by R. Plutchik, H. R. Conte, S. Wilde, and T. B. Karasu, 1994, *Journal of Psychotherapy Practice and Research, 3*, p. 330. Copyright 1994 by American Psychiatric Press. Reprinted with permission.

highly inappropriate. They generally reflect the therapist's anxiety about what is going on, his or her anger at what is being said, or a lack of awareness of what to do in an ambiguous or critical situation. Table 9.2 provides examples of clinicians' responses considered to be highly appropriate interventions. They reflect a sense of honesty between therapist and patient (e.g., "I feel confused about what you are saying"), a desire to explore ideas and issues that arise, and a sense of tactful concern about the patient's feelings.

One interesting aspects of this study was the empirical list of 15 therapist interventions that was finally attained. This list was not concerned with grammatical categories such as "asks a question" or "makes a statement," but was solely concerned with broad content areas. These are shown in Table 9.3. They include categories of therapist behaviors such as gathering information, boosting morale, exploring affects, and searching for purposes. It is important to recognize that not every clinician does everything that is on the list. Different schools and personal styles encourage the use of certain types of interventions and not others. Cognitive–behavior therapists may emphasize educating the client and redirecting his or her

TABLE 9.2

Examples of Clinicians' Responses Considered to Be Highly
Appropriate Interventions

Circumstance	Therapist's response
1. If your patient describes his or her problems . . .	Ask how long he or she has had them.
2. If you do not understand the meaning of a particular communication . . .	Express your confusion or lack of understanding.
3. If your patient constantly complains . . .	Bring this to his or her attention.
4. If your patient expresses sexual feelings toward you . . .	Explore further thoughts, fantasies, and dreams that the patient has about you.
5. If your patient reports a dream . . .	Explore the affect in the dream.
6. If your patient is silent for what appears to be a long time . . .	Comment on that fact.
7. If your patient reveals suicidal ideation . . .	Explore fantasies of what suicide might achieve.
8. If your patient reveals inconsistencies in his or her behavior in similar situations . . .	Ask if the patient is aware of these inconsistencies.
9. If your patient focuses excessively on historical materials . . .	Explore the possibility that this is a way of avoiding present issues.
10. If your patient appears to become overanxious while talking . . .	Inquire about the patient's feelings at that moment.

Note. Appropriate items were selected on the basis of the highest clinician ratings, as well as high agreement (low variability of judgment) among clinicians. From "Strategies of Therapist Interventions: A Preliminary Empirical Study," by R. Plutchik, H. R. Conte, S. Wilde, and T. B. Karasu, 1994, *Journal of Psychotherapy Practice and Research, 3*, p. 329. Copyright 1994 by American Psychiatric Press. Reprinted with permission.

behavior. They may consider that self-disclosure by the therapist is reasonable and appropriate. Dynamic therapists tend to explore affects and the patient–therapist relationship and are inclined to interpret resistances, patterns, and purposes. They generally do not see the task of therapy as one of educating the patient, boosting morale, or redirecting the patient's behavior. All therapists, however, regardless of school, gather information, define the therapeutic structure, and implicitly provide some kind of an educational model of human interactions.

AN INAPPROPRIATE THERAPIST INTERVENTION: THE USE OF
"WHY" QUESTIONS

In ordinary social conversations, people frequently ask other people for the reasons behind their actions or experiences (e.g., "Why do you collect Chinese antiques?" "Why do you like romantic novels?" "Why do you date this man who criticizes your taste in clothes?"). Sometimes a question is put in a negative form; for example, "Why don't you go on vacation with me?" or "Why don't you get married?"

Psychotherapists also use "why" questions. They sometimes ask patients why they came late to a session, why they are depressed, why they cannot enter an elevator, or why they are angry at the therapist.

"Why" questions can be divided into two general categories: (a) those that are concerned with scientific or technical issues and (b) those that are concerned with personal feelings and motivations. An example of the former type would be "Why did your car break down?" The answer might be given in terms of unpaved roads, heavy snow, or worn spark plugs. An example of the latter type would be "Why can't you lose weight?" The answer might be given in terms of a lack of will power, poor habits of eating, or unconscious wishes to punish someone. The comments to follow are solely about the second type of why question.

If we think about it, we discover that why questions concerned with personal feelings and motivations tend to make most individuals to whom they are directed feel uncomfortable or defensive. People tend to become annoyed when asked such questions (e.g., "Why are you late?" "Why can't you eat alone in a restaurant?" "Why are you afraid of insects?"). What is it about such questions that make people feel uncomfortable?

We may understand such questions better if we recognize the settings in which they typically occur. Parents feel free to ask their children why questions ("Why didn't you call?"), whereas children rarely ask such questions of their parents. Teachers normally ask their students why questions ("Why didn't you do your homework?"), whereas students rarely ask their teachers such questions. Supervisors feel free to ask their employees why questions ("Why were you late?"), but employees never ask such questions of their supervisors. Psychotherapists often ask their patients why questions about their feelings and motives ("Why didn't you leave your abusive marriage?" or "Why do you look so upset when you talk about your father?"), whereas patients rarely ask their therapists to explain what they are doing or why they feel certain emotions.

What this suggests is that people who are in higher positions of power or authority usually ask why questions of those who are in lower positions. Implicitly, the asking of a why question of this type is an indirect expression of dominance. When one finds why questions typically being asked by one spouse to another or one friend to another, this is an indirect indication of who feels more dominant or powerful in the relationship. Similarly, dominance is being expressed when psychotherapists ask patients why they felt certain emotions or carried out certain acts.

There is another important aspect to why questions. Most people are so well-socialized and polite that their immediate thought when asked a personal why question is to begin a sentence with "Because." Most people have a strong tendency to want to answer such questions, and this can

TABLE 9.3

An Empirical List of Therapist Intervention Categories and Their Definitions

Intervention category	Definition	Example
1. Educate	Provide specific information to the patient. For example, explain something about normal childhood development to a parent who is upset by a child's behavior.	"It is important for you to talk about your childhood because things that happened then can influence the way you feel now."
2. Gather information	Ask the patient to provide present or past specific biographical information.	"Please tell me about your work history." "Have you ever seriously comtemplated suicide?"
3. Define therapeutic structure	Indicate to the patient what is acceptable and unacceptable behavior in the therapy relationship.	"If you miss sessions you need to pay for them." "I can't accept presents from you."
4. Support self-control	Help the patient set limits on the expression of his or her emotions or thoughts.	"You can think whatever you want, but you don't have to act out your thoughts."
5. Make a self-disclosure	Reveal personal information about yourself (as therapist).	"I'm sorry I'm late, but my car broke down." "Yes, I am married and have three children.
6. Boost morale	Say or do something designed to make the patient feel better.	"You are doing very well." "You showed a lot of courage under the circumstances."
7. Encourage elaboration/ verbalization	Encourage the patient to generate more thoughts and feelings about a given topic.	"Can you tell me more about that?" "Hmm."
8. Explore affects	Ask the patient to elaborate on his or her feelings and emotions.	"How did you feel about that?"

9. Explore patient/therapist relationship	Relate the patient's behavior, thoughts, or feelings to you (as therapist).	"You seem to be angry at me." "I notice that every time I go away on vacation you are late for the next session."
10. Interpret resistance	Make a connection between what the patient is doing, saying, thinking, or feeling at the moment and the fact that therapy is being impeded.	"You always seem to change the subject when I mention your father. I wonder if you are avoiding the topic?"
11. Interpret/search for pattern	Identify repetitive patterns in the patient's behaviors or identify common features underlying different behaviors or feelings.	"You always seem to fall in love with married men."
12. Interpret/search for purpose	Try to determine what the patient's behavior is trying to accomplish.	"Do you think that if you act helpless people will take care of you or not abandon you?" "Do you think that always being late will bring attention to you?"
13. Interpret/search for proximate cause	Try to identify a thought process that connects a recent event with some aspect of the patient's current behavior.	"You seem to be more nervous than usual since you got stuck in the elevator."
14. Bring behavior to patient's attention/sharpen focus	Bring some aspects of the patient's current behavior or verbalizations to his or her attention.	"You sound angry." "You sound like you're ambivalent about your boss."
15. Redirect the patient	Propose that the patient think, feel, or behave differently.	"If people criticize you, stand up for yourself." "I think you should make a list of things to do to help you get a new job."

Note. From "Strategies of Therapist Interventions: A Preliminary Empirical Study," by R. Plutchik, H. R. Conte, S. Wilde, and T. B. Karasu, 1994, *Journal of Psychotherapy Practice and Research*, 3, p. 331. Copyright 1994 by American Psychiatric Press. Reprinted with permission.

create problems for them. One problem is that we do not always know the reason we do things. If a mother says to a child "Why did you knock over my favorite lamp while playing in the living room?" what can the child say? If the child says it was an accident, this does not really answer the mother's question. The child might have a number of other thoughts about it. For example, the child might think, "Because I'm clumsy," or "Because I'm stupid," or "Because I'm mad at you for making me go to bed early." None of these responses, even if true, are acceptable either to the mother or the child. More likely, the child is simply unaware of any plausible reason for the action.

This point is also true for patients in psychotherapy. They often do not know the reasons for the behaviors they engage in or the emotions they have with which they are dissatisfied. They have only the vaguest ideas about why they keep checking to see that the gas is off, why they lose their tempers easily, why they sometimes have suicidal thoughts, or why they feel love (or hate) toward the therapist. Even when a patient can cite what seems like a plausible reason for a feeling or behavior, therapists recognize that all actions are multidetermined and many previous experiences and emotions enter into a single current feeling or behavior. Recognizing one or two components of an event does not mean that the event is fully understood.

Both adults and children feel defensive and uncomfortable when asked why questions. For the most part such questions are put-downs and the implied response is a negative one. Asking an adult "Why didn't you get that promotion?" leads to the feeling "Because I'm not competent." "Why is your room always so sloppy?" implies the response "Because I'm a slob." Thus, why questions often seem to press people to supply an internal stable attribute (or trait) to account for implicitly undesirable actions.

In summary, why questions imply a hierarchical dominance relation between the questioner and the one being questioned, and they have no truly adequate answers. The one being questioned may have to lie to get around them gracefully. It is also likely that the person asking the question is not really interested in the answer but rather in the implied right to ask the question; often there is an implied insult. Because of normal social expectations, most people who are asked why questions try to answer them in some way. However, because motives are not often clear, this may lead to exaggerations or lies.

Sometimes therapists may ask why questions partly because they wish to discover the exaggerations or lies that patients use when faced with an ambiguous or embarrassing situation. However, to assume that a patient's answer to a why question is complete and accurate would be naive. If the ideas that have been presented are correct, does this mean that the therapist should never ask the patient why he or she feels or does things?

As mentioned above, why questions may sometimes provide the therapist with insights into the ways that the patient handles ambiguous or confusing problems. They may reveal something about the patient's personality traits related to hierarchical issues and issues of dominance and submission. They may indirectly reveal something about how the patient handles problems of power and control and what emotions are generated by feelings of embarrassment or defensiveness. These may all be useful insights, but if why questions are used too frequently, they generate anger and distrust in the patient. The question then arises: What alternatives do therapists have in the ways that they interact with patients in the therapeutic dialogue?

APPROPRIATE INTERVENTIONS

Table 9.3 lists 15 types of therapist interventions. Eight of the 15 imply efforts to get the patient to explore, elaborate, identify, generate, and connect ideas and experiences in his or her life. The process of exploration is the alternative to simple why questions. Therapists often ask exploratory questions such as

- Could you talk more about the feelings you have when you think about your father?
- What emotions do you have when you go into an elevator?
- What is it that I said that made you feel uncomfortable?
- What do you feel like doing right now?

In fact, many of the tactics listed in chapter 7 concerned with uncovering emotions may also be used.

In his book *Therapeutic Communication*, Wachtel (1993) described a number of desirable ways of interacting with patients. In general, the goal of the therapist's statements or comments should be to avoid arguing with the patient, criticizing the patient, or blaming the patient. Many therapists believe that answering the patient's questions, giving advice, or indulging the patient's fantasies (e.g., accepting gifts from the patient) is not good practice. Wachtel, like most therapists, considered the emotion of anxiety, with the self-protection, self-deception, and avoidances it generates, as the key issues to be dealt with in psychotherapy.

Wachtel provided a number of clinical examples of both good and bad therapeutic communications. For instance, a woman in group therapy had been silent for a long time. The therapist finally said "I think you're silent because you're trying to hide a lot of anger." Such a comment was experienced as a criticism calling for more defensive behavior. The therapist was really not sure of the reason for the silence because, after all, reality is inherently ambiguous; it could have reflected fear as much as anger, a sense of embarrassment or shame, or more likely some combination of these emotions. A better intervention might have been, "I wonder if you are silent because of all the emotions that are churning around inside of you." A good interpretation tries to convey the message that it is all right to look at one's conflicts if one wishes to and that it is not dangerous for the patient. It also reflects a sense of empathy with the emotions of the patient and a sense that the therapist knows how it feels and will not criticize, rebuke, or blame the patient for her emotions and conflicts.

Good therapist interventions should avoid implicit or direct criticisms of the patient or an implication that the patient is childlike or immature. They should avoid static images that suggest that a person has a fixed personality style that is not likely to change. Rather than say something like "You seem to be a shy person," a better alternative comment might be "I notice you talk more easily at some times than at other times." The aim of the intervention is to help the patient feel that the therapeutic conversation is like a mutual exploration of considerable interest to both parties, rather than an interrogation designed to drag information out of a reluctant witness. "The therapist must help the patient grasp the truth about his life, but the nature of that truth is continually changing" (Wachtel, 1993, p. 157).

Wachtel suggested the following approaches to take when making an intervention:

- Avoid diagnostic terms (e.g., words like narcissistic or borderline).
- Avoid telling the patient what he or she "really" means.
- Describe behavior as temporary or transitional.
- Assume that the patient already knows what you are about to tell him or her (e.g., "As I know you're aware . . . ").
- Clarify for the patient who owns the problem.
- Let the comment point toward implied action (e.g., "It sounds like what you might like to do or say is . . . ").

Most experienced therapists probably use many of these ideas. The key is for the therapist to avoid an adversarial relationship with the patient and not to use power in too obvious a way. The patient should feel that there is nothing more important to the therapist than the attention devoted to the patient during the therapeutic encounter.

CORRECT TREATMENT INTERVENTIONS

Benjamin (1997) identified five categories of correct treatment interventions: those that (a) increase collaboration between the patient and therapist, (b) enable the patient to recognize past and present patterns of behavior and how they may be related, (c) inhibit the expression of undesirable behaviors, (d) decrease the patient's need to maintain anxiety, and (e) facilitate the patient's learning of more adaptive behavior. "If a therapist action does not meet one of these five conditions, it is probably an error" (p. 88).

Benjamin offered a number of suggestions on how to implement correct treatment interventions. With regard to developing a collaborative relationship, she suggested that one way to create a bond is to team up with the patient against "it," the "it" being undesirable aspects of the patient's past behavior and current fears. With regard to learning to recognize one's own maladaptive patterns of behavior, it is important to recognize that insight is not enough. There are at least two reasons for this. One is that insight only reveals what one has been doing that is harmful to the self (e.g., "You keep picking abusive boyfriends because that is what you learned from your father about how men should treat women. You keep hoping that if you can be good enough ... then at last you will be loved;" p. 94). Patients must go beyond insight by developing the desire to change and the strength to begin to modify their own behavior.

The second reason that insight is not enough is that insights often change in the course of therapy. A first insight might be that one's mother was neglectful because she was selfishly preoccupied with her own needs. A second insight might reveal that mother was ignored by her own parents, leading to a desperate search for approval. If insights produce emotional reactions, these may serve as a barometer of the significance of the insights. If little or no emotional reaction occurs, this may reveal to the therapist that the insight is not particularly meaningful to the patient. The expression of emotions may thus act as an indicator of the importance to the patient of revealed material.

CONCLUSION

Social conversation differs considerably from therapeutic communication in terms of goals, emotions, purpose, topics, focus, setting, and roles. Therapeutic communications may be appropriate or inappropriate. Inappropriate ones are those that imply blame or criticism of the patient or deficiencies in his or her personality or family and increase the patient's level of anxiety. Appropriate interventions are largely concerned with tactful exploration of the patient's life, with a focus on emotional reactions to present and past life events.

Most patients enter into therapy because they have emotional problems. These problems may first be clothed as problems in relationships, problems with substances, or problems with work. However, underlying these problems are problems with emotions. The therapist must recognize the importance of the emotions for the therapeutic process and have the knowledge and skills necessary to uncover emotions and to recognize their significance to the individual. Therapeutic communication should reduce anxiety and anger and generate hopefulness and trust, emotions that stay with patients long after the details of the encounter have been forgotten.

EPILOGUE

In this book, I have tried to blend empirical evidence and clinical experience about the role of emotions in psychotherapeutic work. Within this context, I have presented some key ideas about the significance and functions of emotions: (a) that psychotherapy must enlist strong emotional reactions if it is to be a powerful force for change and (b) that most psychological symptoms are about emotions that have gone awry or become dysfunctional. Some emotions (such as panic or depression) are too strong or persistent, whereas others (such as trust and pleasure) are absent or too weak.

A key concept that has been presented is that of the circumplex, or circular structure of relations. Several chapters show that the circumplex is a valid way to describe the relations among emotions, personality traits, personality disorders, and ego defenses. These domains are shown to be systematically related to one another.

Although many theories of emotion are described in the book because they have clinical relevance, the major focus is on the psychoevolutionary theory of emotion. This theory is composed of a structural model, a sequential model, and a derivatives model, each with implications for psychotherapy. These models help clinicians identify many tactics and strategies for uncovering or changing emotions. They have helped us understand the many differences between social conversation and therapeutic communication, and they have provided the theoretical background that has guided the development of tests and scales for measuring emotions, moods, personality traits, ego defenses, and coping styles. These tests (see the appendix) have been used extensively in clinical research and have provided insights into the relations between emotions and such domains as suicide, violence, self-esteem, depression, and anxiety. Some of the empirical work has dealt with the nature of therapeutic interventions and has tried to identify the differences between appropriate and inappropriate interventions. This research has also led to a feedback model of the patient–therapist interaction as well as an empirically determined list of types of therapist interventions.

Some concepts presented in this book may be new or different in focus from what is sometimes taught. This may result in disagreements by the reader with some of the ideas presented here. Such disagreement is inevitable in a field that is said to contain more than 300 different schools of therapy.

In this book, I have not outlined another school of therapy. However, I have examined the many direct and subtle ways that emotions influence and are influenced by psychotherapy. Because all therapists deal with emotions, perhaps this focus may help integrate some of the diverse views of therapy and at the same time facilitate the process of therapy. I hope that the ideas presented here are clear and interesting enough to stimulate serious thought. Perhaps that is the best one can hope for in the complex exchange between writer and reader.

Because of the great diversity of therapeutic theories and styles, this book is necessarily incomplete. For example, in recent years there has been an increasing recognition of the role of evolution in psychology. This developing literature is not only concerned with the issues of nature and nurture and their interactions, but also with how evolutionarily stable adaptations have emerged at different periods of human history and now continue to have an effect on human thought and behavior. This is especially true in the case of maleness and femaleness, but it is also true of more subtle interactions between people. This is a literature that has begun to be extensively explored by many disciplines, but despite some impressive insights, the conclusions are still the source of continued controversy. These theories probably justify more attention than I have devoted to them here.

Therapeutic communication is an extremely complex process, and there is still a great deal that is not known about how it works best. I hope that the ideas in this book stimulate others to continue the process of filling in the missing parts. I hope that the future mosaic will be a design full of beauty and elegance and powerful in its ability to affect human life.

APPENDIX
MEASUREMENT IMPLICATIONS OF
AFFECT THEORY

No clinical evaluation in psychiatry, psychology, or other psychotherapy can be considered complete if it neglects the world of affect
and emotion.

—A. M. Stone

A comprehensive theory of affect should have multiple functions. It
should provide answers to important questions such as "How should emotions be defined?" "What roles do they have in life?" and "How can emotions be changed?" A good theory should have implications for psychotherapy, because psychotherapy is concerned with emotional disorders. It
should also show connections between emotions and other conceptual domains such as personality and personality disorders. Last but not least, a
comprehensive emotion theory should have implications for measurement.
It should identify the most important dimensions and variables that should
be measured and provide some guidelines for constructing appropriate instruments. These points are reiterated to remind the reader of the potentially broad scope of emotion theories.

Appropriate measuring instruments are required before research on
emotions can be attempted. In the course of developing the psychoevolutionary theory, I have constructed or adapted a number of scales to measure different aspects of the complex elements of the emotional chain.
Several of the most important of these scales are described in this appendix.
Clinicians may find some of the measuring instruments useful as part of an
assessment battery.

THE NEED FOR THEORY

How we measure emotions depends on how we define them as well
as on the theories we have about them. Each theory of emotion described

171

in the previous chapters has some implications for assessment of emotions. For example, cognitive theories usually describe the situational and conceptual triggers of emotional reactions, and such reactions are assessed by means of self-reports. Motivational theories are likely to direct the researcher's attention to autonomic changes that occur within the body and to use facial expressions as key indicators of emotion. Evolution-based theories are likely to focus attention on the measurement of expressive behavior of humans and animals, whereas psychoanalytic theories imply that projective and drawing techniques best reflect the unconscious mixed emotional states typical of humans.

However, overlapping theoretical ideas require overlapping measurement techniques as well. It is possible to identify four general approaches to measuring emotions, most of which tend to be used by proponents of all viewpoints.

One method involves the use of self-reports of subjective feelings, a procedure that it useful mainly with human adults. A second method is through ratings made of the behavior of an individual. Such ratings can be used with adults, children, people with mental retardation, and lower animals. A third method is through a rating of the product of someone's behavior (e.g., an individual's handwriting or figure drawings). Finally, emotions may be assessed through the use of recordings of physiological or neural changes.

These methods are described and illustrated in detail in Plutchik (1994) and Plutchik and Kellerman (1989). Rather than summarize this information, I focus here on a number of measurement scales that have been based directly on the psychoevolutionary theory of emotion described in chapter 4.

MOOD SCALES AND ADJECTIVE CHECKLISTS

A number of mood checklists have been described over the past 50 years (reviewed in Plutchik, 1980b). They have been found useful in studying the effects of drugs such as amphetamine, antihistamines, and barbiturates on social and emotional behaviors and in tracking the variations in mood states of college students as well as psychiatric patients.

One such checklist—the Emotion–Mood Index (Plutchik, 1989)— is shown in Table A.1. It consists of 72 terms placed into nine clusters and is based on the psychoevolutionary theory. The first eight groupings of terms reflect the eight basic dimensions of emotion, namely Trust, Dyscontrol, Timidity, Depression, Distrust, Control, Aggression, and Gregarious. The last cluster represents an activation or arousal dimension with terms such as *weak*, *strong*, and *restless*.

An example illustrates its use. The Emotion–Mood Index was ad-

TABLE A.1
The Emotion–Mood Index

Trust	Depression	Aggression
_____ Trusting	_____ Depressed	_____ Aggressive
_____ Friendly	_____ Gloomy	_____ Furious
_____ Obliging	_____ Sad	_____ Bossy
_____ Contented	_____ Empty	_____ Boastful
_____ Cooperative	_____ Lonesome	_____ Annoyed
_____ Tolerant	_____ Helpless	_____ Quarrelsome
_____ Calm	_____ Discouraged	_____ Irritated
_____ Patient	_____ Hopeless	_____ Angry

Dyscontrol	Distrust	Gregarious
_____ Alert	_____ Disgusted	_____ Sociable
_____ Fascinated	_____ Uninterested	_____ Generous
_____ Surprised	_____ Bored	_____ Cheerful
_____ Confused	_____ Distrustful	_____ Affectionate
_____ Attentive	_____ Bitter	_____ Happy
_____ Wondering	_____ Sarcastic	_____ Satisfied
_____ Puzzled	_____ Resentful	_____ Delighted
_____ Bewildered	_____ Fed up	_____ Pleased

Timidity	Control	Activation
_____ Afraid	_____ Hopeful	_____ Slowed-down
_____ Scared	_____ Inquisitive	_____ Sluggish
_____ Nervous	_____ Curious	_____ Relaxed
_____ Timid	_____ Eager	_____ Weak
_____ Worried	_____ Interested	_____ Active
_____ Anxious	_____ Daring	_____ Strong
_____ Shy	_____ Impulsive	_____ Energetic
_____ Cautious	_____ Nosy	_____ Restless

Note. The adjective checklist is theory based. From *Emotion: A Psychoevolutionary Synthesis*, by R. Plutchik (1980a), p. 206. Copyright 1980 by Harper & Row. Reprinted with permission.

ministered weekly to a group of psychiatric inpatients on a research ward. All patients had been carefully screened and were diagnosed as manic–depressive. All had repeated experiences of mania, depression, or both (Platman, Plutchik, Fieve, & Lawlor, 1969).

During the course of the study, 26 patients were judged by the psychiatric staff as being in a manic state, 42 were evaluated as depressed, and 79 were assessed as being in a (temporary) normal state. Comparisons were made between the frequencies of self-reported moods in manic and depressed states for each adjective. It was found that every one of the Trust, Gregarious, and Depression adjectives significantly discriminated between the manic and depressed states. In addition, many adjectives from the other scales also discriminated significantly between these two states.

Separate comparisons were then made between the normal state and the manic or depressed state using the total number of items checked in each scale as the basis for comparisons. It was found that every scale significantly discriminated between the normal and depressed states. Three scales—Depression, Aggression, and Control—discriminated between the normal and manic states. It thus appears that the Emotion–Mood Index is capable of distinguishing among several affective states.

An unpublished study using this adjective checklist was concerned with the conceptions held by people as to what their "best" and "worst" moods are like. To answer this question, 33 evening college students were asked to complete this checklist under three conditions: (a) "How do you feel right now?" (b) "How would you describe the best you have ever felt?" and (c) "How would you describe the worst you have ever felt?"

Results of these self-ratings showed that the best mood is described as one that is high in feelings of cheerfulness, trust, and curiosity and extremely low in feelings of sadness, boredom, fear, and anger. The worst mood is highest in sadness, fearfulness, and boredom (in descending order); it lacks happiness, trust, or interest. In addition, the best mood includes feelings of activity and energy, whereas the worst mood includes feelings of sluggishness and weakness. The product-moment correlation between the best and worst moods is $-.76$, implying that they are essentially opposite in character. The *now* mood correlated .63 with the best mood and $-.24$ with the worst.

If we consider the worst mood these people ever experienced, it appears that the dimension of depression is the most strongly represented. The words that make up this dimension are *depressed, gloomy, sad, empty, lonesome, helpless, discouraged*, and *hopeless*. The experience of loss, separation, and mourning is apparently a more distressing experience than that of fear or worry. A related finding was reported by Plutchik (1970) in a study of ideal and least-liked self images. The major differences between these two kinds of self-descriptions were found to be in the depression and destruction dimensions; that is, individuals liked least the moods of sadness and anger. These findings are only preliminary, but they support the hypothesis that depression may be more distressing than anxiety even though anxiety has often been called the "core" of neurosis. It is also possible that depression is more common in everyday life. The two studies cited here using the Emotion–Mood Index simply illustrate the potential usefulness of a theory-based adjective checklist.

One of the advantages of mood checklists is their comparative brevity. Lubin (1966) has shown that it is possible to reduce the length of several depression checklists from 34 adjectives to 17 and still demonstrate high internal correlations as well as significant correlations with other depression scales. It is also possible to reduce the length of a checklist to a single word per dimension and still discriminate between conditions.

Table A.2 shows such a checklist, which uses one word to represent each of the basic affect dimensions, along with a 5-point intensity scale

TABLE A.2
A Mood Rating Scale Using One Word for Each Affect Dimension

Instructions: For each of the emotions listed below, please indicate how strongly you feel it **right now**.

Right Now Do You Feel	Not at All	Slightly	Moderately	Strongly	Very Strongly
Happy					
Fearful					
Agreeable					
Angry					
Interested					
Disgusted					
Sad					
Surprised					

Note. From *Emotion: A Psychoevolutionary Synthesis*, by R. Plutchik (1980a), p. 208. Copyright 1980 by Harper & Row. Reprinted with permission.

ranging from *not at all* to *very strongly*. It assumes that because words like *sad*, *sorrowful*, or *grief-stricken* all represent different levels of the same basic emotion dimension, repeating them all in a checklist is unnecessarily redundant. Instead, the dimension can be sampled with a single term such as *sad*, and individuals can make an intensity rating for that word.

To test the usefulness of such a brief affect rating scale, I asked a group of 40 college students to complete it at the beginning of each Monday, Wednesday, and Friday class during 1 week (Plutchik, 1966). This represented the control condition. The mood scale was then given just prior to an examination and just after the exams were returned to the students. Analysis of the affect ratings showed that all eight moods remained stable during the control week. Ratings made just before the examination showed highly significant increases in ratings of fearful and interested and highly significant decreases in ratings of happy and agreeable. The other four emotions did not show any significant changes.

On the test return day, the students were given their examination papers and were allowed to see their grades. Affect ratings were then obtained again. Under these conditions, seven of the eight emotions showed highly significant changes in mean self-ratings. There were significant decreases in happy, agreeable, and interested and significant increases in angry, disgusted, sad, and surprised. These findings suggest that these single adjective mood scales are sensitive to stresses, cover a wide range of affect states, and have theoretical relevance (Plutchik, 1966).

This same mood rating scale has been used as part of a battery of tests designed to identify changes in elderly (mostly welfare) tenants in a single-room occupancy hotel in New York City (Plutchik, McCarthy, & Hall, 1975). These tenants were assessed just after a new medical and social services program was introduced directly into the hotel and again assessed 1 year later. Among the changes that took place during that period was a significant increase in feelings of anger and sadness. No significant changes occurred in the other emotions. To explain these results, the authors hypothesized that the tenants' increase in feelings of frustration was associated with their rising expectations. Despite the concerns of the staff, relatively few improvements in living conditions were noted during the 1st year.

Adjective checklists for the measurement of emotional states have come into wide use in recent years. Their advantage is that they are usually brief, have obvious face validity, and can be easily self-administered. They can also be used to provide indices of transient states of emotion or mood as well as long-term emotional dispositions. Their disadvantages include that they are easy to fake and that relatively little validation has been done on clinical populations. In addition, many of the checklists have no theoretical justification for the particular dimensions or scales that are scored. Despite these problems, such checklists represent a useful addition to the other ways of measuring emotions. Russell and Carroll (1999) review some of these issues.

THE EMOTIONS PROFILE INDEX

The Emotions Profile Index (EPI; Plutchik & Kellerman, 1974) is based on the psychoevolutionary theory of emotion and has had wide use both as a measure of emotion and as a measure of certain personality traits. The EPI provides measures of eight basic emotions. It is based on the idea that all interpersonal personality traits can be conceptualized as resulting from a mixture of two or more primary emotions (as discussed in chapter 4). This means that those who described themselves as shy or gloomy are implicitly telling us something about the primary emotions that combine to make up these traits. Shyness, for example, implies frequent feelings of fear, whereas gloominess implies frequent feelings of sadness.

The EPI was developed initially by having 10 clinical psychologists rate the primary emotion components of a large number of traits. Twelve trait terms were finally selected on the grounds of high interjudge consistency on the components and a wide sampling of the trait universe described by factor analytic studies. These terms were then paired in all possible combinations, yielding 66 pairs. Four of the pairs were found to have identical scoring categories and so were dropped, thus leaving 62 pairs of trait terms for the final form of the test.

The EPI is a forced-choice test. The person taking it is simply asked to indicate which of two paired words is more self-descriptive; for example, is he or she more quarrelsome or shy? The choices are scored in terms of the primary emotions implied by the trait word. Each time the respondent makes a choice between two trait words, he or she adds to the score on one or more of the eight basic emotion dimensions. Thus, rather than measure only anxiety, the test also simultaneously measures anger, sadness, joy, and so on. Because the implications of the choices are not always clear to the respondent, the test has something of a projective quality; the respondent does not usually recognize the implicit scoring system. Finally, because of the forced-choice format of the EPI, it tends to reduce response bias associated with a set to choose socially desirable traits. This is true because many of the choices must be made between two equally undesirable or two equally desirable traits. In addition, a bias score is built into the test as a measure of the respondent's tendency to choose socially desirable (or undesirable) traits in those cases in which the items are not matched (Kellerman & Plutchik, 1968).

The following 12 terms are used in the EPI: *adventurous, affectionate, brooding, cautious, gloomy, impulsive, obedient, quarrelsome, resentful, self-conscious, shy,* and *sociable.* A brief definition is provided in the test for each term. The total score for each of the eight primary emotion dimensions is converted into a percentile score on the basis of data obtained from 500 men and 500 women. These people represent a broad range of individuals characterized by a lack of overt pathology or psychiatric hospitalization. The percentile scores are then plotted on a circular diagram, as illustrated in Figure A.1 for patients with severe depression. The center of the circle represents 0 percentile, and the outer circumference of the circle is the 100th percentile. The larger the dark wedge-shaped area, the stronger the emotional disposition that is revealed. Details of scoring and plotting may be found in the published manual (Plutchik & Kellerman, 1974).

Although the EPI has been used in a variety of settings, I present here a brief review of its use in clinical studies. Fahs, Hogan, and Fullerton (1969) showed that the Depression Scale of the EPI discriminated clearly between a group of depressed patients in a hospital and a control group. Conte and Plutchik (1974) demonstrated that those patients who were admitted to a mental hospital after a suicide attempt were significantly higher on the Depression and Aggression Scales of the EPI than a matched group of nonsuicidal patients. A study by Fieve, Platman, and Plutchik (1968) demonstrated that the EPI Depression Scale could be used to assess the effects of two antidepressant drugs, lithium and imipramine.

The EPI has provided the basis for emotion profiles for several clinical groups: narcotic addicts (Sheppard, Fiorentino, Collins, & Merlis, 1969); geriatric patients (Plutchik & DiScipio, 1974); alcoholic individuals with Korsokoff's syndrome (Plutchik & DiScipio, 1974); asthma patients (Plut-

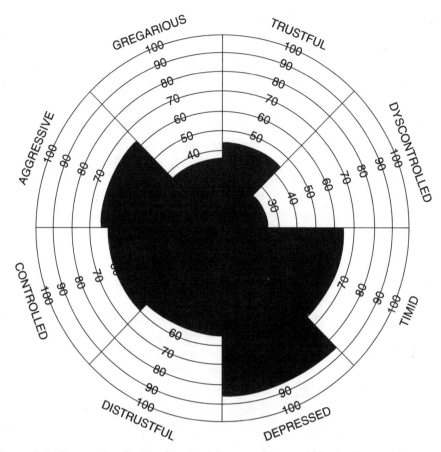

Figure A.1. Depression Profile Obtained From a Group of Manic–Depressive Patients. From *The Psychology and Biology of Emotion* by R. Plutchik, p. 117. Copyright 1994 by Robert Plutchik. Reprinted with permission.

chik, Williams, Jerrett, Karasu, & Kane, 1978), Japanese individuals with schizophrenia, neurosis, or alcoholism (Hama, Matsuyama, Hashimoto, & Plutchik, 1982); women with premenstrual syndrome (Henderson & Whissell, 1997); and patients with acute coronary heart disease (Veselica et al., 1999). A depression profile obtained from a group of manic depressive patients is shown in Figure A.1.

THE PERSONALITY PROFILE

The circumplex concept, which has been described in an earlier chapter, has been used as the basis for tests of personality. One such test is the Personality Profile (Plutchik & Conte, 1989a). The items of this scale were based initially on the angular position of the 171 personality trait terms reported by Conte and Plutchik (1981).

On the basis of the empirical groupings of terms, eight clusters—Aggressive, Assertive, Sociable, Accepting, Submissive, Passive, Depressed, and Rejecting—were identified in sequence around the circumplex. The trait terms *argumentative* and *belligerent* were a part of the Aggressive cluster, *obedient* and *docile* were part of the Submissive cluster, and the Rejecting cluster included such terms as *obstinate*, *stubborn*, and *spiteful*.

The first version of the test was administered to both patient groups and nonpatients; a number of item analyses were carried out, and Conflict and Social Desirability subscales were constructed. Internal reliability of the scales ranged from .76 to .87. Some evidence for construct validity is seen by the fact that a Self-Esteem Scale correlated significantly and negatively with the dimensions of Submissive, Passive, Depressed, Rejecting, and Aggressive and significantly positive with Accepting, Assertive, and Sociable. Normative data are available on 282 nonpatients for each of the eight scales. When several clinical populations were compared with the nonpatients, it was found that patients with affective disorders scored significantly higher than the nonpatients on the Depressed, Passive, and Submissive Scales and significantly lower on the Assertive, Sociable, and Accepting Scales. A group of alcoholic individuals on a detoxification ward were found to be significantly higher than nonpatients on the Passive, Depressed, and Submissive Scales and lower on the Accepting Scale. The highest conflict scores were found in substance abuse outpatients and borderline patients.

The version of the Personality Profile described above was based on ratings made of single personality trait terms. In using the scales with hospital patients, it was found that some terms were unfamiliar to some patients. Therefore, a second version (Conte, Plutchik et al., 1991) of the Personality Profile was constructed using short sentences that defined each trait. Thus, for each of the 89 trait terms on Form A, there are 89 corresponding statements on Form B. Correlations between the corresponding scales of the two forms were high, including those for the Conflict and Social Desirability Scales. Internal reliability as measured by coefficient alpha was also high for each scale. A copy of the scales is included in Table A.3.

To provide a measure of the discriminant validity of the Personality Profile, three groups were compared: 74 nonpatients, 144 psychiatric outpatients, and 60 psychiatric inpatients at a large municipal hospital. Analysis of variance showed that the outpatients scored highest of all groups on the scales of Submissive, Passive, Depressed, Rejecting, and Conflict. The inpatients were significantly less aggressive, sociable, and conflicted than either the nonpatients or the outpatients. Only on the Assertiveness Scale did the nonpatients score higher than the inpatients or the outpatients. These findings make clinical sense.

Another study using the Personality Profile, Form B was concerned

TABLE A.3
Personality Profile (Form B)

Name _____ Sex _____ Age _____ Date _____

Instructions

Please indicate how often each statement describes your behavior or feelings by putting a check in the appropriate space.

	Never	Rarely	Some-times	Often	Very Often
1. I am easy to get along with					
2. I do what I am told					
3. I can't get things done					
4. I feel isolated from people					
5. I get jealous					
6. I argue with others					
7. I enjoy doing things that are risky					
8. I am kind					
9. I don't mind it when people have opinions different from mine					
10. I do what other people want me to do					
11. I feel like giving up					
12. I get depressed and feel low					
13. It is difficult to get me to do something I don't want to do					
14. I let people know what is wrong with their opinions					
15. I am sure of myself					
16. I like to be with other people					
17. When someone does something for me I feel I should do something in return					
18. I am a quiet person					
19. I have little motivation to do anything					
20. I can't help myself					

TABLE A.3 (*Continued*)

	Never	Rarely	Some-times	Often	Very Often
21. It's difficult to get me to change my mind					
22. I get into fights with other people					
23. I say what I want to					
24. I am a warm and caring person					
25. I do a job the best I can					
26. I am easily led by other people					
27. I don't have strong opinions					
28. I look and feel sad					
29. I am selfish					
30. I look down on people					
31. I have lots of energy and get things done					
32. I am a happy person					
33. I am accepting of other people					
34. I avoid calling attention to myself					
35. I don't believe in planning ahead					
36. I feel blue					
37. I act in a mean way					
38. I get angry very easily					
39. I like to take chances in new situations					
40. I am a giving person					
41. I like to help others to get something done					
42. I don't allow myself to do many of the things I want to do					
43. I am not sure of myself					
44. I worry about things a lot					

TABLE A.3 (*Continued*)

	Never	Rarely	Some-times	Often	Very Often
45. I tend to change my personal attachments					
46. I make remarks designed to hurt other people's feelings					
47. I have a lot of energy					
48. I treat people nicely					
49. I feel calm					
50. I keep my feelings and thoughts to myself					
51. I make decisions with difficulty					
52. I feel upset and jumpy					
53. I don't like to give anything to anyone					
54. I get angry quickly					
55. I say what I think					
56. I have good manners					
57. I go along with other people's wishes					
58. I avoid taking risks					
59. I can't make up my mind					
60. I look at the bad side of things and expect the worst					
61. I want more than my share					
62. I like to tell everybody what to do					
63. I have faith in myself					
64. I don't mind changes					
65. I try to be of service to others					
66. I get embarrassed easily					
67. I don't care much how things turn out					
68. I act sad					

TABLE A.3 (*Continued*)

	Never	Rarely	Some-times	Often	Very Often
69. I feel angry and insulted					
70. My critical opinions prevent people from carrying out their plans					
71. I show my true feelings and opinions					
72. I am considerate of others					
73. I stay cool when others get excited					
74. I am afraid to show my feelings					
75. I let things be done without taking part					
76. I am unhappy					
77. I don't accept new ideas or people easily					
78. I complain about lots of things					
79. I make up my mind easily					
80. I am easily affected by other people's feelings					
81. I feel very discouraged					
82. I doubt the reasons people give for doing what they do					
83. I am grumpy					
84. I get excited about many things					
85. I don't get upset easily					
86. I feel that things are bad and the future won't be any better					
87. I get impatient with people who believe in different things than I do					
88. I am unfriendly					
89. I can only see the dark side of things					

Note. © Learning Foundation, Inc. 1999.

with the extent to which personality traits can be used to predict the outcome of psychotherapy (Conte, Plutchik, Buck, Picard, & Karasu, 1991). In this study, 96 patients who were newly admitted to a psychiatric outpatient clinic attended a median of 14 therapy sessions and completed the Personality Profile, Form B after registering at the clinic and prior to their psychiatric evaluations. Only the dimension of rejection was found to be negatively correlated with the outcome measures. However, there was a significant positive correlation between scores on the dimensions of Rejection, Aggression, Conflict, and Passivity and the number and extent of symptoms and problems with which these patients presented at the outpatient clinic.

A second study (Conte, Plutchik, Buck, Picard, & Karasu, 1991) investigated the relations between ego functions and personality traits. Four ego function scales—Judgment, Synthetic–Integrative Functioning, Mastery–Competence, and Ego Strength Scales—were used based on Bellak's (1984) descriptions of ego functions. Correlations between these various dimensions and the eight personality dimensions were obtained. Generally the dimensions of submissive, passive, depressed, rejecting, aggressive, and conflict all correlated negatively and significantly with the four ego functions. Acceptance, assertiveness, and sociability all correlated positively with the ego functions. The highest correlation that was found (.68) was between assertiveness and ego strength. It thus appears that ego functions, as conceptualized within a psychodynamic tradition, correlated highly with personality dimensions.

Conte, Plutchik, Picard, Galanter, and Jacoby (1991) provide an example of the use of the Personality Profile, Form B to study personality traits and coping styles of hospitalized alcoholic individuals. In this study, 40 inpatients on an alcohol detoxification unit of a large municipal hospital were administered a battery of tests consisting of the Personality Profile, Form B; a coping styles test; a Depression Scale; and the Brief MAST, a measure of alcohol-related behavior (Vaillant, 1983). A demographically comparable group of 40 outpatients attending the medical screening clinic of the same hospital also completed the battery.

Results showed that those in the alcoholic group as a whole described themselves as considerably more passive, conflicted, and depressed. Alcoholic women scored significantly higher than the alcoholic men on the dimensions of passivity, aggressiveness, depression, and conflict. Alcoholic women were also more submissive, passive, and depressed than the nonalcoholic women in the comparison group. Overall, the results suggest that hospitalized alcoholic women were considerably more dysfunctional than either nonalcoholic women or alcoholic men. These differences may be seen in the Personality Profile, Form B scoring circumplex shown in Figure A.2.

PERSONALITY PROFILE INDEX

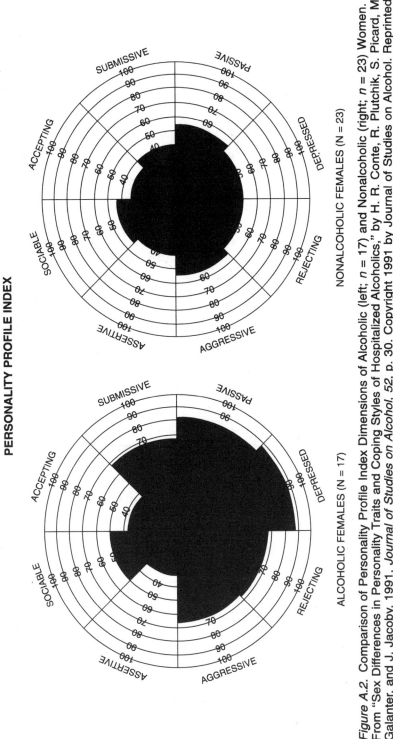

ALCOHOLIC FEMALES (N = 17)

NONALCOHOLIC FEMALES (N = 23)

Figure A.2. Comparison of Personality Profile Index Dimensions of Alcoholic (left; *n* = 17) and Nonalcoholic (right; *n* = 23) Women. From "Sex Differences in Personality Traits and Coping Styles of Hospitalized Alcoholics," by H. R. Conte, R. Plutchik, S. Picard, M. Galanter, and J. Jacoby, 1991, *Journal of Studies on Alcohol, 52*, p. 30. Copyright 1991 by Journal of Studies on Alcohol. Reprinted with permission.

THE MEASUREMENT OF EGO DEFENSES
(THE LIFE STYLE INDEX)

The third scale to be described as part of the family of scales implied by the psychoevolutionary theory of emotion measures ego defenses. The details of test construction and evaluation have been presented elsewhere (Conte & Apter, 1995; Plutchik, 1995; Plutchik et al. 1979), and so only a general overview is described here.

Most clinicians, even those who are unsympathetic to psychoanalytic theory, have come to accept and find useful the concept of ego defenses. This is true even though there is considerable controversy around certain issues related to defenses (Plutchik, 1995; Westen, 1998). For example, experts disagree about the number of ego defenses that exist and the question of which defenses are most primitive. Nevertheless, there is considerable agreement that some defenses are more similar to each other and some less similar and that polarities exist (e.g., introjection vs. displacement). There is also agreement that defenses are usually unconscious.

These ideas have led to the notion that a circumplex can describe the relations among defenses. The theory (described in chapter 6) also implies that defenses are derivatives of emotion and that for each basic emotion there is a basic defense mechanism. These ideas have provided the bases for the development of a set of scales designed to measure certain basic defenses.

The scales that make up the Life Style Index (Conte & Apter, 1995) are self-report measures (see Table A.4). They are designed to provide insight into unconscious states on the basis of the derivatives of the unconscious states. For example, a person who strongly insists that he is free of prejudice may be using denial as an ego defense. To confirm this idea, a group of experienced clinicians were asked by our research group to rank the items of the scales in terms of relevancy to each scale. Their results are illustrated in Exhibit A.1. Internal reliability of the scales is moderate and test–retest scores are highly correlated (Conte & Apter, 1995).

A number of studies have revealed the validity of the Life Style Index. For example, all but one of the scales correlate significantly with anxiety scores and negatively with self-esteem scores. Psychiatric patients, on average, score higher than control participants on most scales. Suicide risk in psychiatric patients was found to be positively correlated with regression and displacement, and it was negatively correlated with denial, whereas risk of violence (as measured by a separate test) was positively correlated with projection and denial.

Depressed patients have significantly higher-than-normal scores on the repression, regression, and reaction-formation scales. Ego strength correlates positively with intellectualization and negatively with displacement and denial. Normal elderly women are more likely to use reaction-

TABLE A.4
Life Style Index

Name _____ Sex _____ Age _____ Date _____

Instructions

Please indicate whether each of the following statements describes the way you *usually* feel or act. If the statement does describe you, place a check in the first column marked **YES**; if the statement *does not* describe you, check **NO**.

	Yes	No
1. I am a very easy person to get along with		
2. When I want something, I just can't wait to get it		
3. There has always been a person whom I wished I were like		
4. People do not consider me to be an emotional person		
5. I feel outraged at dirty movies		
6. I rarely remember my dreams		
7. People who boss other people around make me furious		
8. I sometimes have an urge to push my fist through a wall		
9. I'm annoyed by the fact that people show off too much		
10. In my daydreams, I am always the center of attention		
11. I am the type that never cries		
12. Using public bathrooms is very upsetting to me		
13. I am always willing to listen to all sides of an argument		
14. I "fly off the handle" easily		
15. When someone shoves me in a crowd, I feel like kicking the person		
16. People admire many things about me		
17. I believe it's better to think things out than to get angry		
18. I get sick a lot		
19. I have a bad memory for faces		
20. When I've been rejected by someone, I've sometimes felt suicidal		
21. When I hear dirty jokes, I feel very embarrassed		
22. I always see the bright side of things		

TABLE A.4 (*Continued*)

	Yes	No
23. I hate hostile people		
24. I have trouble getting rid of anything that belongs to me		
25. I have trouble remembering people's names		
26. I tend to be too impulsive		
27. People who try to get their way by yelling and screaming make me sick		
28. I am free from prejudice		
29. I have a strong need to have people tell me that I am appealing		
30. When I go on a trip, I plan every detail in advance		
31. Sometimes I wish that an atom bomb would destroy the world		
32. Pornography is disgusting		
33. When I become upset I eat a lot		
34. I never feel fed up with people		
35. I cannot remember many things about my childhood		
36. I frequently take work with me when I go on vacation		
37. In my fantasies I accomplish great things		
38. Most people annoy me because they are too selfish		
39. Touching anything slimy makes me feel nauseous		
40. If someone bothers me, I don't tell it to him but I tend to complain to someone else		
41. I believe people will take advantage of me if I am not careful		
42. It takes me a long time to see bad qualities in other people		
43. When I read or hear about a tragedy, it never seems to affect me		
44. In arguments, I'm usually more logical than the other person		
45. I have a strong need to be complimented		
46. Promiscuity is disgusting		
47. When I drive a car, I sometimes get an urge to hit another car		
48. When things don't go my way, I sometimes sulk		
49. When I see someone who is bloody, it almost never bothers me		

TABLE A.4 (*Continued*)

	Yes	No
50. I get irritable when I don't get attention		
51. People tell me I'll believe anything		
52. I wear clothes that hide my bad points		
53. It is very difficult for me to use dirty words		
54. I seem to have a lot of arguments with people		
55. One of the things I hate about people is that they are insincere		
56. People tell me I'm too objective about everything		
57. My moral standards are higher than those of most people I know		
58. When I can't cope, I feel like crying		
59. I can't seem to express my emotions		
60. When someone bumps into me, I get furious		
61. I put things that I don't like out of my mind		
62. I very seldom feel affectionate		
63. I hate people who always try to be the center of attention		
64. I collect a lot of different things		
65. I work harder than most people in order to be good at what I'm interested in		
66. Hearing a baby cry does not bother me		
67. I have been so angry that I have wanted to smash things		
68. I'm always optimistic		
69. I lie a lot		
70. I feel a greater commitment to doing tasks than I do to socializing		
71. Most people are obnoxious		
72. I would never go to a movie that was X-rated		
73. I am irritated because people can't be trusted		
74. I will do anything to make a good impression		
75. I don't understand why I do some of the things I do		

	Yes	No
76. I go out of my way to see movies that show a lot of violence		
77. I think the world situation is much better than most people think it is		
78. When I am disappointed, I act very moody		
79. The way people dress on beaches these days is indecent		
80. I do not let my emotions run away with me		
81. I plan for the worst so that I will not be caught off guard		
82. My life is so great that a lot of people wish they were in my shoes		
83. I have hit or kicked something so hard when I was angry that I accidentally hurt myself		
84. People with low moral standards make me sick		
85. I hardly remember anything about my early years in school		
86. When I become upset, I can't help acting childishly		
87. I am more comfortable discussing my thoughts than my feelings		
88. I can't seem to finish anything that I start		
89. When I hear about atrocities, it doesn't bother me		
90. People in my family almost never disagree with one another		
91. I yell at people a lot		
92. I hate people who step on others in order to get ahead		
93. When I'm upset, I often get drunk		
94. I am lucky to have fewer problems than most people		
95. When something is bothering me, I sleep more than usual		
96. I think it's disgusting the way most people lie to get ahead		
97. I use dirty words a lot		

Note. From © Learning Foundation, Inc. 1999.

formation and regression than are normal elderly men. The women also report experiencing a greater number of life problems. Life problems and total ego defense score correlated highly.

Another study (Greenwald, Reznikoff, & Plutchik, 1994) correlated

EXHIBIT A.1
Items Ranking Highest on Relevancy for the Eight Ego Defense Scales

Compensation
  In my dreams, I'm always the center of attention.
Denial
  I am free of prejudice.
Displacement
  If someone bothers me, I don't tell it to him, but I tend to complain to
    someone else.
Intellectualization
  I am more comfortable discussing my thoughts than my feelings.
Projection
  I believe people will take advantage of you if you are not careful.
Reaction Formation
  Pornography is disgusting.
Regression
  I get irritable when I don't get attention.
Repression
  I rarely remember my dreams.

Life Style Index scores with personality disorder diagnoses obtained from the Millon Clinical Multiaxial Inventory (Millon, 1987). The population consisted of a group of 74 hospitalized alcoholic individuals. It was found that each personality disorder diagnosis correlated highest with a particular ego defense (for six of the eight scales) in such a way as to be consistent with the theory of defenses as derivatives of emotion (described in chapter 6). For example, histrionic personality disorder correlated highest with denial, whereas paranoid personality disorder correlated highest with projection (Greenwald, Reznikoff, & Plutchik, 1994).

In recent years, the Life Style Index has been translated into Dutch, Norwegian, Russian, Hebrew, and Chinese. One of the studies from Israel may be used to illustrate what the scoring profiles look like. A total of 130 adolescent patients at a psychiatric hospital in Israel were tested with the Life Style Index and several other scales. Forty of the 130 patients had been admitted subsequent to a suicide attempt. Comparable data were obtained from a group of nonsuicidal high school students (control group). Results showed that the suicidal patients scored significantly higher than the control group on repression, regression, and total defense score. The pattern of results for the suicidal patients is presented in Figure A.3.

When the suicidal patients were compared with the nonsuicidal inpatients, it was found that the suicidal patients had the highest ego defense scores, the nonsuicidal inpatients had intermediate defense scores, and the control group had the lowest ego defense scores. It appears that the patients admitted for a suicide attempt were more disturbed and in greater conflict than the other two groups.

Figure A.3 shows that the suicidal patients are considerably above the

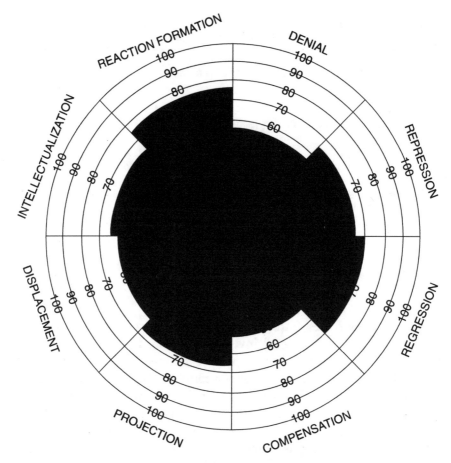

Figure A.3. Percentile Scores on the Life Style Index of 40 Suicidal Adolescents. From "The Life Style Index: A Self-Report Measure of Ego Defenses" (p. 195), by H. R. Conte and A. Apter, 1995. In *Ego Defenses: Theory and Measurement*, edited by H. R. Conte and R. Plutchik. Copyright 1995 by John Wiley & Sons. Reprinted with permission.

norm (the 50th percentile) on reaction formation, regression, projection, and intellectualization. From a clinical point of view, high scores on reaction formation suggest that the suicidal patients believe that they have high moral standards, particularly in relation to sex (i.e., use of obscene language, viewing of pornography, and promiscuity). This image is supported by their high scores on intellectualization, implying that they do not easily express emotion or affection and that they see themselves as being more rational and objective than most people.

The conflict in these suicidal adolescents becomes more evident when we see their simultaneous high scores on projection and regression. Such scores mean that the patients tend to project their own unacceptable impulses onto others (e.g., they report "hating hostile people"). Their high scores on regression implies that they are impulsive, moody, and act child-ishly when frustrated. These scale scores thus provide a picture of conflicted young people who described themselves as high-minded and mature and at the same time, angry and childish.

The Life Style Index appears to be a reasonable way to measure the conscious derivatives of unconscious defense mechanisms. It is easy to ad-minister and score and has revealed some interesting relations between ego defenses and anxiety, self-esteem, alcoholism, suicidality, violence, and other clinical variables. It is based on theory and is part of the family of scales implied by affect theory.

THE AECOM COPING SCALES

The last of the family of emotion-related scales to be described is the AECOM Coping Scales (Plutchik, 1989). (I chose the acronym AECOM because the scales were developed during my tenure at the Albert Einstein College of Medicine.) As elaborated in chapter 6, coping styles are related to ego defenses, but whereas defenses are generally unconscious attempts to deal with anxiety and life problems carried out by an immature ego, coping styles generally are conscious attempts used by mature individuals to solve problems. It is important to emphasize that coping styles do not have any connotation of psychopathology, as do ego defenses. They are common, garden-variety methods that all people use to varying degrees in order to deal with life problems. They are general enough to be applicable to almost any problem an individual may encounter, although some work better than others. It is also possible for an adult to use certain coping styles and certain defenses at the same time.

The derivatives model of the psychoevolutionary theory of affect pos-its that a coping style exists as a conscious parallel to each basic defense. For example, for the ego defense of repression, there exists a parallel coping style in which the individual deliberately inhibits certain classes of behav-ior in order to avoid anxiety and frustration. The terms *suppression* and *avoidance* are suggested as the conscious coping style for the unconscious mechanism of repression. Similarly, the unconscious mechanism of denial may be the precursor to a conscious coping mechanism that tries to min-imize the significance of a stressful event. This coping style is therefore called *minimization*. The model of coping styles being proposed assumes that for each of the eight basic emotions there is a related ego defense and a derivative coping style. The various coping styles have been given the following names (with the related defenses listed in parentheses): *suppres-sion* (repression), *minimization* (denial), *reversal* (reaction formation), *map-ping* (intellectualization), *substitution* (displacement), *blame* (projection), *re-*

placement (compensation), and *help-seeking* (regression). These concepts have been defined in chapter 6.

A group of five clinicians met regularly to construct items that reflected the many ways that people use to cope with problems. It became increasingly evident that the coping methods could be grouped into a relatively few categories. The schema proposed here of eight basic coping styles that correspond to eight basic ego defenses seemed to be both general and parsimonious.

After consensus had been arrived at among the members of the group, the items were then presented to an independent group of 10 psychiatrists, who were asked to indicate the extent to which each item adequately reflected each of the eight basic coping styles as defined by the theoretical model. On the basis of their responses, several items were dropped and the wording of others was changed.

The 95 items of the scales, labeled the AECOM *Coping Scale*, were incorporated into a format in which the respondent indicated on a 4-point scale how frequently he or she felt or acted in the ways described (see Table A.5). For example, the coping style of minimization is reflected by such items as "When something bothers me, I can ignore it" and "I feel that problems have a way of taking care of themselves." *Suppression* is expressed by such items as "I try not to think about unpleasant things" and "I avoid funerals." *Help-seeking* is defined by such items as "When I have a problem I try to get others to help me" and "I try to be associated with people who take charge of a situation."

The AECOM Coping Scales have been administered to several nonpatient and patient groups and has been modified so that the present version contains 87 items. Preliminary norms from a sample of 120 college students are available. No sex differences have been found in coping styles in this college population. The internal reliabilities of the eight coping scales as measured by coefficient alpha varied from .58 to .79, with an average of .70. The use of the scales as a teaching device in a series of workshops on professional burnout is described by Wilder and Plutchik (1982).

In an unpublished study (Plutchik & Lang, 1990), 199 prisoners in a Canadian penitentiary were asked to complete the AECOM Coping Scales along with several other instruments. A group of 76 Canadian college students also completed the same battery of tests. It was found that the college students scored significantly higher than the prisoners on the coping styles of minimization, replacement, and reversal and scored significantly lower on suppression, help-seeking, and mapping. When these coping styles of the prisoners were correlated with parenting styles of their parents, it was found that high maternal rejection and depression were associated with the tendency of the prisoners to use help-seeking as a coping style for solving problems. The fathers' degree of sociability was found

TABLE A.5
AECOM Coping Scales

Name _____ Sex _____ Age _____ Date _____

Instructions

Here is a list of statements describing how people behave in different situations or how they feel about various things. Please indicate how often each statement describes your behavior or feelings by putting a check in the appropriate space.

	Never	Rarely	Some-times	Often
1. I'm an optimist				
2. I avoid thinking about unpleasant things				
3. When I have a problem, I try to get others to help me				
4. If an illness or accident prevented me from doing my usual work, I would still find useful things to do				
5. If other people stopped making decisions for me, I could make my own				
6. When I get upset, I look for something to eat				
7. I get as much information as I can before I make decisions				
8. I try to see the funny side of upsetting situations				
9. I don't worry in advance about problems that are likely to occur				
10. I try not to think about my problems				
11. I try to be involved with people who can take care of things better than I can				
12. I exercise regularly to try to improve the shape of my body				
13. When things go wrong for me, it is someone else's fault				
14. I read fiction to take my mind off my problems				
15. When I have a problem, I try to think of all the different ways to take care of it				

	Never	Rarely	Some-times	Often
16. I make an extra effort to be nice to people I don't like				
17. I feel that things are not as bad as they seem to others				
18. I avoid funerals				
19. When I feel upset, I like to be taken care of				
20. If I lose a friend, I try to make another one				
21. I would get more done if people didn't bother me				
22. When I get angry, I work it off by doing physical activities				
23. I try to carefully analyze every problem				
24. When I get angry, I try to hide my feelings				
25. I ignore aches and pains				
26. I do not look at disturbing scenes in movies				
27. When I'm sick, I like to get in bed and be waited on				
28. When I do poorly at something, I try to improve				
29. Because other people interfere, I can't get my work done				
30. When I feel nervous, I go for a walk				
31. I try to figure out the possible good and bad outcomes before making any decision				
32. If I feel shy in a group, I still force myself to approach people				
33. I feel that problems have a way of taking care of themselves				
34. I avoid visiting people in the hospital				
35. I get someone else's opinions before I buy anything important				

	Never	Rarely	Some-times	Often
36. When I feel sad, I try to do something that interests me				
37. I'd be better off if people stopped interfering in my life				
38. When I feel tense, I like to work with my hands				
39. I spend a lot of time thinking about how to solve my problems				
40. When I am in a tense or unpleasant situation, I try to think of something funny to say				
41. I have to be very sick to see a doctor				
42. I avoid unhappy movies				
43. When I'm upset, I try to find someone to talk to about what is bothering me				
44. If someone close to me died, I would keep busy to take my mind off the loss				
45. Other people cause my problems				
46. When I have a problem, I try to figure out all the steps necessary to solve it				
47. I am the kind of person who does not complain				
48. I don't worry about things in advance because I'm sure that everything will turn out all right				
49. I avoid talking about death				
50. I avoid being alone when I feel upset				
51. I work hard to overcome my weaknesses				
52. I'd get along better with people if they didn't argue so much				
53. When things get to be too much for me, I daydream				
54. If a doctor told me I had a serious illness, I would try to learn as much about it as I could				

TABLE A.5 (*Continued*)

	Never	Rarely	Some-times	Often
55. Even if I felt nervous about saying what was on my mind in a group, I would speak up anyway				
56. When something bothers me, I can ignore it				
57. I avoid visiting a person who is in mourning				
58. I ask other people for their advice when I am not sure about something				
59. When I feel unhappy, I try to do something that will cheer me up				
60. If others were kinder to me, I could get more done				
61. When I'm upset, reading calms me down				
62. When I have many decisions to make, I decide which is most important before I do anything				
63. When I'm in an embarrasing situation, I try to act as if I am comfortable				
64. I feel that there is very little that is worth worrying about				
65. I try to avoid unpleasant situations				
66. When things go wrong, I feel sorry for myself				
67. If someone close to me died, I would help other people who had lost someone				
68. If my doctor knew more, I would be more willing to take his advice				
69. When I get tense, I call people on the phone				
70. When I feel sad, I try to hide it with a smile				
71. I believe that regular health check-ups are a waste of my time				
72. I avoid reading unpleasant news				

TABLE A.5 (*Continued*)

	Never	Rarely	Some-times	Often
73. When I'm upset, I let people know how bad I feel				
74. If I can't do something at first, I am willing to spend a lot of time to learn				
75. I'd get along better with other people if they didn't take advantage of me				
76. When I'm worried or upset, I take a couple of drinks to relax				
77. If I wanted to engage in a sport that I thought was dangerous, I would make myself try it				
78. No matter how bad things seem, I don't let them upset me				
79. I take tranquilizers when I feel very nervous				
80. When I have a problem, I go to pieces				
81. I buy clothes that minimize unattractive parts of my body				
82. I eat when I feel depressed				
83. I'm not afraid to take risks because when your number is up it's up				
84. I avoid thinking about making a will				
85. I watch my diet so that I will not gain weight				
86. I avoid going to cemeteries				

Note. From © Learning Foundation, Inc. 1999.

to be negatively correlated with the coping style of suppression. In other words, fathers who did not socialize warmly with their children tended to have children who avoided many social encounters (at least in this prison population).

In a study of 74 middle managers in the Bell telephone system (Bunker, 1982), correlations were found between coping scales scores and levels of stress, as well as other test data. Those managers who were rated as having many psychological symptoms were significantly higher on the defense of denial and the coping style of blame than were those managers who had few psychological symptoms. They were also judged to be less effective managers. Managers evaluated as effective copers had relatively high scores on mapping. When the managers rated low on stress were compared to those rated high, it was found that the low-stress individuals were relatively lower on most of the coping styles, with the exception of suppression and mapping, whereas the high-stress individuals were high on everything except reversal and help-seeking. These patterns indicate that the presence of psychological symptoms and level of functioning on the job are related to patterns of coping.

Another study (Conte, Plutchik, Picard, Galanter, & Jacoby, 1991) compared 40 alcoholic inpatients on a detoxification ward with 40 control patients with the same general social background but who came to an emergency room screening clinic for treatment of minor physical ailments. All patients took a battery of tests that included the coping scales.

Figure A.4 shows the coping style profile of the 40 alcoholic inpatients. They appeared to have a strong tendency to use suppression as a way of dealing with life stresses. They also were very likely to blame other people for their problems, and they had a strong tendency to seek help from others. (Perhaps this tendency is the basis for describing alcoholic individuals as dependent personalities.) The alcoholic individuals were significantly higher on these coping dimensions than those in the matched control group.

Conte, Plutchik, Schwartz, and Wild (1983) used the AECOM Coping Scales in an effort to predict change in hospitalized individuals with schizophrenia after discharge. In this investigation, a group of inpatients with schizophrenia completed a battery of self-report questionnaires designed to measure dimensions of personality, affect, conflict, ego defenses, and coping styles. Similar ratings were made by each patient's primary therapist. Those patients who were rehospitalized during the next 2 years were identified. It was found that the best predictors of readmission to the hospital included two ego defenses, denial and displacement, and the coping style of suppression. This latter finding is consistent with the prisoner study in which the prisoners were also found to use suppression significantly more than did the control group.

Josepho and Plutchik (1994) investigated the relations between interpersonal problems, coping styles, and suicide risk. The study sample consisted of 71 adult psychiatric inpatients from a large municipal hospital. One-fourth of the patients (25%) were admitted because of a suicide attempt, and approximately two-fifths (40%) of the patients had suicidal ideation included as a reason for admission.

Each patient was asked to complete a suicide risk scale, a problem checklist, and the AECOM Coping Scales. Results showed that the number of interpersonal problems was significantly and positively related to

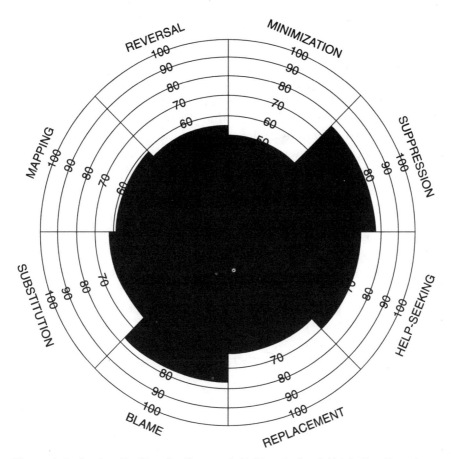

Figure A.4. Coping Profile of a Group of 40 Hospitalized Alcoholics Based on Sex Differences in Personality Traits and Coping Styles of Hospitalized Alcoholics. From "Sex Differences in Personality Traits and Coping Styles of Hospitalized Alcoholics," by H. R. Conte, R. Plutchik, S. Picard, M. Galanter, and J. Jacoby, 1991, *Journal of Studies on Alcohol, 52*, p. 29. Copyright 1991 by the Journal of Studies on Alcohol. Reprinted with permission.

suicide risk. Those who attempted suicide had significantly more problems than the comparison groups (i.e., those patients who had suicidal ideation only, and those with no suicidal symptoms) and were significantly higher on the coping style of suppression. They were also significantly lower on the coping styles of replacement (i.e., improving limitations that exist in oneself or in the situation). In addition, partial correlation analyses indicated that the greater the tendency to minimize (i.e., assuming the problem is not as important as other people think it is), the lower the suicide risk. When the coping measures as a group were added to the problem stress measure, a large improvement in the prediction of suicide risk was obtained.

SUMMARY

This appendix has described a number of tests and scales that may be used to measure moods, emotions, personality traits, ego defenses, and coping styles. The scales included here are all based on the psychoevolutionary theory of affect in the sense that the basic dimensions to be measured are all basic emotions or derivatives of the eight basic emotions. All the scales also use the circumplex model. The most adequate measures are those derived from theory so that the outcome of the measurement operations may contribute to the enhancement or modification of the theory. Theory-based measures also have a wider nomological network than do purely empirical measures. For each test described in this chapter, some empirical data are given to show the usefulness of these instruments in clinical settings. The diversity of measuring instruments implies that the measurement of emotions is a much broader problem than is the measurement of subjective feelings by means of adjective checklists (Plutchik & Conte, 1989b; Plutchik & Van Praag, 1998). The field of emotion study comprises a vast array of phenomena, and the ideal measures of emotion and its derivatives are those that are diverse, theory-based, and systematically related to these complex phenomena.

REFERENCES

Akhtar, S. (1992). *Broken structures: Severe personality disorders and their treatment.* Northdale, NJ: Jason Aronson.

Alexander, R. D. (1987). *The biology of moral systems.* Hawthorne, NY: Aldine De Gruyter.

Allen, B., & Potkay, C. R. (1981). On the arbitrary distinction between states and traits. *Journal of Personality and Social Psychology, 4,* 916–928.

American Psychiatric Association. (1967). *Diagnostic and statistical manual of mental disorders* (2nd ed.). Washington, DC: Author.

American Psychiatric Association. (1980). *Diagnostic and statistical manual of mental disorders* (3rd ed.). Washington, DC: Author.

American Psychiatric Association. (1987). *Diagnostic and statistical manual of mental disorders* (3rd ed., rev.). Washington, DC: Author.

American Psychiatric Association. (1994). *Diagnostic and statistical manual of mental disorders* (4th ed.). Washington, DC: Author.

American Thesaurus of Slang. (1953). New York: Cravell.

Arieti, S. (Ed.). (1974). *American handbook of psychiatry.* New York: Basic Books.

Averill, J. R. (1975). A semantic atlas of emotional concepts. *Catalog of Selected Documents in Psychology, 5,* 330 (Ms. No. 421).

Barkow, J. H., Cosmides, L., & Tooby, J. (1992). *The adapted mind: Evolutionary psychology and the generation of culture.* New York: Oxford University Press.

Bellak, L. (1984). The flexibility of EFA. In L. Bellak & L. A. Goldsmith (Eds.), *The broad scope of ego function assessment* (pp. 6–19). New York: Wiley.

Bellak, L., Hurvich, M., & Gediman, H. K. (1973). *Ego functions in schizophrenics, neurotics, and normals.* New York: Wiley.

Benjamin, L. S. (1993). *Interpersonal diagnosis and treatment of personality disorders.* New York: Guilford Press.

Benjamin, L. S. (1996). *Interpersonal diagnosis and treatment of personality disorders* (2nd ed.). New York: Guilford Press.

Bibring, G. L., Dwyer, T. F., Huntington, D. S., & Valenstein, A. F. (1961). A study of the psychological processes in pregnancy and in the earliest mother–child relationship. Appendix B. Glossary of defenses. *Psychoanalytic Study of the Child, 16,* 62–72.

Blashfield, R. K. (1986). Structural approaches to classification. In T. Millon & G. L. Klerman (Eds.), *Contemporary directions in psychopathology: Toward the DSM–IV* (pp. 363–380). New York: Guilford Press.

Bogdan, R. J. (1997). *Interpreting minds.* Cambridge, MA: Bradford Books.

Bond, M., Gardner, S. T., Christian, J., & Sigal, J. J. (1983). Empirical study of self-rated defense styles. *Archives of General Psychiatry, 40,* 333–338.

Brenner, C. (1974). On the nature and development of affects: A unified theory. *Psychoanalytic Quarterly, 43,* 532–556.

Brenner, C. (1975). Affects and psychic conflict. *Psychoanalytic Quarterly, 44,* 5–28.

Buirski, P., Plutchik, R., & Kellerman, H. (1978). Sex differences, dominance, and personality in the chimpanzee. *Animal Behavior, 26,* 123–129.

Bull, N. (1952). The attitude theory of emotion. *International Record of Medicine, 165,* 216–220.

Bull, N., & Gidro-Frank, L. (1950). Emotions induced and studied in hypnotic subjects, II. *Journal of Nervous and Mental Disease, 112,* 97–120.

Bunker, K. A. (1982). *Comparisons of marketing subjects high and low in psychological symptoms* (Rep. No. CA2059, 114). New York: American Telephone & Telegraph Co. Assessment Center.

Cannon, W. B. (1929). *Bodily changes in pain, hunger, fear and rage* (2nd ed.). New York: Appleton.

Cantor, N., & Harlow, R. E. (1994). Personality, strategic behavior, and daily-life problem solving. *Current Directions in Psychological Science, 3,* 169–172.

Carson, R. C. (1996). Seamlessness in personality and its derangements. *Journal of Personality Assessment, 66,* 240–247.

Chapman, A. H. (1967). *Textbook of clinical psychiatry: An interpersonal approach.* Philadelphia: Lippincott.

Clore, G. I., Ortony, A., & Foss, M. A. (1987). The psychological foundations of the affective lexicon. *Journal of Personality and Social Psychology, 53,* 751–766.

Conte, H. R., & Apter, A. (1995). The Life Style Index: A self-report measure of ego defenses. In H. R. Conte & R. Plutchik (Eds.), *Ego defenses: Theory and measurement* (pp. 179–201). New York: Wiley.

Conte, H. R., & Plutchik, R. (1974). Personality and background characteristics of suicidal mental patients. *Journal of Psychiatric Research, 10,* 181–188.

Conte, H. R., & Plutchik, R. (1981). A circumplex model for interpersonal traits. *Journal of Personality and Social Psychology, 2,* 823–830.

Conte, H. R., Plutchik, R., Buck, L., Picard, S., & Karasu, T. B. (1991). Interrelations between ego functions and personality traits: Their relation to psychotherapy outcome. *American Journal of Psychotherapy, 45,* 69–77.

Conte, H. R., Plutchik, R., Picard, S., Galanter, M., & Jacoby, J. (1991). Sex differences in personality traits and coping styles of hospitalized alcoholics. *Journal of Studies on Alcohol, 52,* 26–32.

Conte, H. R., Plutchik, R., Schwartz, B., & Wild, K. (1983, May). *Psychodynamic variables related to outcome in hospitalized schizophrenics.* Paper presented at the 91st annual convention of the American Psychiatric Association, Anaheim, CA.

Corruble, E., Ginestet, D., & Guelfi, J. D. (1996). Comorbidity of personality disorders and unipolar major depression: A review. *Journal of Affective Disorders, 37,* 157–170.

Darwin, C. (1965). *The expression of the emotions in man and animals.* Chicago: University of Chicago Press. (Original work published 1872)

Davitz, J. R. (1970). A dictionary and grammar of emotion. In M. Arnold (Ed.). *Feelings and emotions: The Loyola symposium.* New York: Academic Press.

Dictionary of American Slang. (1975). New York: Cravell.

Dix, T. (1991). The affective organization of parenting: Adaptive and maladaptive processes. *Psychological Bulletin, 110,* 3–25.

Ellis, A. (1962). *Reason and emotion in psychotherapy.* New York: Lyle Stuart.

Ellis, A. (1981). Misrepresentation of behavior therapy by psychoanalysts. *American Psychologist, 36,* 798–799.

English, O. S., & Finch, S. M. (1964). *Introduction to psychiatry.* New York: Norton.

Ewalt, J. R., & Farnsworth, D. L. (1963). *Textbook of psychiatry.* New York: McGraw-Hill.

Fahs, H., Hogan, T. P., & Fullerton, D. T. (1969). Emotional profile of depression. *Psychological Reports, 25,* 18.

Fava, M., Alpert, J. E., Borus, J. S., Nierenberg, A. A., Pava, J. A., & Rosenbaum, J. F. (1996). Patterns of personality disorder comorbidity in early-onset versus late-onset major depression. *American Journal of Psychiatry, 153,* 1308–1312.

Fenichel, O. (1946). *The psychoanalytic theory of neurosis.* London: Routledge & Kegan Paul.

Fieve, R. R., Platman, S. R., & Plutchik, R. (1968). The use of lithium in affective disorders: I. Acute endogenous depression. *American Journal of Psychiatry, 125,* 487–491.

Fisher, G. A. (1997). Theoretical and methodological elaborations of the circumplex model of personality traits and emotions. In R. Plutchik & H. R. Conte (Eds.), *Circumplex models of personality and emotions* (pp. 245–269). Washington, DC: American Psychological Association.

Fisher, G. A., Heise, D. R., Bohrnstedt, G. W., & Lucke, J. F. (1985). Evidence for extending the circumplex model of personality trait language to self-reported moods. *Journal of Personality and Social Psychology, 49,* 233–242.

Fisher, S., & Greenberg, R. P. (1996). *Freud scientifically appraised: Testing the theories and therapy.* New York: Wiley.

Frances, A., Widiger, T., & Fyer, M. R. (1990). The influence of classification methods on comorbidity. In J. D. Maser & C. K. Cloninger (Eds.), *Comorbidity of mood and anxiety disorders* (pp. 41–59). Washington, DC: American Psychiatric Press.

Frankl, V. E. (1975). *The unconscious God: Psychotherapy and theology.* New York: Simon & Schuster.

Freud, A. (1946). *The ego and the mechanisms of defense.* New York: International Universities Press. (Original work published 1936)

Freud, S. (1957). Analysis terminable and interminable. In J. Strachey (Ed. and Trans.), *The standard edition of the complete psychological works of Sigmund Freud*

(Vol. 23, pp. 216–253). London: Hogarth Press. (Original work published 1937)

Freud, S. (1957). Repression. In J. Stracey (Ed. and Trans.), *The standard edition of the complete psychological works of Sigmund Freud* (Vol. 14, pp. 146–158). London: Hogarth Press. (Original work published 1915)

Freud, S. (1959). Inhibitions, symptoms and anxiety. In J. Strachey (Ed. and Trans.), *The standard edition of the complete psychological works of Sigmund Freud* (Vol. 20, pp. 77–175). London: Hogarth Press. (Original work published 1926)

Freud, S. (1963). Introductory lectures on psycho-analysis. In J. Strachey (Ed. and Trans.), *The standard edition of the complete psychological works of Sigmund Freud* (Vol. 16, pp. 243–483). London: Hogarth Press. (Original work published 1916)

Freud, S. (1964). Constructions in analysis. In J. Strachey (Ed. and Trans.), *The standard edition of the complete psychological works of Sigmund Freud* (Vol. 23, pp. 257–269). London: Hogarth Press. (Original work published 1937)

Freud, S., & Breuer, J. (1936). *Studies on hysteria* (A. A. Brill, Trans.). New York: Nervous and Mental Disease Publication Company. (Original work published 1895)

Fridlund, A. J. (1994). *Human facial expression: An evolutionary view*. San Diego, CA: Academic Press.

Furman, B., & Ahola, T. (1992). *Solution talk: Hosting therapeutic conversations*. New York: Norton.

Gardner, R. (1988). Psychiatric syndromes as infrastructure for intra-specific communication. In M. R. A. Chance (Ed.), *Social fabrics of the mind* (pp. 197–225). Hove, UK: Erlbaum.

Glover, E. (1949). *Psycho-analysis: A handbook for medical practitioners and students of comparative psychology*. New York: Norton.

Greenberg, L. S. (1993). Emotion and change process in psychotherapy. In M. Lewis & J. M. Haviland (Eds.). *Handbook of emotion* (Vol. 99, 499–510). New York: Guilford Press.

Greenberg, L. S., & Korman, L. (1994). Assimilating emotion into psychotherapy integration. *Journal of Psychotherapy Integration, 3*, 249–265.

Greenberg, L. S., & Paivio, S. C. (1997). *Working with emotions in psychotherapy*. New York: Guilford Press.

Greenberg, L. S., Rice, L. N., & Elliott, R. (1993). *Facilitating emotional change: The moment-by-moment process*. New York: Guilford Press.

Greenberg, L. S., & Safran, J. D. (1990). Emotion-change processes in psychotherapy. In R. Plutchik & H. Kellerman (Eds.), *Emotion, psychopathology, and psychotherapy* (Vol. 5, pp. 59–88). New York: Academic Press.

Greenwald, D. J., Reznikoff, M., & Plutchik, R. (1994). Suicide risk and violence risk in alcoholics: Predictors of aggressive risk. *The Journal of Nervous and Mental Disease, 182*, 3–8.

Grilo, C. M., Becker, D. F., Fehon, D. C., Edell, W. S., & McGlashan, J. H. (1996).

Conduct disorder, substance abuse disorders, and coexisting conduct and substance abuse disorders in adolescent patients. *American Journal of Psychiatry, 153*, 914–920.

Gurin, G., Veroff, J., & Field, S. (1960). *Americans view their mental health* (Joint Commission on Mental Illness and Health, Monograph Series No. 4). New York: Basic Books.

Gurtman, M. B. (1997). Studying personality traits: The circular way. In R. Plutchik & H. R. Conte (Eds.), *Circumplex models of personality and emotions* (pp. 81–102). Washington, DC: American Psychological Association.

Haan, N. (1977). *Coping and defending: Processes of self-environment organization.* New York: Academic Press.

Hahn, M. E., & Simmel, E. C. (1976). *Communicative behavior and evolution.* New York: Academic Press.

Haley, J. (1980). *Leaving home: The therapy of disturbed young people.* New York: McGraw-Hill.

Haley, J. (1984). *Ordeal therapy: Unusual ways of changing people.* San Francisco: Jossey-Bass.

Hama, H., Matsuyama, Y., Hashimoto, E., & Plutchik, R. (1982). Emotion profiles of Japanese schizophrenics, neurotics, and alcoholics. *Psychologia, 25*, 144–148.

Hauser, M. D. (1996). *The evolution of communication.* Cambridge, MA: Bradford Press.

Heider, F. (1958). *The psychology of interpersonal relations.* New York: Wiley.

Henderson, B., & Whissell, C. (1997). Changes in women's emotions as a function of emotion valence, self-determined category of premenstrual distress, and day in the menstrual cycle. *Psychological Reports, 80*, 1272–1274.

Henry, W. P. (1997). The circumplex in psychotherapy research. In R. Plutchik & H. R. Conte (Eds.), *Circumplex models of personality and emotions* (pp. 385–410). Washington, DC: American Psychological Association.

Herpertz, S., Steinmeyer, E. M., & Sass, H. (1994). Patterns of comorbidity among *DSM–III–R* and ICD–1 personality disorders as observed with a new inventory for the assessment of personality disorders. *European Archives of Psychiatry and Clinical Neuroscience, 244*, 161–169.

Hill, C. E., & O'Grady, K. E. (1985). List of therapist intentions illustrated in a case study and with therapists of varying theoretical orientations. *Journal of Counseling Psychology, 32*, 3–22.

Hogan, R. (1983). A socioanalytic theory of personality. In *Nebraska symposium on motivation 1982. Personality—current theory and research* (pp. 55–89). Lincoln: University of Nebraska Press.

Horney, K. (1948). *Neurosis and human growth.* New York: Norton.

Horowitz, L. M., Dryer, D. C., & Krasnoperova, E. N. (1997). The circumplex structure of interpersonal problems. In R. Plutchik & H. R. Conte (Eds.), *Circumplex models of personality and emotions* (pp. 347–384). Washington, DC: American Psychological Association.

Horowitz, L. M., Rosenberg, S. E., Baer, B. A., Ureno, G., & Villasenor, V. S. (1988). Inventory of interpersonal problems: Psychometric properties and clinical applications. *Journal of Consulting and Clinical Psychology, 56,* 885–892.

Ihilevich, D., & Gleser, G. C. (1991). *Defenses in psychotherapy: The clinical application of the Defense Mechanisms Inventory.* Odessa, FL: Psychological Assessment Resources.

James, W. (1884). What is emotion? *Mind, 19,* 188–205.

James, W. (1890). *The principles of psychology.* New York: Holt, Rinehart & Winston.

Josepho, S. A., & Plutchik, R. (1994). Stress, coping, and suicide risk in psychiatric inpatients. *Suicide and Life Threatening Behavior, 24,* 48–57.

Kaplan, H. I., & Sadock, B. J. (Eds.). (1989). *Comprehensive textbook of psychiatry.* New Haven, CT: Yale University Press.

Karasu, T. B. (1992). *Wisdom in the practice of psychotherapy.* New York: Basic Books.

Karasu, T. B., & Plutchik, R. (1978). Research problems in psychosomatic medicine and psychotherapy of somatic disorders. In T. B. Karasu & R. I. Steinmuller (Eds.), *Psychotherapeutics in medicine* (pp. 311–338). New York: Grune & Stratton.

Keller, M., & Shapiro, R. W. (1982). "Double depression": Superimposition of acute depressive episodes on chronic depressive disorders. *American Journal of Psychiatry, 139,* 438–442.

Kellerman, H. (1979). *Group therapy and personality: Intersecting structures.* New York: Grune & Stratton.

Kelly, V. (1996). Affect and the redefinition of intimacy. In D. L. Nathanson (Ed.), *Knowing feeling: Affect, script, and psychotherapy* (pp. 55–104). New York: Norton.

Kemper, T. D. (1987). How many emotions are there? Wedding the social and the autonomic components. *American Journal of Sociology, 93,* 263–289.

Kiesler, D. J. (1983). The 1982 Interpersonal Circle: A taxonomy for complementarity in human transactions. *Psychological Review, 90,* 185–214.

Kiesler, D. J. (1986). The 1982 Interpersonal Circle: An analysis of *DSM–III* personality disorders. In T. Millon & G. Klerman (Eds.), *Contemporary directions in psychopathology: Toward DSM–IV* (pp. 571–597). New York: Guilford Press.

Kiesler, D. J., Schmidt, J. A., & Wagner, C. C. (1997). A circumplex inventory of impact messages: An operational bridge between emotion and interpersonal behavior. In R. Plutchik & H. R. Conte (Eds.), *Circumplex models of personality and emotions* (pp. 221–244). Washington, DC: American Psychological Association.

Klein, D. N., Lewinsohn, P. M., & Seeley, J. R. (1996). Hypomanic personality traits in a community sample of adolescents. *Journal of Affective Disorders, 38,* 135–143.

Kleinginna, R. R., & Kleinginna, A. M. (1981). A categorized list of emotion definitions, with suggestions for a consensual definition. *Motivation and Emotion, 5*, 345–379.

Knapp, P. (1981). Core processes in the organization of emotions. *Journal of the American Academy of Psychoanalysis, 9*, 415–434.

Krebs, J. R., Davies, N. B., & Parr, J. (1993). *An introduction to behavioural ecology* (3rd ed.). Oxford, UK: Blackwell Scientific Publications.

Kulka, R. A., Veroff, J., & Douvan, E. (1979). Social class and the use of professional help for personal problems: 1957 and 1976. *Journal of Health and Social Behavior, 20*, 2–17.

Kurschner, M. G., & Beitman, B. D. (1990). Panic attacks without fear: An overview. *Behavior Research and Therapy, 28*, 469–479.

Labouvie, E., Miller, K. J., Langenbucher, J., & Morgenstern, J. (1997). The comorbidity of alcoholism and personality disorders in a clinical population: Prevalence and relation to alcohol typology variables. *Journal of Abnormal Psychology, 106*, 74–84.

Langs, R. (1990). *Psychotherapy: A basic text.* Northvale, NJ: Jason Aronson.

Lazarus, A. A. (1997). *Brief but comprehensive psychotherapy: The multimodal way.* New York: Springer.

Lazarus, R. S. (1966). *Psychological stress and the coping process.* New York: McGraw Hill.

Lazarus, R. S. (1991). *Emotion and adaptation.* New York: Oxford University Press.

Lazarus, R. S., & Folkman, S. (1984). *Stress, appraisal, and coping.* New York: Springer.

Lazarus, R. S., & Lazarus, B. N. (1994). *Passion and reason: Making sense of our emotions.* New York: Oxford University Press.

Leary, T., & Coffey, H. S. (1955). Interpersonal diagnosis: Some problems of methodology and validation. *Journal of Abnormal and Social Psychology, 50*, 110–124.

Lewis, M., & Haviland, J. M. (Eds.). (1993). *Handbook of emotions.* New York: Guilford Press.

Liberman, R. P., Mueser, K. T., & Wallace, C. J. (1986). Social skills training for schizophrenic individuals at risk for relapse. *American Journal of Psychiatry, 143*, 523–526.

Loewenstein, R. M. (1967). Defensive organization and autonomous ego function. *Journal of the American Psychoanalytic Association, 15*, 795–809.

Loranger, A. W. (1996). Dependent personality disorders: Age, sex, and Axis I comorbidity. *Journal of Nervous and Mental Disease, 184*, 17–21.

Lougeay, D. C. (1986). *Relationship of jealousy to defensiveness and anxiety: A correlation-descriptive study.* PhD Dissertation. San Diego, CA: United States International University.

Lubin, B. (1966). Fourteen brief depression adjective checklists. *Archives of General Psychiatry, 15*, 205–208.

Mahoney, M. J. (1996). Emotionality and health: Lessons from and for psychotherapy. In D. L. Nathanson (Ed.), *Knowing feeling: Affect, script, and psychotherapy* (pp. 241–253). New York: Norton.

Maranhao, T. (1986). *Therapeutic and Socratic dialogue*. Madison, WI: University of Wisconsin Press.

Marshall, J. R. (1996). Comorbidity and its effects on panic disorder. *Bulletin of the Menninger Clinic, 60*(2, Suppl. A), 39–53.

Masterson, J. F. (1976). *Psychotherapy of the borderline adult*. New York: Basic Books.

McGlashan, T. H., & Miller, G. H. (1982). The goals of psychoanalysis and psychoanalytic psychotherapy. *Archives of General Psychiatry, 39,* 377–388.

Meichenbaum, D. (1994). *A clinical handbook/practical therapist manual for assessing and treating adults with post-traumatic stress disorder (PTSD)*. Waterloo, Ontario, Canada: Institute Press.

Millon, T. (1987). *Manual for the MCMI–II* (2nd ed.). Minneapolis, MN: National Computer Systems.

Millon, T. (1994). Personality disorders: Conceptual distinctions and classification issues. In P. J. Costa & T. A. Widiger (Eds.), *Personality disorders and the five-factor model of personality* (pp. 279–301). Washington, DC: American Psychological Association.

Mishne, J. M. (1993). *The evolution and application of clinical theory*. New York: Free Press.

Moore, B. E., & Fine, B. D. (Eds.). (1990). *Psychoanalytic terms and concepts*. New Haven, CT: Yale University Press.

Myllyniemi, R. (1997). The interpersonal circle and the emotional undercurrents of human sociability. In R. Plutchik & H. R. Conte (Eds.), *Circumplex models of personality and emotions* (pp. 271–298). Washington, DC: American Psychological Association.

Nathanson, D. L. (Ed.). (1996). *Knowing feeling: Affect, script, and psychotherapy*. New York: Norton.

Nesse, R. M. (1991). Psychology. In M. Maxwell (Ed.), *The sociological imagination*. Albany: State University of New York Press.

Novaco, R. W. (1976). The functions and regulation of the arousal of anger. *American Journal of Psychiatry, 133,* 1124–1128.

Noyes, A. P., & Kolb, L. C. (1963). *Modern clinical psychiatry*. Philadelphia: Saunders.

Okasha, A., Omen, A. M., Lotaief, F., Ghanem, M., Seif el Dawla, A., & Okasha, T. (1996). Comorbidity of Axis I and Axis II diagnoses in a sample of Egyptian patients with neurotic disorders. *Comprehensive Psychiatry, 37,* 95–101.

Parker, S. T. (1985). A social technological model for the evolution of language. *Current Anthropology, 26,* 617–639.

Pasquarelli, B., & Bull, N. (1951). Experimental investigations of the mind–body continuum in affective states. *Journal of Nervous and Mental Disease, 113,* 512–521.

Perry, J. C. (1990). *Defense mechanism rating scales* (5th ed.). Boston: Harvard Medical School.

Pfeffer, C. R., & Plutchik, R. (1989). Co-occurrence of psychiatric disorders in child psychiatric patients and nonpatients: A circumplex model. *Comprehensive Psychiatry, 30,* 275–282.

Picard, R. W. (1997). *Affective computing.* Cambridge, MA: MIT Press.

Pincus, A. L., & Wiggins, J. S. (1990). Interpersonal problems and conceptions of personality disorders. *Journal of Personality Disorders, 4,* 342–352.

Pinker, S. (1994). *The language instinct: How the mind creates language.* New York: Harper Perennial.

Platman, S. R., Plutchik, R., Fieve, R. R., & Lawlor, W. (1969). Emotion profiles associated with mania and depression. *Archives of General Psychiatry, 20,* 210–214.

Plutchik, R. (1962). *The emotions: Facts, theories, and a new model.* New York: Random House.

Plutchik, R. (1967). The affective differential: Emotion profiles implied by diagnostic concepts. *Psychological Reports, 20,* 19–25.

Plutchik, R. (1970). Emotions, evolution, and adaptive processes. In M. Arnold (Ed.), *Feelings and emotions: The Loyola Symposium* (pp. 1–14). New York: Academic Press.

Plutchik, R. (1977). Cognitions in the service of emotions: An evolutionary perspective. In D. K. Candland, J. P. Fell, E. Keen, A. I. Leshner, R. Plutchik, & R. M. Tarpy (Eds.), *Emotion* (pp. 189–212). Monterey, CA: Brooks/Cole.

Plutchik, R. (1980a). *Emotions: A psychoevolutionary synthesis.* New York: Harper & Row.

Plutchik, R. (1980b). A general psychoevolutionary theory of emotion. In R. Plutchik & H. Kellerman (Eds.), *Emotion: Theory, research, and experience: Vol. 1. Theories of emotion.* New York: Academic Press.

Plutchik, R. (1983). Emotions in early development: A psychoevolutionary approach. In R. Plutchik & H. Kellerman (Eds.), *Emotion: Theory, research, and experience: Vol. 2. Emotions in early development* (pp. 221–258). New York: Academic Press.

Plutchik, R. (1984). Emotions: A general psychoevolutionary theory. In K. R. Scherer & P. Ekman (Eds.), *Approaches to emotion* (pp. 197–220). Hillsdale, NJ: Erlbaum.

Plutchik, R. (1987). Evolutionary bases of empathy. In N. Eisenberg & J. Strayer (Eds.), *Empathy and its development* (pp. 38–46). New York: Cambridge University Press.

Plutchik, R. (1988). The nature of emotions: Clinical implications. In M. Clynes & J. Panksepp (Eds.), *Emotions and psychopathology* (pp. 1–20). New York: Plenum Press.

Plutchik, R. (1989). Measuring emotions and their derivatives. In R. Plutchik & H. Kellerman (Eds.), *Emotion: Theory, research, and experience: Vol. 4. The measurement of emotions* (pp. 1–35). San Diego, CA: Academic Press.

Plutchik, R. (1990). Emotions and psychotherapy: A psychoevolutionary perspective. In R. Plutchik & H. Kellerman (Eds.), *Emotions, psychopathology, and psychotherapy* (Vol. 5, pp. 3–41). New York: Academic Press.

Plutchik, R. (1992, May). *Personality, ego defenses and coping styles in relation to health and disease*. Paper presented at the symposium New Perspectives in Cardiology, sponsored by The Russek Foundation, Boca Raton, FL.

Plutchik, R. (1993). Emotions and their vicissitudes: Emotions and psychopathology. In M. Lewis & J. M. Haviland (Eds.), *Handbook of emotions* (pp. 53–66). New York: Guilford Press.

Plutchik, R. (1994). *The psychology and biology of emotion*. New York: Harper-Collins.

Plutchik, R. (1995). A theory of ego defenses. In H. R. Conte & R. Plutchik (Eds.), *Ego defenses: Theory and measurement* (pp. 13–37). New York: Wiley.

Plutchik, R. (1997). The circumplex as a general model of the structure of emotions and personality. In R. Plutchik & H. R. Conte (Eds.), *Circumplex models of personality and emotions* (pp. 17–46). Washington, DC: American Psychological Association.

Plutchik, R. (2000). Aggression, violence, and suicide. In R. Maris, L. Berman, & M. Silverman (Eds.), *Comprehensive textbook of suicidology and suicide prevention* (pp. 407–423). New York: Guilford Press.

Plutchik, R., & Conte, H. R. (1985). Quantitative assessment of personality disorders. In R. Nickols, J. O. Cavenar, Jr., & H. K. H. Brodie (Eds.), *Psychiatry* (Vol. 7, pp. 1–13). Philadelphia: J. B. Lippincott.

Plutchik, R., & Conte, H. R. (1989a). Measuring emotions and their derivatives: Personality traits, ego defenses, and coping styles. In S. Wetzler & M. Katz (Eds.), *Contemporary approaches to psychological assessment* (pp. 239–269). New York: Brunner/Mazel.

Plutchik, R., & Conte, H. R. (1989b). Self-report scales for the measurement of depression. *Psychiatric Annals, 19*, 367–371.

Plutchik, R., & Conte, H. R. (1994, June). *The circumplex structure of personality disorders: An empirical study*. Paper presented at the annual meeting of the Society for Psychotherapy Research, York, England.

Plutchik, R., & Conte, H. R. (Eds.). (1997). *Circumplex models of personality and emotions*. Washington, DC: American Psychological Association.

Plutchik, R., Conte, H. R., Wilde, S., & Karasu, T. B. (1994). Strategies of therapist interventions: A preliminary empirical study. *Journal of Psychotherapy Practice and Research, 3*, 325–332.

Plutchik, R., & DiScipio, W. S. (1974). Personality patterns in chronic alcoholism (Korsakoff's syndrome), chronic schizophrenia, and geriatric patients with chronic brain syndrome. *Journal of the American Geriatrics Society, 22*, 514–516.

Plutchik, R., & Kellerman, H. (1974). *Manual of the Emotions Profile Index*. Los Angeles: Western Psychological Services.

Plutchik, R., & Kellerman, H. (Eds.). (1989). *The measurement of emotions*. New York: Academic Press.

Plutchik, R., Kellerman, H., & Conte, H. R. (1979). A structural theory of ego defenses and emotions. In C. E. Izard (Ed.), *Emotions in personality and psychopathology* (pp. 229–257). New York: Plenum Press.

Plutchik, R., & Landau, H. (1973). Perceived dominance and emotional states in small groups. *Psychotherapy: Theory, Research, and Practice, 10*, 343–344.

Plutchik, R., McCarthy, M., & Hall, B. T. (1975). Changes in elderly welfare hotel residents during a one-year period. *Journal of the American Geriatrics Society, 23*, 265–270.

Plutchik, R., & Platman, S. R. (1977). Personality connotations of psychiatric diagnoses. *Journal of Nervous and Mental Disease, 165*, 418–422.

Plutchik, R., & Van Praag, H. M. (1989). The measurement of suicidality, aggressivity, and impulsivity. *Progress in Neuro-Psychopharmacology and Biological Psychiatry, 13*, 23–24.

Plutchik, R., & Van Praag, H. M. (1998). Interrelations among anxiety, depression, aggression, impulsivity and suicidality: An evaluation of the comorbidity concept. In M. Maes & E. F. Coccaro (Eds.), *Neurobiology and clinical views on aggression and impulsivity* (pp. 129–134). New York: Wiley.

Plutchik, R., Williams, M. H., Jr., Jerrett, I., Karasu, T. B., & Kane, C. (1978). Emotions, personality, and life stresses in asthma. *Journal of Psychosomatic Research, 22*, 425–431.

Prochaska, J. O., Norcross, J. C., & DiClemente, C. C. (1994). *Changing for good*. New York: William Morrow & Co.

Rado, S. (1969). *Adaptational psychodynamics: Motivation and control*. New York: Science House.

Rado, S. (1975). *Psychoanalysis of behavior*. New York: Grune & Stratton.

Rapaport, D. (1950). *Emotions and memory*. New York: International Universities Press.

Reich, J. (1996). The morbidity of *DSM–III–R* dependent personality disorder. *Journal of Nervous and Mental Disease, 184*, 22–26.

Rodriguez Torres, A., & Del Porto, J. A. (1995). Comorbidity of obsessive–compulsive disorders: A Brazilian controlled study. *Psychopathology, 28*, 322–329.

Rogers, C. R. (1951). *Client-centered therapy: Its major practice, implications, and theory*. Boston: Houghton-Mifflin.

Rogers, C. R. (1965). *Client-centered therapy*. Boston: Houghton-Mifflin.

Romney, D. M., & Bynner, J. M. (1989). Evaluation of a circumplex model of *DSM–III* personality disorders. *Journal of Research in Personality, 23*, 525–538.

Russell, J. A. (1989). Measures of emotion. In R. Plutchik & H. Kellerman (Eds.), *The measurement of emotions* (pp. 83–112). New York: Academic Press.

Russell, J. A., & Carroll, J. M. (1999). On the bipolarity of positive and negative affect. *Psychological Bulletin, 125*, 3–30.

Schaefer, E. S. (1997). Integration of configurational and factorial models for family relationships and child behavior. In R. Plutchik & H. R. Conte (Eds.), *Circumplex models of personality and emotions* (pp. 133–154). Washington, DC: American Psychological Association.

Schafer, R. (1954). *Psychoanalytic interpretation in Rorschach testing*. New York: Grune & Stratton.

Schur, M. (1968, May). *Introduction to the colloquium on affect and cognition*. Paper presented at the meeting of the American Psychoanalytic Society convention, Boston, MA.

Seyforth, R. M., Cheney, D. L., & Marler, P. (1980). Monkey responses to three different alarm cells: Evidence of predator classification and semantic communication. *Science, 210*, 801–803.

Sheppard, C., Fiorentino, D., Collins, L., & Merlis, S. (1969). Comparison of emotion profiles as defined by two additional MMPI profiles in male narcotic addicts. *Journal of Clinical Psychology, 25*, 186–188.

Shields, S. A. (1984). Distinguishing between emotion and nonemotion: Judgments about experience. *Motivation and Emotion, 8*, 355–369.

Sim, J. P., & Romney, D. M. (1990). The relationship between a circumplex model of interpersonal behaviors and personality disorders. *Journal of Personality Disorders, 4*, 329–341.

Sjoback, H. (1973). *The psychoanalytic theory of defensive processes*. New York: Wiley.

Skodol, A. E., Oldham, J. M., Hyler, S. E., Stein, D. J., Hollander, E., Gallager, P. E., & Lopez, A. E. (1995). Patterns of anxiety and personality disorder comorbidity. *Journal of Psychiatric Research, 29*, 361–374.

Spalletta, G., Troisi, A., Saracco, M., Ciani, N., & Pasini, A. (1996). Symptom profile, Axis II comorbidity, and suicidal behavior in young males with *DSM–III–R* depressive illness. *Journal of Affective Disorders, 39*, 141–148.

Sperling, S. J. (1958). On denial and the essential nature of defense. *International Journal of Psychoanalysis, 39*, 25–38.

Spezzano, C. (1993). *Affect in psychoanalysis: A clinical synthesis*. Hillsdale, NJ: Analytic Press.

Stevens, A., & Price, J. (1996). *Evolutionary psychiatry: A new beginning*. New York: Routledge.

Stiles, W. B. (1979). Verbal response modes and psychotherapeutic technique. *Psychiatry, 42*, 49–62.

Stone, A. M. (1996). Clinical assessment of affect. In D. L. Nathanson (Ed.), *Knowing feeling: Affect, script, and psychotherapy* (pp. 22–36). New York: Norton.

Storm, C., & Storm, T. (1987). A taxonomic study of the vocabulary of emotions. *Journal of Personality and Social Psychology, 53*, 805–816.

Strack, S., Lorr, M., & Campbell, L. (1990). An evaluation of Millon's circular model of personality disorders. *Journal of Personality Disorders, 4*, 353–361.

Strayhorn, J. M. (1988). *The competent child: An approach to psychotherapy and preventive mental health*. New York: Guilford Press.

Strongman, K. (1987). *The psychology of emotion*. New York: Wiley.

Szajnberg, N. M. (Ed.). (1992). *Educating the emotions: Bruno Bettelheim and psychoanalytic development*. New York: Plenum Press.

Taurke, E., Flegenheimer, W., McCullough, L., Winston, A., Pollack, J., & Trujillo, M. (1990). Change in affect-defense ratio from early to late sessions in relation to outcome. *Journal of Clinical Psychology, 46,* 657–668.

Tomkins, S. S. (1962). *Affect, imagery, and consciousness: Vol. 1. Positive affects*. New York: Springer.

Tomkins, S. S. (1980). Affect as amplification: Some modifications in a theory. In R. Plutchik & H. Kellerman (Eds.). *Emotion: Theory, research, and experience: Vol. 1. Theories of emotion* (pp. 141–164). New York: Academic Press.

Tomkins, S. S. (1992). *Affect, imagery, and consciousness: Vol. 4. Cognition*. New York: Springer.

Tomkins, S. S. (1995). Script theory: Differential magnification of affects. In V. Demos (Ed.), *Exploring affect: Selections from the writings of Silvan S. Tomkins* (pp. 312–410). New York: Cambridge University Press.

Tracey, T. J. G., & Rounds, J. B. (1997). Circular structure of vocational interests. In R. Plutchik & H. R. Conte (Eds.), *Circumplex models of personality and emotions* (pp. 183–204). Washington, DC: American Psychological Association.

Trower, P., & Gilbert, P. (1989). New theoretical conceptions of social anxiety and social phobia. *Clinical Psychology Review, 9,* 19–35.

Vaillant, G. E. (1971). Theoretical hierarchy of adaptive ego mechanisms. *Archives of General Psychiatry, 24,* 107–118.

Vaillant, G. E. (1975). Natural history of male psychological health: III. Empirical dimensions of mental health. *Archives of General Psychiatry, 32,* 420–426.

Vaillant, G. E. (1976). Natural history of male psychological health: The relation of choice of ego mechanism of defense to adult adjustment. *Archives of General Psychiatry, 33,* 535–545.

Vaillant, G. E. (1983). *The natural history of alcoholism: Courses, patterns, and paths to recovery*. Cambridge, MA: Harvard University.

Vaillant, L. M. (1997). *Changing character: Short-term anxiety-regulating psychotherapy for restructuring defenses, affects, and attachments*. New York: Basic Books.

VandenBos, G. R. (1996). Outcome assessment of psychotherapy. *American Psychologist, 51,* 1005–1006.

Verwoerdt, A. (1972). Psychopathological responses to the stress of physical illness. In Z. J. Lipowski (Ed.), *Psychosocial aspects of physical illness* (Advances in Psychosomatic Medicine, 8, pp. 111–116). Basel, Switzerland: Karger.

Veselica, K. C., Amidyic, V., Durijancek, J., Kozmar, D., Sram, M., Glavas, B., & Catipovic, B. (1999). Association of heart rate and heart-rate variability with scores on the Emotion Profile Index in patients with acute coronary disease. *Psychological Reports, 84,* 433–442.

Viederman, M., & Perry, S. W. (1980). Use of a psychodynamic life narrative in the treatment of depression in the physically ill. *General Hospital Psychiatry, 3,* 177–185.

Wachtel, P. L. (1993). *Therapeutic communication: Knowing what to say when.* New York: Guilford Press.

Webster's International Unabridged Dictionary. (1971). New York: G & C Merriam Co.

Weisman, A. D. (1965). *The existential core of psychoanalysis: Reality sense and responsibility.* Boston: Little, Brown.

Westen, D. (1998). The scientific legacy of Sigmund Freud: Toward a psychodynamically informed psychological science. *Psychological Bulletin, 124,* 333–371.

White, R. W. (1963). *Ego and reality in psychoanalytic theory.* New York: International Universities Press.

Widiger, T. A., & Hagemoser, S. (1997). Personality disorders and the interpersonal circumplex. In R. Plutchik & H. R. Conte (Eds.), *Circumplex models of personality and emotions* (pp. 299–325). Washington, DC: American Psychological Association Press.

Wiggins, J. S. (1982). Circumplex models of interpersonal behavior in clinical psychology. In P. Kendall & J. Butcher (Eds.), *Handbook of research methods in clinical psychology* (pp. 183–221). New York: Wiley.

Wiggins, J. S., & Trobst, K. K. (1997). When is a circumplex an "interpersonal circumplex"? The case of supportive actions. In R. Plutchik & H. R. Conte (Eds.), *Circumplex models of personality and emotions* (pp. 57–80). Washington, DC: American Psychological Association.

Wilder, J. S., & Plutchik, R. (1982). Preparing the professional: Building prevention of burnout into professional training. In W. Payne (Ed.), *Job stress and burnout* (pp. 113–129). Beverly Hills, CA: Sage.

Wilson, E. O. (1975). *Sociobiology: The new synthesis.* Cambridge, MA: Harvard University Press.

World Health Organization. (1994). *International statistical classification of diseases, tenth revision* (ICD-10). Geneva, Switzerland: Author.

Yalom, I. (1980). *Existential psychotherapy.* New York: Basic Books.

Yalom, I. (1989). *Love's executioner and other tales of psychotherapy.* New York: Basic Books.

Yalom, I. (1995). *The theory and practice of group psychotherapy* (4th ed.). New York: Basic Books.

Young, P. T. (1961). *Motivation and emotion.* New York: John Wiley & Sons.

AUTHOR INDEX

Fridlund, A. J., 150
Fullerton, D. T., 177
Furman, B., 33
Fyer, M. R., 87

Galanter, M., 9, 184, 185, 200
Gardner, R., 31
Gardner, S. T., 112
Gediman, H. K., 116
Gidro-Frank, L., 98
Gilbert, P., 77
Ginestet, D., 84
Gleser, G. C., 114
Glover, E., 113
Greenberg, L. S., 6, 16, 18, 57, 58, 66, 138
Greenberg, R. P., 60
Greenwald, D. J., 190, 191
Grilo, C. M., 86
Guelfi, J. D., 84
Gurin, G., 22
Gurtman, M. B., 71

Haan, N., 115
Hagemoser, S., 85
Hahn, M. E., 150
Haley, J., 30, 140
Hall, B. T., 176
Hama, H., 178
Harlow, R. E., 76
Hashimoto, E., 178
Hauser, M. D., 70, 149, 150
Haviland, J. M., 16
Heider, F., 5, 41, 43
Heise, D. R., 71
Henderson, B., 178
Henry, W. P., 102
Herperks, S., 84
Hill, C. E., 158
Hogan, R., 141
Hogan, T. P., 177
Horney, K., 147
Horowitz, L. M., 101, 102
Huntington, D. S., 112
Hurvich, M., 116

Ihilevich, D., 114

Jacoby, J., 9, 184, 185, 200
James, W., 5, 41, 42
Jerrett, I., 178
Josepho, S. A., 9, 200

Kane, C., 178
Kaplan, H. I., 112
Karasu, T. B., 25, 27, 35, 66, 138, 151, 157, 158, 159, 160, 163, 178, 184
Keller, M., 87
Kellerman, H., 9, 87, 115, 118, 120, 140, 172, 176, 177
Kelly, V., 66
Kemper, T. D., 62
Kiesler, D. J., 84, 101
Klein, D. N., 85
Kleinginna, A. M., 39
Kleinginna, R. R., 39
Knapp, P., 17
Kolb, L. C., 116
Korman, L., 57
Krasnoperova, E. N., 102
Krebs, J. R., 150
Kulka, R. A., 22
Kuschner, M. G., 35

Labouvie, E., 84
Landau, H., 140
Langenbucher, J., 84
Langs, R., 18
Lawlor, W., 173
Lazarus, A. A., 151
Lazarus, B. N., 56
Lazarus, R. S., 5, 35, 55, 56
Leary, T., 83
Lewinsohn, P. M., 85
Lewis, M., 16
Liberman, R. P., 146
Loewenstein, R. M., 114
Loranger, A. W., 86
Lorr, M., 96
Lougeay, D. C., 115
Lubin, B., 174
Lucke, J. F., 71

Mahoney, M. J., 26
Maranhao, T., 26, 27, 32, 155

Marler, P., 75
Marshall, J. R., 84
Masterson, J. F., 29
Matsuyama, Y., 178
McCarthy, M., 176
McGlashan, J. H., 86
McGlashan, T. H., 36
Meichenbaum, D., 14
Merlis, S., 177
Miller, G. H., 36
Miller, K. J., 84
Millon, T., 76, 96, 171
Mishne, J. M., 27, 28
Moore, B. E., 112
Morgenstern, J., 84
Mueser, K. T., 146
Myllyniemi, R., 71

Nathanson, D. L., 16, 29
Nesse, R. M., 74
Norcross, J. C., 36, 37
Novaco, R. W., 77
Noyes, A. P., 116

O'Grady, K. E., 158
Okasha, A., 86
Ortony, A., 40

Paivio, S. C., 6, 18, 58, 66, 138
Parker, S. T., 150
Parr, J., 150
Pasini, A., 86
Pasquarelli, B., 98
Perry, J. C., 112, 113
Perry, S. W., 142
Pfeffer, C. R., 90, 91
Picard, R. W., 19
Picard, S., 9, 184, 185, 200
Pincus, A. L., 96
Pinker, S., 150
Platman, S. R., 87, 88, 96, 173, 177
Plutchik, R., 9, 25, 33, 35, 39, 44, 60,
    62, 63, 65, 66, 70, 72, 73, 74,
    75, 82, 86, 87, 88, 90, 91, 96,
    97, 98, 106, 115, 118, 119, 120,
    121, 140, 147, 157, 158, 159,
    160, 163, 172, 173, 174, 175,
    176, 177, 178, 179, 184, 185,

186, 190, 191, 193, 194, 200,
    202
Potkay, C. R., 63
Price, J., 30, 31
Prochaska, J. O., 36, 37

Rado, S., 5, 27, 47, 48
Rapaport, D., 75
Reich, J., 86
Reznikoff, M., 190, 191
Rice, L. N., 16, 57
Rodriguez Torres, A., 84
Rogers, C. R., 17, 29
Romney, D. M., 96
Rosenberg, S. E., 101
Rounds, J. B., 71
Russell, J. A., 82, 176

Sadock, B. J., 112
Safran, J. D., 58
Saracco, M., 86
Sass, H., 84
Schafer, R., 112
Schmidt, J. A., 101
Schwartz, B., 200
Seeley, J. R., 86
Seyforth, R. M., 75
Shapiro, D., 27, 33
Shapiro, R. W., 87
Sheppard, C., 177
Shields, S. A., 40
Sigal, J. J., 112
Sim, J. P., 96
Simmel, E. C., 150
Sjoback, H., 111, 112, 116
Skodol, A. E., 86
Spalletta, G., 86
Sperling, S. J., 112
Spezzano, C., 5, 17, 19, 32, 43, 51, 52,
    66, 70, 76, 108, 151
Steinmeyer, E. M., 84
Stevens, A., 30, 31
Stiles, W. B., 158
Stone, A. M., 30
Storm, C., 40
Storm, T., 40
Strack, S., 96
Strayhorn, J. M., 36, 37
Strongman, K., 39

Szajnberg, N. M., 151

Taurke, E., 54
Tomkins, S. S., 5, 19, 29, 53
Tooby, J., 60
Tracey, T. J. G., 71
Trobst, K. K., 71
Troisi, A., 86
Trower, P., 77

Ureno, G., 101

Vaillant, G. E., 113, 115, 116, 184
Vaillant, L.M., 5, 16, 19, 25, 29, 49, 54,
    55, 70, 136, 137, 151
Valenstein, A. F., 112
VandenBos, G. R., 22
van Praag, H. M., 86, 147, 202
Verwoerdt, A., 113
Veroff, J., 22
Veselica, K. C., 178

Viederman, M., 142
Villasenor, V. S., 101

Wachtel, P. L., 154, 165, 166
Wagner, C. C., 101
Wallace, C. J., 146
*Webster's International Unabridged
    Dictionary*, 15
Weisman, A. D., 16, 25, 66, 108
Westen, D., 60, 61, 186
Whissell, C., 178
White, R. W., 116
Widiger, T., 85, 87
Wiggins, J. S., 71, 84, 89, 96
Wild, K., 200
Wilde, S., 157, 158, 159, 160, 163
Wilder, J. S., 194
Williams, M. H., Jr., 178
Wilson, E. O., 150

Yalom, I., 23, 25, 28, 33, 35, 36, 37, 110,
    138, 143, 144, 147
Young, P. T., 67

SUBJECT INDEX

Circumplex model. *See also* Psychoevolutionary theory
  axes question, 100–101
  clinical practice application, 101–103
  ego defenses, 118–121
  emotion derivatives, 70–73
  and emotion sequence, 64–70
  impulses to action, 97–100, 104–106
  personality disorders, 86–97
  Personality Profile test, 178–179
  personality traits, 70–71
  in structural model, 62–64
Client-centered therapy, 17–18
Clients, 17–18
Cognitive appraisal, 35
Cognitive-behavior therapy, 159–160
Cognitive coping, 56
Cognitive theory, 16, 41, 43
Collaborative therapeutic relationship, 166–167
Color relationships, emotions similarity, 62–63
Communication, 149–151. *See also* Therapeutic communication
Comorbidity, personality disorders, 84–87
Compensation (defense mechanism)
  circumplex model, 118–120
  corresponding coping style, 122
  Life Style Index assessment, 191–192
  underlying structure, 119
Complementarity theory, 101
Conflict
  emotional components, 129
  and impulse to action, 98
Control relationships
  existential issues, 140–141
  symptoms link, 30
  and territoriality, 141
Coping response, Lazarus's theory, 55–57
Coping styles, 107–126
  characteristics, 121–126
  ego defenses relationship, 115, 121–125
  measurement scale, 9–10
  therapeutic tactics, 132–133
Core conflicts, 135
Core relational theme, 56

Darwinian theory, 41–42, 60

Death anxiety, 143–144
Deception, 107–126
  as clinical issue, 110
  and evolutionary psychology, 108–110
  facial expression in, 108
  Freudian theory, 110
  self-deception association, 109
Defense mechanisms. *See* Ego defenses
Denial (defense mechanism)
  circumplex model, 118–121
  corresponding coping style, 122
  death anxiety reaction, 143
  Life Style Index assessment, 191–192
  underlying structure, 119
Dependent personality disorder
  circumplex model, 91–97
  DSM–IV affect disturbances, 24
  as emotion derivative, 83
  personality traits link, 85
Depression
  adjective checklists, 172–174
  and Brenner's ego psychology, 49–51
  Emotions Profile Index, 177–178
  function of, 76–77
  grief differences, 142–143
  and hierarchical relationships, 140
  therapeutic tactics, 134–135
Derivatives model, 70–73
  and coping styles, 193
  ego defenses, 117–118
  and personality, 70–73
  in psychoevolutionary theory, 70–73
Dickinson, Emily, 13
Digital coding, of speech, 150
Disgust (basic emotion)
  circumplex model, 64
  derivatives, 73, 83
  personality disorders link, 83
  sequential model, 69
"Disidentification," 144
Displacement (defense mechanism)
  circumplex model, 118–121
  corresponding coping style, 122
  Life Style Index assessment, 191–192
  underlying structure, 119
Dominance hierarchies, 140–141
Drives
  affects link, 52–54
  and symptoms, 27

structural model, 63–65
Mood scales, 172–176
Motivation, affects role, 53–54
Mourning, 142

Narcissistic personality disorder
    circumplex model, 91–97
    DSM–IV affect disturbance, 25
    as emotion derivative, 83
    personality traits link, 85
Neurological tradition, 41–42
Neurotic character, 34

Obsessive-compulsive disorder
    DSM–IV affect disturbances, 24
    personality traits link, 85
Obsessive-compulsive personality disorder
    circumplex model, 91–97
    DSM–IV affect disturbances, 24
    as emotion derivative, 83

Panic
    anxiety relationship, 49
    and DSM–IV affect disturbances, 24
Paranoid personality disorder
    circumplex model, 91–97
    DSM–IV affect disturbances, 25
    as emotion derivative, 83
    personality traits link, 85
Parenting, emotions functional role, 75
Passive-aggressive personality disorder
    circumplex model, 91–97
    personality traits link, 85
Patient-therapist communication. See
        Therapeutic communication
Patients, 17–18
Personality disorders, 81–106
    changing definitions of, 93–95
    circumplex model, 86–97
    comorbidity problem, 84–87
        implications, 86–87
    derivatives model, 72–73, 82–84
    DSM–IV description, 82
    ego defenses correlation, 191
    personality traits link, 84–85
Personality Profile, 9, 178–185
    alcoholism trait measure, 184–185

circumplex model basis of, 178–179
psychometric characteristics, 179
in psychotherapy outcome prediction,
    184
Personality traits
    circumplex model, 70–71
    clinical approach, 135–136
    derivatives model, 70–73
    emotional states link, 63–64, 70–73
    function, 75–77, 135–136
    personality disorders link, 83–85
    psychoanalytic theory, 52–53
    and structural model, 63–64
Pleasure principle, 49
Polarity dimension
    ego defenses, 116–117, 120–121
    in structural model, 61–63
Posttraumatic stress, metaphors, 14
Posture, and emotional feelings, 98
Power relationships
    existential issues, 140–141
    in therapeutic communication, 152
    symptoms link, 30
Primary appraisals, 56
Primary dyads, 63–64
Primary emotions, structural model, 62–
    64
Primary anxiety, 45
Primate vocalizations, function, 75
Primitive defenses, classifications, 112–
    114
Problem-focused coping, 56
Projection (defense mechanism)
    circumplex model, 118–121
    corresponding coping style, 122
    Life Style Index assessment, 191–192
    underlying structure, 119
Psychoanalytic theory. See Psychody-
        namic approaches
Psychodynamic approaches
    and ego defenses, theory, 111
    emotion theory, 17, 44–55
    historical tradition, 41, 43
    psychoevolutionary theory influence of,
        60
    symptom meanings, 27–28
    therapeutic tactics, affect in, 160

Psychoevolutionary theory, 59–79. *See also* Circumplex model
  clinical tactics basis, 127–138
  derivatives model in, 70–73
  ego defenses, 107–126
  emotions definition, 77–79
  functional perspective, 74–77
  origins, 60–61
  sequential model in, 64–70
  structural model in, 61–64
Psychological services, 22
Psychopathology, functional perspective, 76
Psychophysiology, history, 41–42
"Psychosomatic equivalent," 35
Psychotherapy goals, and symptoms, 35–37
Psychotherapy outcome predictors
  affect expression as, 54
  Personality Profile test in, 184

Rado, Sandor, emergency affects theory, 46–48
Rational-emotive therapy, 17
Reaction formation (defense mechanism)
  circumplex model, 118–120
  corresponding coping style, 122
  Life Style Index assessment, 191–192
  underlying structure, 119
Regression (defense mechanism)
  circumplex model, 118–121
  corresponding coping style, 122
  Life Style Index assessment, 191–192
  underlying structure, 119
Replacement
  AECOM Coping Scales assessment, 193–201
  as coping style, 122
Repression (defense mechanism)
  and Brenner's ego psychology, 48–51
  circumplex model, 118–121
  corresponding coping style, 122
  Freudian theory, 44–46
  Life Style Index assessment, 191–192
  symptom origin, 27
  underlying structure, 119
Reversal
  AECOM Coping Scales assessment, 193–201

as coping style, 124
Role playing
  in restructuring of emotion, 58
  value of, 138

Sadness (basic emotion)
  adaptive and maladaptive forms, 49, 55
  circumplex model, 64
  derivatives, 73, 83
  function, 76
  personality disorders link, 83
  sequential model, 68–69
    feedback loop, 68
Schizoid personality disorder
  circumplex model, 91–97
  DSM–IV affect disturbances, 25
  personality traits link, 85
Schizophrenia
  coping style profile, 200
  DSM–IV affect disturbances, 24
Schizotypal personality disorder
  circumplex model, 91–97
  DSM–IV affect disturbances, 25
Secondary appraisals, 56
Self-deception, 107–126
  as clinical issue, 110
  ego defenses link, 111
  and evolutionary psychology, 108–110
Self-disclosure, 152–153
Self-ratings, 172–176
Sequential model, 64–70
  assumptions, 68–70
  in psychoevolutionary theory, 64–70
Short-term integrative therapy
  affect restructuring, 54–55
  core themes, 29
Similarity dimension
  ego defenses, 116–117, 120–121
  in structural model, 61–63
Social anxiety, function of, 76–77
Social conversation, 151–154
Social skills training, 146, 148
Speech, and communication, 150
Spezzano, Charles, affect theory, 51–53
Stress
  coping response, 55–57
  redefinition of, 128–129
  therapeutic tactics, 128–129, 134–135

Structural Analysis of Social Behavior, 102

Structural model
dimensions in, 61–63
in psychoevolutionary theory, 61–64

Studies on Hysteria (Freud & Breuer), 43

Substitution
AECOM Coping Scales assessment, 193–201
as coping style, 125

Suicide
coping style profile, 200–201
ego defense measure, 191–193
risk factors, 146–147
two-stage model, 147

Suppression
AECOM Coping Scales assessment, 193–201
as coping style, 193

Surprise (basic emotion)
circumplex model, 64
derivatives, 72–73, 83
personality disorders link, 83
sequential model, 69

Symbols, symptoms as, 32

Symptoms, 21–37
"affect scripts" role in, 29–30
Brenner's ego psychology, 50–51
definitions, 22–26
in *DSM–IV*, 23–25
evolutionary theory, 30–32
existential therapy approach, 28–29
patients' perspective, 25–26
and power relationships, 30
psychodynamic approaches, 27–28, 50–52
and psychotherapy goals, 35–37
short-term integrative approach, 29
as symbols, 32

theoretical models, 26–33

Temporality, 142–144
Territoriality, 141
Therapeutic communication, 149–168
appropriate forms of, 165–167
feedback system, 156–158
model of, 155–160
versus social conversation, 151–154
and "why" questions, 160–165

Therapeutic Communication (Wachtel), 154, 165

Tomkins, Sylvan S., emotion theory, 53–54

"Transference neurosis," 28

Ultimate rescuer belief, 143–144

Unconscious
Freudian theory, 45–46
and psychoevolutionary theory, 60
and symptoms, 28

The Unconscious (Freud), 46

Uncovering emotions, 127–138

Vaillant, Leigh McCullough, 54–55
affect restructuring theory, 54–55
core themes of symptoms theory, 29
uncovering emotion interventions, 136–137

"Why" questions, 160–165
Worry, 49

Yalom, I., 143–144

ABOUT THE AUTHOR

Robert Plutchik, PhD, is professor emeritus of psychiatry and psychology at the Albert Einstein College of Medicine. Formerly, he was associate director of the psychiatry department at the Bronx Municipal Hospital Center in New York City, as well as director of program development and clinical research at the Bronx Psychiatric Center. He has written extensively on the subject of emotion as well as on the subjects of psychotherapy, suicide, and violence. He is the author or the coauthor of over 260 professional journal articles and 45 chapters in edited books. He has written six books and coedited nine others, including *Circumplex Models of Personality and Emotions* (APA, 1997) coedited with Hope Conte. Currently, he is involved in clinical research and is adjunct professor of psychology at the University of South Florida, where he teaches the psychology of emotions.